Conquistador's Wake

CONQUISTADOR'S WAKE

Tracking the Legacy of Hernando de Soto in the Indigenous Southeast

DENNIS B. BLANTON

University of Georgia Press
Athens

Published with the generous
support of Fernbank

Athens, Georgia 30602
www.ugapress.org

Designed by Erin Kirk New
Set in Garamond Premier Pro
Printed and bound by Integrated Books International
The paper in this book meets the guidelines for
permanence and durability of the Committee on
Production Guidelines for Book Longevity of the
Council on Library Resources.

Most University of Georgia Press titles are
available from popular e-book vendors.

Printed in the United States of America
19 20 21 22 23 P 5 4 3 2 1

Library of Congress Cataloging-in-Publication Data
Names: Blanton, Dennis B., author.
Title: Conquistador's wake : tracking the legacy of Hernando de Soto
in the indigenous Southeast / Dennis B. Blanton.
Description: Athens : University of Georgia Press, [2020] |
Includes bibliographical references and index.
Identifiers: LCCN 2019030451 | ISBN 9780820356358 (hardcover) |
ISBN 9780820356372 (paperback) | ISBN 9780820356365 (ebook)
Subjects: LCSH: Soto, Hernando de, approximately 1500–1542. |
Indians of North America—Georgia—Dodge County—Antiquities.
| Excavations (Archaeology)—Georgia—Dodge County. | Glass Site
(Ga.) | Georgia—Discovery and exploration—Spanish. |
Dodge County (Ga.)—Antiquities.
Classification: LCC E125.S7 B56 2020 | DDC 975.8/532—dc23
LC record available at https://lccn.loc.gov/2019030451

For South Georgia,

and everyone who makes it a special place

and

in respectful appreciation for the people

who knew the Glass Site as home

Contents

Contents

List of Figures

Acknowledgments

My archaeological adventure with the Glass Site has hardly been a solitary undertaking, and the interactions I have had along the way with so many wonderful people have been tremendously rewarding. In the course of it all, I have many times been awed and embarrassed by demonstrations of generosity in its purest form. The kindness of people in South Georgia, especially, has taken my breath away. And everyone who has participated, whether for an hour or for years, has made a meaningful contribution of some kind. Absolutely nothing I have been able to find or learn archaeologically, or to put down in this book, would have been possible without that support. There is no way I can repay the debts that are owed, but perhaps the book will stand as one small reward beyond the feeble recognition I will muster here. And as is customary, I take ultimate responsibility for what has been done and what I have claimed.

I must first recognize the enduring support of Fernbank Museum of Natural History and the rich collaboration I have had with many of the staff there. The project began with the blessing of the museum, and my tie to Fernbank remains strong. The former president and CEO, Susan Neugent, deserves special thanks. She believed in what I wanted to do and persuaded many others that it was worthwhile. Other people formerly or still affiliated with Fernbank who also enriched the experience are Jennifer Grant-Warner, Chris Bean, Bobbi Hohmann, Wil Grewe-Mullins, Mike Brown, Hampton Morris, Mallory Costen, and Kathryn Ruedrich. I was also fortunate to receive grant support from the National Geographic Society when I was at the museum (NGS-CRE Grant No. 8765-10).

The project was extraordinarily fortunate to find its targets on the property of supportive landowners. Glass Land and Timber Company permitted the work at Coffee Bluff and the Glass Site and cheered us along every step of the way. I have special appreciation and affection for the late Pat (Glass) and Wilson Thorpe, and for Anne (Glass), Craig, and Andrew Hilliard. Jennifer Thorpe has only perpetuated the family's kindness. The company and the project were fortunate to have the steady guidance and input of the GLT manager, Kenny Powell. The Georgia Department of Natural Resources also allowed our work to expand to its holdings in Coffee County, and I am especially grateful for help with those arrangements from David Crass.

Equally meaningful was the opportunity the project afforded me to work closely with Frankie Snow. I, personally, and the project at large are better for it, and readers will recognize right away how central Frankie was to so much of what has happened. Frankie pioneered Big Bend archaeology, and I have the utmost respect for his tireless efforts to bring the region's story to the fore.

My local alma mater, South Georgia State College, was also enormously supportive. I especially want to single out the help I received from Virginia Carson, Jim Cottingham, Chris Trowell, and Amy Hancock.

I recognized long ago that my competences are limited, and to compensate I have relied on several fine archaeologist colleagues for expert help. Jeffrey Glover at Georgia State University applied his skill with total station mapping and GIS analysis, Spencer Barker showed us all what metal detecting can be, and Chet Walker brought his geophysical knowledge and skills to bear. Meg Gaillard served as project photographer in 2010. Staff with the Orianne Society, Mr. Wayne Taylor, Brannon Knight, and Jeff Brewer, mechanically cleared underbrush at the site, as did Jimmy and Terrence Slacks, who additionally operated a backhoe. Kate Singley worked her artifact conservation magic to ensure centuries-old metal will survive another few hundred years. Jakob Lyman and Rachael Vannatta prepared the maps for the book and Meredith Whitt and Kimberly Watters the illustrations. And I have my old friend Bill Walker to thank for making incisive editorial comments on an early draft.

Other professional or uniquely skilled colleagues have made critical contributions. They include Frank Lee, Brian and Danielle Floyd, Julian Williams, John Kantner, Don Thieme, Doug Tarver, Christine Neal, Bob Entorf, Dorothy Peteet, Frederick Rich, Melanie DeVore, Charles Lagoueyte, Keith Stephenson, Michael Robertson, Michael Forrester, Terri Lisman,

Robert DeVillar, Daniel Deacampo, Kathleen Deagan, Chester DePratter, Jim Legg, Clay Mathers, Jeff Mitchem, Donna Ruhl, Louie Harper, Marvin Smith, Ian Brown, and Gifford Waters.

Each season I worked alongside a field assistant charged with helping me handle logistics, technical details, crew training, and decision making. These vital project members carried much of the day-to-day load in the field. My special thanks is due to all of them: Brian Floyd, Irina Franklin, Caryn Lobdell, Erin Andrews, James Stewart, Inger Wood, Rachel Hensler, Wes Patterson, and Tyler Stumpf.

The field teams have consisted of professionals, students, public program participants, and volunteers. I will probably fail to recognize them all by name, but over the years they have included Tim Warnock, Tom McRae, Jack Kilgore, Furney Hemingway, Pat LoRusso, Doug Tarver, Dick Brunelle, Pennie Moses, Becky Mobley, John Perloff, David Kasriel, Rachel Vykukal, Chad Horton, Melanie Wing, Irene Frankofsky, Eugene Chapman, Leslie Perry, James Thomas, Meg Gaillard, Rachel Hensler, Chris Judge, Richard Moss, Amy Nash, Keith Bailey, Lilly Bakhtiari, Paniz Edjlali, Marissa Finnegan, Chris Glover, Crissey Phillips, Sally Phipps, Jenna Pirtle, Hazel Sanchez, Halley Stoutzenberger, Melissa Webb, Andrea Palmiotto, Kenneth McPherson, Kevin Kiernan, Russell Wright, Whitt Perrin-Wright, Tom McRae, Rick and Sonja Sellers, Dennis Karapov, Doug Walker, Gail Tarver, Scott Goodlow, Terry Hynes, David Noble, Andrew Carlin, Melissa Finnegan, Lyn Kirkland, Tom Peard, Leslie Perry, Crissey Phillips, Tony Fitzpatrick, Willard Andrews, Joel Jones, Tom McCrae, Missy Stedmen ,Candace Clark, Margaret Kilgore, Melissa Best, Brian Best, Elena Thompson, Laura Stults, Christine Turple, Susan Geoffrey, Christopher Azbell, Tobie King, Donna Beaver, Kathy Mills, John Mills, Bonnie Mills, Katherine Healan, Allen Vegotsky, Tyler Patterson, Julia Withers, Allison Bailey, Emily Detmer, Ashton Antinazi, Dustin Mullis, Bruce Defoor, Jamie Zimmer-Dauphne, Bobsie Turner, Bernard Huber, Nancy Robinson, John Perloff, Jeff Bragg, John Vaughn, Andrew Vaughn, and Bonnie Beck.

Conquistador's Wake

I

On a Mission

Nearly five hundred years ago, decades before Jamestown and Plymouth were even imagined, a foreign expeditionary force of hundreds, led by a seasoned conquistador, rammed through what is now Georgia on its way to an ignoble end. A thousand miles and several years away, the desperate and demoralized survivors would turn themselves over to the Mississippi, whose currents swept their makeshift flotilla into the Gulf of Mexico and eventual haven at Veracruz.

Originally, that expedition had found inspiration in the exploits of a young Spanish mercenary enticed by the possibilities of newfound continents (figure 1.1). A child of *la conquista*, the teenaged Hernando de Soto committed himself in 1514 to the New World, honing his soldierly skills throughout Central America before attracting the attention of Francisco Pizarro, conqueror of the great Incan empire. Having trained his sights on the Andean realm, Pizarro recruited the daring Soto in 1531 to his cadre of trusted officers. In that role the young adventurer did not disappoint.

More than once, outnumbered Spanish contingents led by Soto managed to prevail over throngs of Inca warriors. Choosing to capitulate in the face of repeated defeats, the Inca king, Atahualpa, received counsel from Soto, who had insinuated himself as a go-between to Pizarro. But in a sinister turn the king was murdered no sooner had he arranged to pack a large room in the Cuzco palace with gold and silver. Rewarded for his valiant service, Soto returned to Spain in 1536 with a generous cut of the treasure and to prospects of a courtly existence . . . at least for a while.

Restless and greedy to a fault, and perhaps deeply affected by his battlefield experiences, Soto could not resist the temptation of another campaign

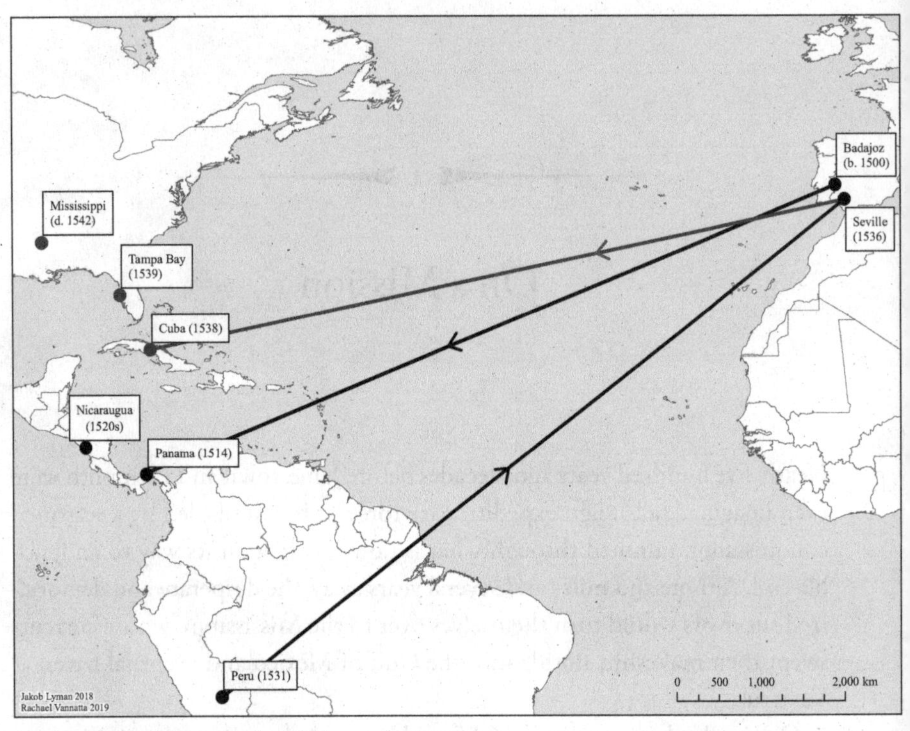

1.1 Biographical geography of Hernando de Soto

in the Americas. Rumors of Native riches in the northern continent were rife, and driven more by avarice than by facts, he pursued the prize he decided was waiting somewhere in the vast territory then known as La Florida and to us today as the southeastern United States. The Spanish royals approved his proposal for a Floridian *entrada* in 1537, conditioned on the terms that he fund it himself, turn over a fifth of any extracted wealth, and complete the exploration within four years. He was allowed a seventh share of any remaining spoils. In a stunning act of arrogance, he accepted the terms, no doubt buoyed by his prior record and the status conveyed by a new title, governor of Florida. Soto parlayed a personal fortune into ships and supplies and tempted a legion of would-be explorers to his scheme, and his ships carried an intimidating force to peninsular Florida, where it disembarked at Tampa Bay at the end of May in 1539.

Well aware of the tactical advantages that "shock and awe" afforded in the New World arena, Soto plunged into the interior of the Deep South backed by some six hundred men. They were an armored, clanking horde outfitted with swords, crossbows, lances, and rudimentary firearms called arquebuses, with many astride the 250-odd horses they had off-loaded. In the mix Soto included skilled tradespeople such as blacksmiths, farriers, and carpenters, along with the few assigned to official duties. And of course, they were all validated in principle and in spirit by the participation of no less than seven Catholic clerics.

The small army marched for more than three years on a circuitous path through the Southeast, making it as far north as Appalachia in today's North Carolina and Tennessee before heading southwest to reach as far as Texas (figure 1.2). Operating under a get-rich strategy requiring exploitation of indigenous people, Soto and his group were the first Europeans to make contact with dozens of native Indian groups, most of which were elements of sophisticated Mississippian cultures. Though the entrada's legacy is ugly, accounts of the expedition provide a glimpse of indigenous societies that is of inestimable value. As anthropologist Charles Hudson persuasively argued, getting the Soto story straight is as much or more about getting the pre-contact Native story right as it is about charting the prologue to our national narrative.[1]

Those events and Hudson's aims are the jumping-off points for this book. Truth be told, it was archaeological fates that forced me into the perpetual scholarly fray that surrounds Soto. It has been a task I ultimately owe to serendipitous discoveries near the Ocmulgee River in southern Georgia, and I've chosen to engage with it as much from a sense of obligation as from design.

But this should not be taken to mean that I have ever been ambivalent about the project. Historical clarity around the initial pass through Georgia of Soto's force has long been hobbled by uncertainties, created in no small part by a complete lack of compelling material evidence. How could a small army that tore through the southern half of the state for weeks be so hard to track? Challenges like this can keep an archaeologist up at night, but they are also the calls to action most of us live for.

Yet looking back, I could argue that this story is one of failure. Not because it ended badly, to be sure, but because some of my original questions are still left hanging. Thus I see added value in the story because it serves to convey how research really works. Yes, good scholarship begins with a good question,

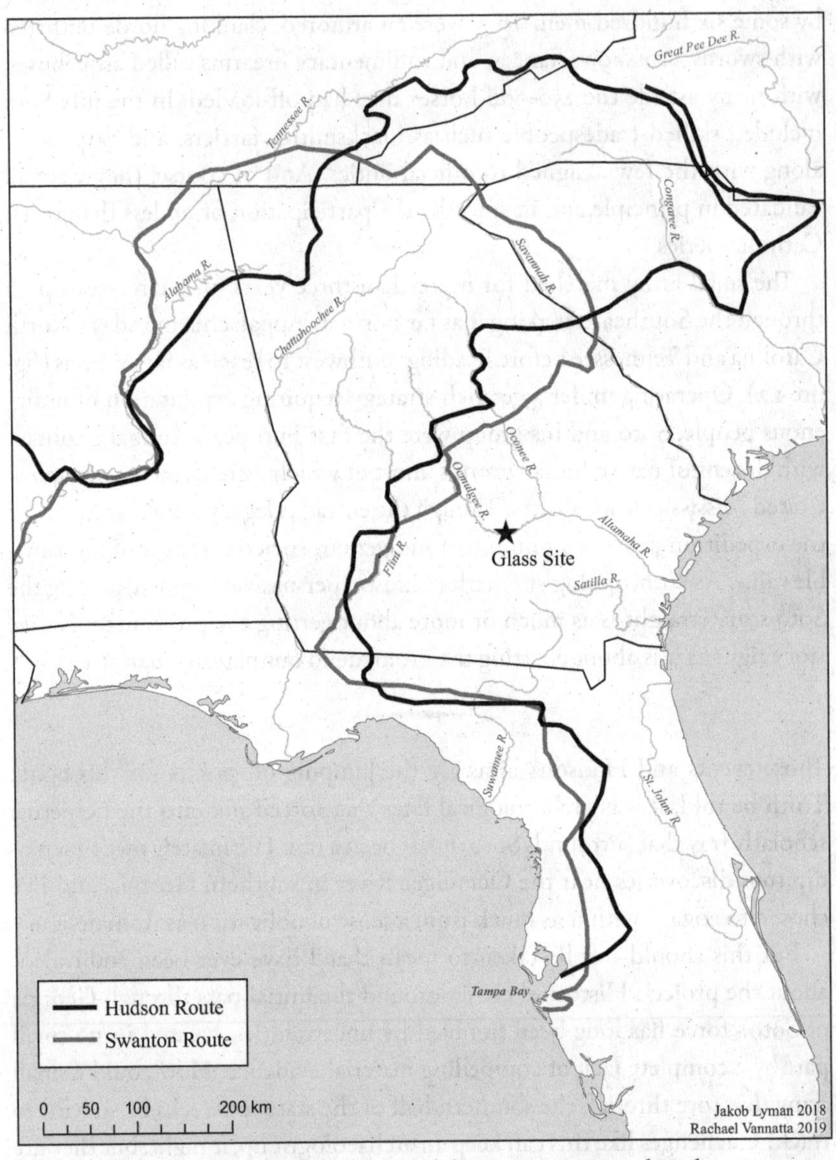

1.2 Projections of Hernando de Soto's path (after Swanton 1985 and Hudson 1997; only through Alabama)

and that I had. But pursuit of a good "problem" often leads down the proverbial rabbit hole where there exists a branching warren of possibilities. It was that kind of experience that caused me to abandon an original quest and to set off on a different archaeological journey that has run more than a decade.

This is also a story about the relationship of history and archaeology. Or, more to the point, what we do and can know about our past, and how we come to know it. Archaeological and historical sources both have their flaws, and although respective practitioners are painfully aware of the shortcomings, tension can surround cherished views of which has primacy over the other. It is a dangerous conceit to be dismissive of one or the other sources of information, and with this case I aim to demonstrate how it is better to fuse documentary clues with those that come from the ground.

I also demonstrate with this example that "history" is not fully set down. It is something best appreciated in the active voice. That history will forever be a work in progress seems universally unappreciated. Much of the time I sense a confidence that we've got the story in the bag, that we know now all that we'll ever know—or can know—about local, regional, and national events, or at least all that matters. Certainly there's a powerful, common narrative at work that implies that kind of closure. But most of the time, the prevailing story line hangs only on a framework, and it is tainted by a range of mythic portrayals. In practice, the framework lends sufficient structure for telling a compelling story, but yawning chinks in it give huge license for interpretation. My concern is to bring new precision to a sliver of the historical record, to shore up the scaffolding, namely, in the shadowy era of initial exploration and colonization in the southeastern United States.

We can also be deceived by the way the popular narrative of national history assigns huge emphasis to just a small number of locations. Think Plymouth and Jamestown, Boston and Philadelphia, the Alamo and San Francisco, and so on. Lost in the condensed tellings are pivotal events, many with long trajectories that played out elsewhere, in places today we want to view as inconsequential at best and backward at worst. It is exactly in those less familiar places that so much of the Spanish colonial story of the Deep South, along the "borderlands," unfolded. So, yes, this is an explicit attempt to balance the telling of history, even if it serves as only a fleeting reminder. I want us to acknowledge that history is where you find it and not only where you make it. And this includes South Georgia.

So what is the crux of my story? It began as a search for one of the most obscure of all Spanish Catholic missions, dating to the early 1600s, in what today is one of the most obscure corners of Georgia. It resulted not in a celebration of a mission's relocation but in the opportune discovery of some of the most elusive archaeological evidence there is, the calling cards of the infamous conquistador, Hernando de Soto, who meandered through the region a century before the mission was established. Still, I cannot claim, even after a decade of intensive study, that full closure has been achieved. Numerous questions linger. But such is the nature of this kind of endeavor, and a time comes when the obligation to share results outweighs an interest in getting every detail right. Historical investigations will almost always amount to works in progress, but the operative word is *progress*, and what follows is a kind of interim report that helps move the historical ball, just a bit.[2]

II

Possessed by Passions

My hunt for the mission was sparked long before 2005, but I'll begin the account of it with events during and around that year. About the time I was beginning to feel settled in a new role as director of archaeology at Shirley Plantation in Virginia, I received an inquiry from old colleagues about my interest in a job in Atlanta. It involved curation of one of the most important archaeological collections in the Southeast, at Fernbank Museum of Natural History, where it had recently been transferred. The prospect was hugely attractive on both personal and professional levels. Intellectually, the stature of the collection was a draw. It was the outcome of standard-setting research, and it had become deeply influential to our understanding of the Spanish mission period, not to mention millennia of Native development preceding it. I relished the opportunity to secure the collection's future and publically tell its story. The work would carry extra meaning because I had the fortune of working on the St. Catherines Island project in its first decade, during the early 1980s, helping excavate and document some of the evidence shipped to Fernbank in hundreds of boxes. But perhaps best of all, the job would bring me back to my archaeological home, Georgia. I eagerly accepted the position.

Although I am native to South Carolina, and it was there that my archaeological predispositions were first nourished, I learned to be an archaeologist in neighboring Georgia. My family moved in 1975, when I was a junior in high school, from the red clay hills of the Carolina Piedmont to the small and languorous hamlet of Alma in the southeastern corner of the state (figure 2.1). It is a chunk of the world that even to Georgians is akin to the Outback. The compact town grid consisted of as many unpaved as paved streets, and a

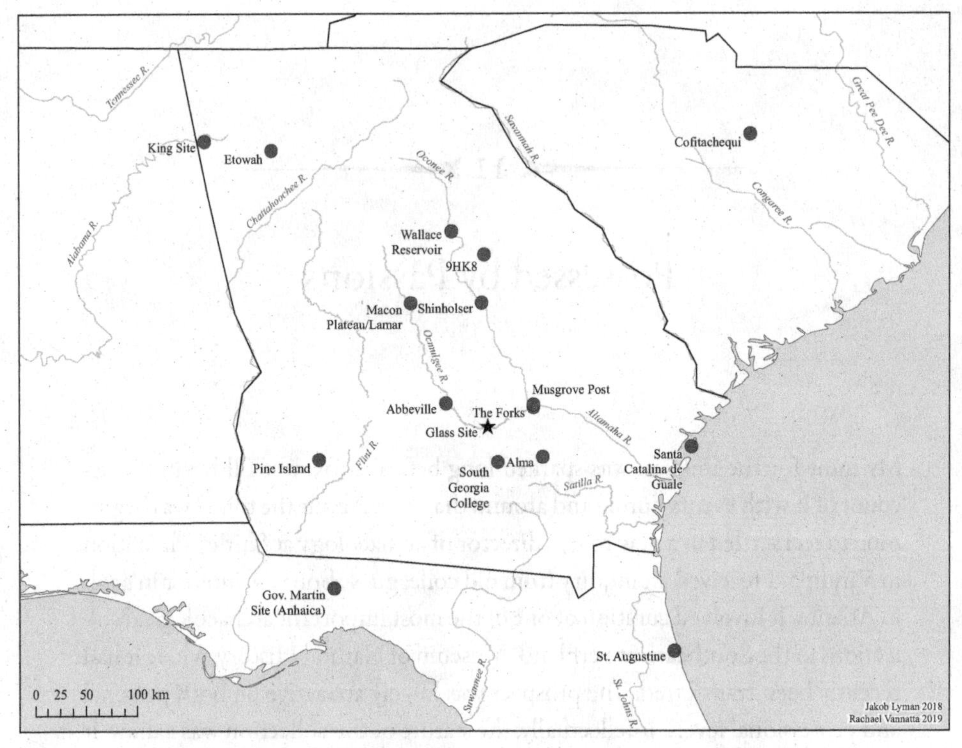

2.1 Map of key places mentioned in the text

principal landmark was a single traffic signal that could do nothing but blink. A hundred years ago Alma had been whittled out of the monotonous "pine barrens" as a railroad stop, but today, like so many places in South Georgia, it is losing as many people as it attracts.

Much about my relocation to Alma was challenging, especially at that age, but the move also allowed me to dedicate myself to a preoccupation, archaeology. Enjoying a certain anonymity, I could devote more time than ever to it without the risk of neglecting lifelong buddies. Almost daily I would disappear into books or the countryside where I considered the real action to be. That was plenty satisfying to a point, but I was starved for more. Local libraries didn't offer much, friends with the same intense interest were nonexistent, and opportunities for organized pursuits were unheard of. Yet almost miraculously, chances to feed my appetite eventually presented themselves.

Small towns being what they are, word got around of my unusual interests. My brother's middle school teacher, Tim Warnock, sent notice that he was curious about what I had begun to discover since he, too, harbored curiosity about local history and archaeology. Once we connected, Tim would orchestrate excursions to seek out new archaeological sites. Usually in the company of his students, he and I would organize outings, taking advantage of his intimate knowledge of people and geography and my growing "expertise" in local prehistory. For me, those expeditions were everything, cruising the backside of southeastern Georgia in his old Datsun wagon looking for cool stuff. Fortunately, Tim was natural educator enough, and worldly enough, to take an interest in my direction. A veteran of Vietnam and the Peace Corps, and a graduate-degree holder, he was the perfect mentor for ambitious but unworldly me.

My circle of South Georgia archaeological acquaintances soon widened to include Chris Trowell and Frankie Snow, who lived in nearby Douglas. Tim had heard of those two and their more sophisticated archaeological sleuthing, and he arranged for us to meet with them at South Georgia College, where Chris was a professor. I remember that first meeting very well and the two things I learned from it: I really didn't know very much, and the archaeology of the area was far more interesting than I had ever imagined. Within minutes my head was vibrating from their tales of recording sites by the hundreds, some with spectacular evidence of Native prehistory, and also from the pile of academic literature they had laid out. It was a rapturous moment. Better still, Chris and Frankie encouraged me to continue my separate explorations. It was like lighting a fuse. Those two saw a lot of me after that, and still today they are friends and respected mentors.

Shortly thereafter I graduated from Bacon County High School and with guidance from Tim Warnock committed myself to college-level study of archaeology. Perhaps he saw in me some aptitude for it, but at the very least he got that archaeology was my obsession. University schooling, he argued, would likely be miserable unless I was pursuing something relevant on a personal level, and it was also obvious the training would be essential if I had any chance of a career in the field. My parents could understand that too and didn't resist the plan, but they were somewhat dubious of my chances of success. Because I had not been a stellar high school student and because our family couldn't boast of university graduates, they believed I would do better to study a trade. So out of convenience and to keep down costs, it was decided I would launch my uncertain college career at, no surprise, South Georgia College. It was only a half hour's drive away across the flatwoods, and as a commuter student, I could find work in Alma—and continue my local explorations. I passed the trial enrollment by excelling in my first term at South Georgia. As a Dean's List student I demonstrated to everyone, not least of all myself, that I just might have had what it took to get where I wanted to go. And that confidence boost was really the key, another nudge toward the life I was determined to have.

South Georgia College had no courses specifically in anthropology or archaeology, much less a program devoted to them, and it was at lunchtime rather than class time that I learned the most about those subjects. My pattern for much of the two years I attended was to wander around midday to the dining hall, where Chris Trowell would frequently join me. I had never enjoyed quality time with an academic before, and it was during our chats that the ins and outs of a scholarly existence were laid out. In fact, one of the most terrifying, yet also satisfying, experiences was his mandate that I present a scholarly paper and then publish it, based on the results of my local studies. Sure enough, I did so in 1979 and now see to it that the same advice is issued to my own promising students.

But the only script to those dining-hall conversations was mutual interests, and most of the time I was content simply to listen to the stories. It was somewhere in Chris's meandering downloads that I learned of the Spanish mission called Santa Isabel de Utinahica. It was mentioned more or less in the same breath as a trading fort near The Forks operated by none other than Mary Musgrove, the Creek Indian "queen."[1] This was all of great interest because by that point my archaeological radius beyond Alma had reached the Altamaha River, about forty-five minutes north. The Altamaha is an area rich in archaeological sites, many of which were made visible for the first time by rapacious logging and pine-tree planting. The Forks marks the confluence of the Oconee and the Ocmulgee Rivers that forms the Altamaha, and because the Altamaha is a major artery to the coast, it had for thousands of years served as a corridor of travel to and from the interior. This gave The Forks great strategic importance as the gateway to even deeper interior travel. It was no accident then that a seventeenth-century Spanish mission and the eighteenth-century trading fort were both sited there. At every opportunity I would point my banana pudding–colored '62 Chevy pickup in that direction to see what I could find.

I didn't get much specific information about the Spanish mission in those days because, especially then, there was precious little known about it. But the idea that the site of a Spanish outpost ever existed in my effective backyard was unforgettable. I didn't devote much effort to finding it, however. The tale had an almost mythical quality to it that made it seem foolish to pursue. Relocating mounds plundered by C. B. Moore at the turn of the century proved more fruitful.[2] But there it was, the germ of an idea that took thirty years to fully develop.

The 1970s were an interesting time in Georgia archaeology, as they were nationwide. A new generation of archaeologists, encouraged by new paradigms and new federal historic preservation laws, were enjoying a burst of research not seen since the New Deal projects of the 1930s.[3] Also, what was and still is the most influential Spanish mission project was launched at that time on privately owned St. Catherines Island. David Hurst Thomas, under the auspices of the American Museum of Natural History, began a decades-long, comprehensive investigation of the Eden-like barrier island.[4] By 1981 he and his Big Apple team had succeeded in pinpointing the location of Santa Catalina de Guale, a mission site that had eluded the searches of others. Not many of us in southern Georgia knew quite what to make of the Yankee posse, but we learned quickly enough that the brand of archaeology being practiced on that inaccessible island was something special. In the meantime there was also work under way at the now famous King Site in mountainous northwestern Georgia, a place where unequivocal evidence of contact between exploring Spanish and Native people occurred in the sixteenth century.[5]

During that era of exciting new work, much of it intersecting the Spanish story, I completed an associate's degree at South Georgia College and transferred to the University of Georgia. In the fall of 1978, when I started at UGA, Charles Hudson had dedicated himself to a fresh look at the Hernando de Soto entrada, supported by a pair of stellar graduate students, Marvin Smith and Chester DePratter. Hudson was just coming off publication of his now-classic *The Southeastern Indians*, and it was thrill enough to share some of the same air with him. But it was doubly exciting to be around the anthropology department in Baldwin Hall and witness, even from a distance, trench-level scholarship. The deliberations about Soto's path and the evidence for it often infused classroom discussions, not to mention chats in the corridors and after hours. So by osmosis and through lectures, I became conversant in Georgia's early Spanish story.

In the meantime I was still in regular contact with Chris Trowell. He knew by then that I was in archaeology for the long haul, and as usual made sure my eyes were open and my feet were on the ground. Chris is honest and direct if nothing else, and at some point during my UGA stint he explained, "This BA in anthropology you're about to receive, and a dime, won't get you anything but a phone call." Gulp. "So if you're serious about all this you had best make up your mind right now to go to graduate school." Gulp. But any anxiety I harbored was again smothered by my determination, and I was more excited to act on his advice than not.

Suffice it to say, I went on to complete my master's degree at Brown University in 1983. There my focus was not at all on Spanish-era archaeology but on prehistoric Native cultures, and particularly what we could learn from their stone tools. I had wanted to do something completely new, and while I was not uninterested in the Spanish topic, it seemed to me it was already in good hands. Time in the Northeast became another formative period in my development, in large measure because of the strong influence of my advisor at Brown, Richard Gould. It also exposed me to new people and possibilities, not to mention supplied a new credential. But what didn't change was my unshakable interest in southeastern archaeology. I was perfectly content to take all that I had learned in New England and practice it back home.

Case in point, a fellow Brown graduate student, Steve Mrozowski, managed to get a small grant from the American Museum of Natural History for his own research on parasites in privies. In talking about the AMNH program, he reminded me of its project on St. Catherines. I wanted to be a part of that work, made the necessary contacts, and was selected for the fall 1983 field crew. What a marvelous experience it was. First of all, the team operated an uptown field camp if I ever saw one: a menu that included leg of lamb, fresh artichokes, and high-dollar ice cream, and accommodations in nicely renovated, tabby slave quarters. New Yorkers in Georgia—a brave new world for me. And the archaeology was equally marvelous. Our focus was the newly discovered Santa Catalina mission site and the three buildings that made up its religious compound, the church, the friary, and the kitchen. I spent most of my time at the *convento* and the kitchen, documenting enthralling evidence of intimate interaction during the seventeenth century between a handful of Franciscan missionaries and an entire Native community. In the process I even excavated one of the most evocative pieces of the evidence, a fragment of a bronze bell bearing the image of the Madonna.

Yet following those weeks on the island my career developed along a very different path. Over the course of twenty years, I found fulfillment in the world of "compliance" archaeology, practicing it with private consulting firms, at the Center for Archaeological Investigations at Southern Illinois University, and then from 1989 to 2005 co-directing and directing the Center for Archaeological Research at the College of William & Mary. It was immediately after my long spell at William & Mary, having taken on a new program at Shirley Plantation, that St. Catherines Island returned to my life.

All those seemingly disconnected experiences culminated in my unplanned—and still ongoing—search for a Spanish mission. It's the sort of outcome some would describe as destiny. I don't know if that's the appropriate term for it, but I appreciate in retrospect that, even personally, history matters. We, as individuals, are the product of experiences, direct and indirect, that steer us in certain directions.

III

Never Say Never

As I've mentioned already, my deliberate search for the ephemeral Catholic mission known as Santa Isabel de Utinahica didn't begin until 2005. When I joined its staff, Fernbank renewed a program of archaeological research, and the mission initiative was central to it. I argued that discovery of Santa Isabel would provide an important complement to the story of Mission Santa Catalina that the museum planned to tell with its newly acquired collection. I also conceived of the Santa Isabel search as a context for a new public archaeology program that would enhance the educational dimension of the museum. And, all the better, it would satisfy my abiding curiosity about a quasi-mythical place I had been introduced to long before in a college dining hall.

In its day Santa Isabel de Utinahica was everything that Santa Catalina de Guale was not. That, for me, is what made it an appealing subject. Santa Isabel was the most remote of all the forty-odd religious outposts in the La Florida mission system of the seventeenth century. Established, as we are led to believe, at or near The Forks, it was the northernmost and interior-most unit in the system, standing literally at the frontier of the frontier. Santa Catalina, by contrast, was located in the mainstream of the system, perched at the coastline only a short sail from the capital of St. Augustine. It was, by all accounts, among the richest, if not *the* richest, of all the region's missions. Santa Isabel was short-lived and perhaps only intermittently staffed at that. It just might have been the poorest of all the missions. Hazy accounts of it indicate a lifespan of only a few decades, roughly between 1610 and 1640. Santa Catalina was unusually long-lived, having been scouted as early as the 1580s and persistent through most of the seventeenth century.[1]

Those realities of Santa Isabel's existence translate, archaeologically speaking, into a serious challenge. No maps even approximate its location, and surviving written descriptions of its whereabouts are vague in the extreme.[2] Some of the best clues come from an account of a *visitation* undertaken by Fray Luis Geronimo de Ore in 1616, the purpose of which was to take stock of conditions at numerous missions in what is now Florida and Georgia (figure 3.1).[3]

The mission's relatively brief history is another hindrance to discovery. Duration often translates into visibility: the longer an occupation the greater the opportunity to litter. Moreover, a poorly supplied mission outpost, occupied by a single Franciscan friar, was the epitome of impoverishment. Even after years, a European living under those conditions, disconnected most of the time from peers, would leave paltry material evidence—things that would survive for an archaeologist to discover.

Because those limitations apply in differing degrees to most former mission locations, a standard archaeological strategy has evolved for finding them, pioneered in part by Dave Thomas's Santa Catalina search.[4] Much of the time the very first step involves paper documents. If you don't know it already, archaeologists are not at all averse to research that takes them indoors—into libraries, archives, and the like. Better still, they collaborate with skilled historical researchers. Intensive documentary research is an essential aspect of "historical archaeology," the branch of the discipline concerned with places occupied when Europeans were making records of them. Fortunately, the Spanish were usually fastidious about it. So in the case of a mission search, part of the job is to ferret out all the original information about the place that you can reasonably find. Almost always the records fall short of what you want them to be, frequently lacking maps, good descriptions of landmarks, and so on, but they will often narrow the field of possible locations, if only down to tens of square miles.

The second element of the strategy is to find an appropriate Indian settlement. Missions were always established within or very close to Indian communities, and it is far easier to find evidence of an intensively occupied Indian town than debris generated by one or just a few poor churchmen. The key is to understand what Native artifacts of the late prehistoric era, or early "contact" era, look like. If you can find a place with appreciable amounts of Indian pottery that was made in the style unique to the 1600s, in the area you believe the mission was established, it becomes the obvious starting point of the search unless you already have Spanish artifacts to work from.

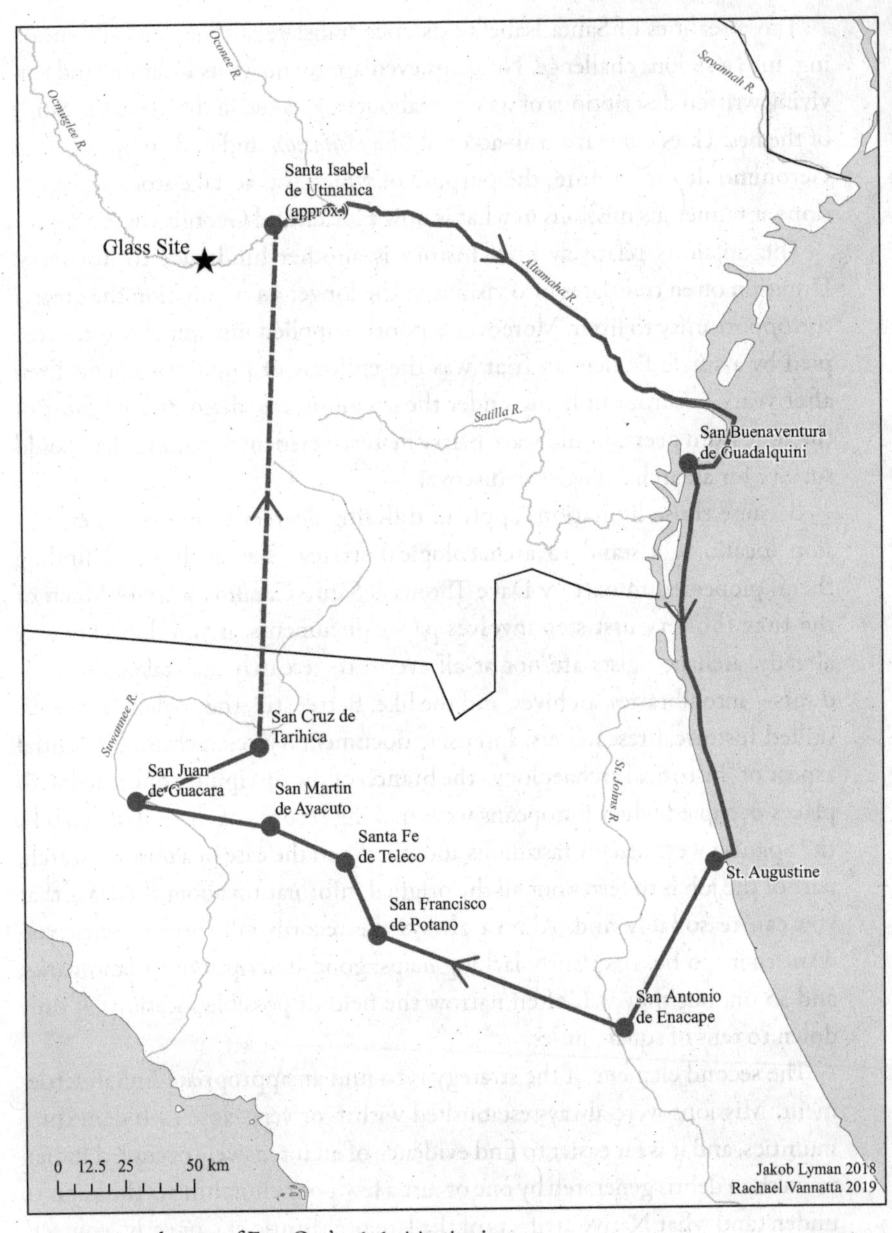

3.1 Estimated route of Fray Ore's 1616 *visitation* journey

The third aspect of the strategy is purely archaeological, and it means taking into account accumulated field experience. For example, the outcomes of successful mission searches elsewhere in La Florida teach that mission compounds were created in accordance with an idealized model. The three essential buildings were a church (*iglesia*), a friar's residence (*convento*), and a kitchen (*cocina*), and they were arranged in a compact, orderly grouping with an orientation about forty-five degrees off true north-south. Very often one or more water wells were also present. Past fieldwork demonstrates, too, that the mission buildings were constructed in a hybrid, vernacular style, defined by rectangular European floor plans but assembled in the wattle and daub Indian fashion, their wood frames plastered over with local clay. Unlike more durable mission buildings in the West, such as in Arizona, New Mexico, and California, where today you can still worship inside a mud brick or stone church, the La Florida structures were thoroughly biodegradable—and flammable. As a result, no aboveground traces survive for us to admire. But armed with this basic design knowledge and appropriate archaeological methods, we can discover telltale signs that persist below ground. Specifically, a combination of high-tech geophysics and traditional excavation permits mission buildings to stand out against the background of Indian evidence.[5]

The tried and true three-pronged approach is precisely the one I adopted in the Santa Isabel search. Yet documentary sources barely murmur descriptions of where this mission was, what it looked like, and how it functioned. That's not to say that one day new and better records won't be discovered, but the diligent work of my predecessors still left little to work with beyond a box on a map that encompasses up to five hundred square miles around The Forks. Something more was necessary before a realistic hunt could be undertaken.

For that I plunged into step two of the strategy: find candidate Indian sites. On one hand, the area I was about to search was familiar, but on the other, I didn't have all the latest and best information to work from. I had been working and living outside Georgia for years at that point and knew there was strong likelihood of new and relevant discoveries over the last few decades. To get myself up to speed on the archaeological state of affairs, there was really only one credible source to consult: Frankie Snow.

I still put as much stock in Frankie's guidance as I had in the early years at South Georgia College. The man literally wrote the book on the archaeology of the lower Ocmulgee River—exactly where I was aiming to get to work.[6] Frankie is a formally trained scientist, in botany, and a brilliant observer. Those talents, combined with his predilection for local archaeology, made him an essential source. His writings are based on a literal lifetime of scouring the area for archaeological sites and drawn from the astonishingly detailed records of them he has captured in a series of journals. Although Frankie published a summary work in 1977, his studies continue unabated, and the body of data grows ever larger. With time he has emerged as the local sage for anyone who has stumbled across something he or she doesn't understand. He's constantly sought out by area residents to pass judgment on one discovery or another, be it a plant, an animal, or an artifact, and some turn out to be important. The Glass Site came to his attention by one such contact.

My immediate goal was to put together a short list of about a half-dozen sites that were the best-known candidates for the Santa Isabel location or at least one of the Indian villages affiliated with it. They would define the starting point of my mission search. Call them the low-hanging archaeological fruit. Working from Frankie's earlier reports, I could already see a couple of worthy candidates, but I called him and asked for fresh input. He proposed a list of six Indian sites, all within an area measuring closer to one hundred rather than five hundred square miles (figure 3.2). On four of them, probable mission-era artifacts had already been found among the Indian artifacts, things like glass "trade" beads and the occasional piece of foreign metal. Two of the stronger candidate sites proved to be a challenge to gain access to, but the others were on property, both state- and privately owned, that we were welcomed to search.

On that short list was the Glass Site, but Frankie had included it almost as an afterthought. It happened to exist on a large property with a more promising site called Coffee Bluff, where, in fact, the project was first started. The Glass Site had been reported to him by members of the local hunt club, and in typical fashion he paid a visit, made a small collection from the surface, and dutifully recorded it. By the time of that visit, he suspected that the site was probably related somehow to the occupation at Coffee Bluff. The Indian pottery at both places was of a very late date and perhaps overlapping with the Spanish period. But because no actual Spanish artifacts were then known from the Glass Site, it didn't compete with the places where they had been discovered previously. All to say, the site that became our eventual focus made

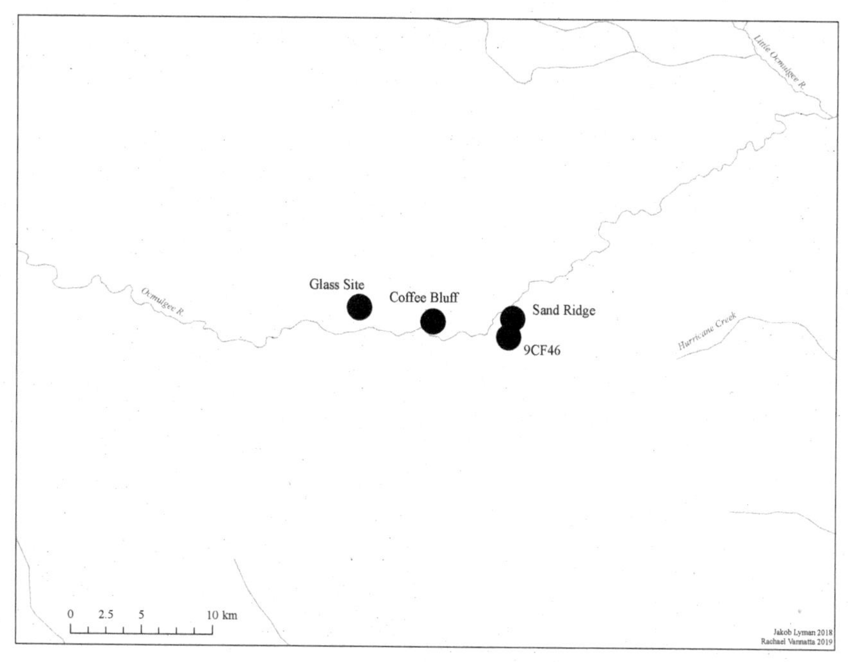

3.2 Project-related archaeological sites in the Ocmulgee Big Bend area

the original list almost out of convenience. We were already on the property to look at Coffee Bluff so why not consider Glass if we had the time?

You need to appreciate that putting a site on a wish list is one thing, but getting permission to do the archaeology is another. This is especially true of sites on private property. The sacred status we accord rights of ownership in this country, together with landowner paranoia about government overreach, often kills requests from archaeologists. Lots of doors get slammed in our faces; lots of phone calls are cut short. Many if not most of the rejections result from erroneous notions about the consequences of an archaeological discovery, that it would automatically translate into legal restrictions on the freedom to use a property. Truth is, this just isn't so. Our government strongly guards the rights of private property owners. Landowners literally possess the archaeology, the same as they would belowground mineral rights. The one exception is human burials; they *are* legally protected under almost any circumstance. So having suffered through plenty of negative encounters, I was not entirely sanguine about the prospects for gaining permission to work on all our candidate sites. But there was much to gain if we could arrange it.

Once again, Frankie's local connections proved to be critical. He knew the manager of the property on which Coffee Bluff and Glass were located. The two of them lived in the same town, Douglas, and they enjoyed a lifelong acquaintance. By that bridge I connected with the land manager, Kenny Powell, and he helped set up a meeting in Eastman with the property owners, Pat and Wilson Thorpe and Ann and Craig Hilliard. That in itself was major progress. I made the two-and-a-half-hour drive from Atlanta to Eastman one fall day in 2005, with my boss, Susan Neugent, director and CEO of Fernbank Museum of Natural History, and the chair of the museum's board of trustees, Hampton Morris. We wanted the Thorpes and the Hilliards to know that Fernbank was serious and appreciative.

Our meeting was in the small house on a side street that served as headquarters for Glass Land and Timber Company. Pine trees are still a principal money crop in this part of Georgia, and numerous business concerns, from local to international in scale, own enormous tracts for the purpose of growing and harvesting them. The Glass family enterprise was among the older of the local timber operations, having been founded by Albert Glass Sr. in the 1940s, then as much for turpentine as for wood. The company was now operated jointly by his three children, but they had transitioned to management of pine "plantations" for pulpwood. The tract we were interested in was located just east of the desolate old steamboat town of Jacksonville. It encompassed nearly four thousand acres and reached from the Ocmulgee River northward beyond the old "river road."

The tone and the outcome of the meeting exceeded my wildest expectations. In fact, I don't believe any of us wanted it to end. The Glass "girls," Pat and Ann, and their spouses, along with Kenny, were far more gracious than they had to be. But the best part of it was the enthusiasm. The idea of a Spanish mission site on *their* land was almost more than they could process, and by the time we parted ways, they were as determined as I was to find it. "What are we waiting for?" they declared. From the office we migrated to the main-street diner for a buffet lunch, and in spite of the cornbread, collards, and fried chicken, we managed to iron out details of our arrangement. It was an auspicious beginning.

Fieldwork began at Coffee Bluff on 15 April 2006. As the name implies, the site commands a view of the Ocmulgee River from atop a sheer, eroding bank on the outside of a looping meander. On the opposite side is a giant, shimmering sandbar. Mississippi and swallow-tailed kites seem ever present overhead. Regrettably it's the collapsing riverbank that captures your gaze after a while. Since Frankie first recorded this site in 1984, the riverbank has migrated some 20 m (65 ft), gobbling chunks of the old village as it moves. The river's appetite will not be sated, so capturing what we could of the vanishing archaeology was, alone, a strong motivation.

But as is true of most sites Frankie has recorded, this one was revealed to him by human rather than natural forces. Ramped-up commercial timber operations, beginning in the 1970s, had clear-cut vast swaths of native growth to replace it with ranks of loblolly or slash pines. The planted seedlings were modified genetically as fast-growing "supertrees," destined to become fodder for pulp and paper factories. Industrial-scale cutting and clearing precede an operation that, by turns, removes and burns stumps and "slash," usually in parallel rows up to a mile long, and then beds the soil with huge plows pulled behind bulldozers. Pine seedlings are then planted in the new beds. After they are grown and harvested, the process is repeated all over again. All that scraping and slicing and turning of the soil, often marking the first-ever mechanical alteration of the ground, has obvious bad effects on archaeological sites. But for Frankie it afforded an opportunity, imperfect as it was, to see and record an ancient cultural landscape that, arguably, would otherwise still be lost to us.

What Frankie observed on the scarified surface of that clear-cut area, just back from the river bluff on a hint of higher ground, was a semicircular spread of Indian artifacts, consisting mainly of the distinctive kind of pottery known to date late in prehistory and into the era of European contact. The pottery has been given the name Lamar, after a famous site upstream near Macon, and it signifies an entire culture that archaeologists have given the same name.[7] Made and decorated in unique ways, varieties of it can serve as a signpost for mission-period occupations. Across the scatter, artifacts were concentrated at five different places (figure 3.3). These "midden" patches stood out against the brown, sticky floodplain soil, not only because of the unusually high density of pottery in them but also because of darker soil coloration and the inclusion

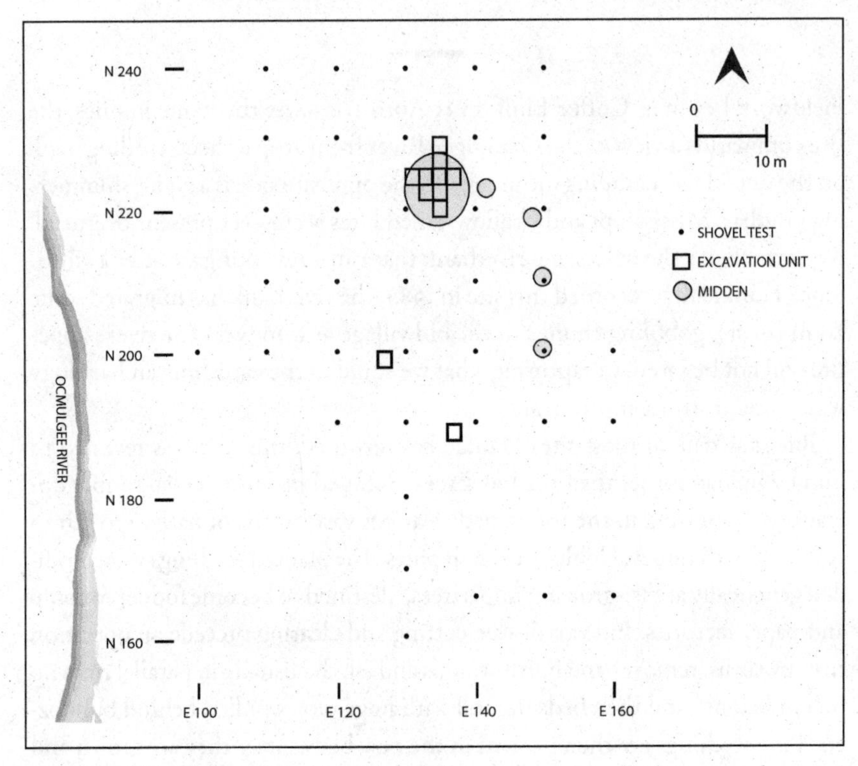

3.3 Coffee Bluff (9TF115) site plan. The midden patches originally documented by Frankie Snow are shown with gray shading.

of things like mussel shells that Indians had taken from the river for food. In effect, the surface evidence was revealing in fairly clear detail the configuration of an abandoned community, about a football field's length across, that just might have been visited by Spanish missionaries.

That possibility was underscored at Coffee Bluff by the discovery of a solitary artifact. In the course of collecting things in the new clear-cut, an acquaintance of Frankie picked up a two-inch-square fragment of Spanish majolica in the heart of one of the midden patches. Majolica was the Spanish cousin of delft-type ceramic ware, and it was made in a range of distinctive types, usually identifiable by painted decoration. But this piece is perfectly plain, and while it did confirm suspicions of a Spanish presence in the area, it was impossible to carry the inference any further. The chances of narrowing the timing of the Spanish-Indian interaction at Coffee Bluff, based on this one piece, is next to zero. The best estimate would be sometime between about 1525 and 1640.

When I started the new round of investigation at Coffee Bluff twenty years later, Frankie's prior observations were of obvious value. At the same time, I didn't want to presume we understood all the parameters of the site. My strategy called, first, for a round of systematic shovel testing to confirm, or not, the original sense of its extent, depth, and condition. Our results, by then obtained in the midst of picket-like lines of planted pine trees, generally duplicated Frankie's. With that, the next phase of work entailed closer investigation of a few of the artifact hotspots, presumably marking points of relatively intensive activity such as around dwellings.

Surely it's no mystery why the midden area where the Spanish majolica was found became a major focus of the follow-up study. My research questions all surrounded the story of Mission Santa Isabel, and the proverbial smoking guns that could verify its existence would be more Spanish artifacts. In the course of three weeks that first season, during which forty-two small tests and four larger units were opened, not another hint of Spanish presence was recovered. Plenty of mission-era Indian artifacts filled our bags, but nothing made in Europe at about the same time joined them.

Still, I elected to return for a second season at Coffee Bluff in 2008. On the positive side, the area called Midden 1, where the majolica had turned up, appeared as if it had been created just off the slope of a low, artificial mound. Such a feature could have been constructed during the occupation to support a dwelling, and I wanted to know if this was the case. I was also exasperated. I just couldn't accept the idea that a single fragment of majolica bowl was the sole trace of a Spanish presence on the site. How could a vessel like that break without leaving conjoining fragments, or how could it exist without other companion things of European origin? Perhaps with more excavation our luck would change.

Once again, we reaped new information about the Indian community, but seven more carefully controlled excavation units, plus additional shovel tests, had produced nothing in the way of mission-related artifacts. Ultimately, we could not confirm the presence of a low mound, but there was plenty of evidence to indicate that the midden was associated with an Indian-built structure. Concentrations of clay daub, broken pottery, and isolated lenses of midden were all common on the suspicious bump out there in the floodplain. Yet to this day, the lack of other Spanish artifacts at Coffee Bluff confounds me.

It was disappointment in the first season's results at Coffee Bluff that led us to begin work at the Glass Site. The plan I had defined for sites on the list involved subjecting them all, over multiple seasons, to a similar level of investigation. Ideally, we would complete a basic evaluation of two places each year. Having nothing new, at least in the way of mission artifacts, to show for the effort at Coffee Bluff, and because it was on the same property where we had enthusiastic landowner support, I shifted the operation about two and a half miles to Glass. Frankly, I was not terribly enthusiastic about our odds, given the limited information we had to go on, but it was a convenient option and useful to fulfill the two-sites-a-season research quota.

My first visit to the Glass Site had been during the previous winter in the company of Frankie and Kenny. It occupies a fairly nondescript patch of South Georgia country. In fact, the better description then was probably scruffy. About five years prior, this area, too, had been clear cut. Native bottomland hardwoods were harvested to make way for a market-worthy crop of pine trees. This meant we arrived to glare at the weeds and whippy saplings that had voluntarily sprung up in the clearing. A tangle of brush, about as tall as the young pines, had overtaken the clearing where hunters, and then Frankie, had once seen an abundance of Indian artifacts on the surface. The day of my visit it was hard to see bare ground at all. But it was telling of the site's potential that pieces of pottery and other artifacts could still be spied even on the floor of the thicket. That kind of sign would persist only where there had been an intensively occupied Indian settlement.

Based on Frankie's recollections of the original surface evidence, the patchy observations made the day of our visit, and the results from a few preliminary shovel tests, we chose to lay out a line of five 1 x 2 m test units in a part of the site that seemed to hold particular promise (figure 3.4). It was a place where artifacts seemed to be concentrated and, here and there in the furrows created by the giant bedding plow, were exposures of a fine gray ashy residue, not to mention a few pieces of animal bone. Admittedly, we made an educated guess about where to begin because we needed and wanted to gain a basic sense,

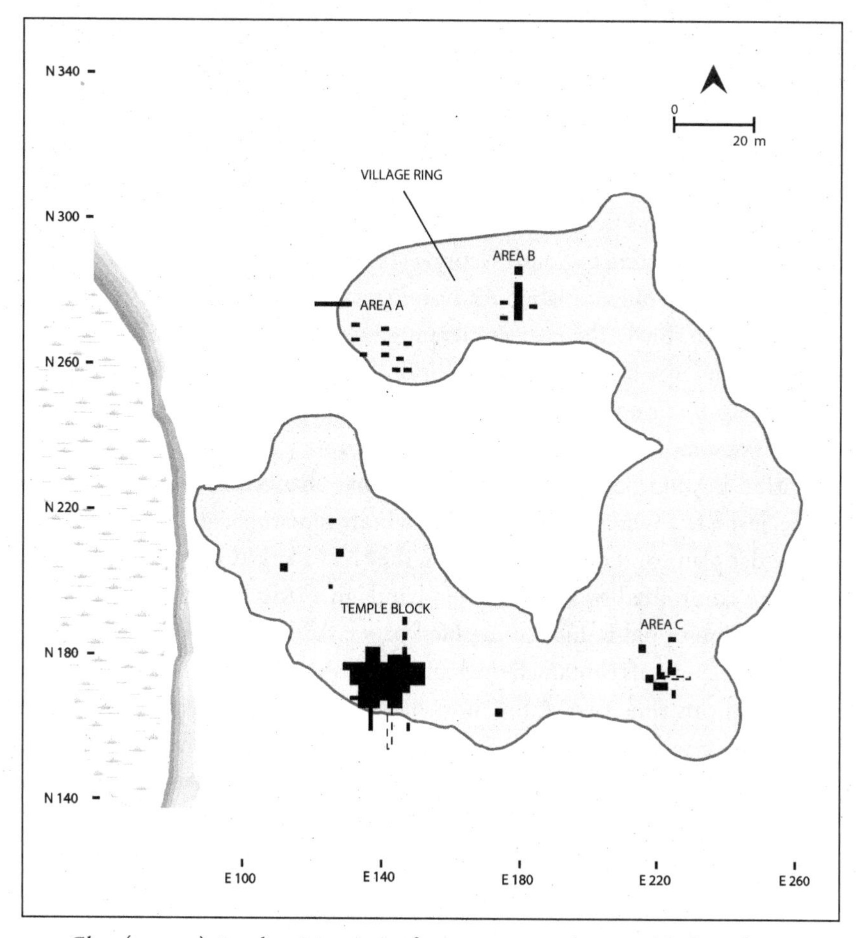

3.4 Glass (9TF145) site plan. Locations of excavations are shown in black, and the village ring, signified archaeologically by high artifact density, is depicted with gray shading.

sooner rather than later, of what the site was all about. We were trying to move beyond the disappointment of Coffee Bluff.

That initial excavation was organized as a discontinuous line of rectangular units spanning a total distance of 18 m. Imagine a broken trench running north to south. The project team, consisting of me and two paid assistants, eight adult students in our public archaeology program, and two local volunteers, was divided among the separate rectangles. Progress was slow. Archaeology is that way just about all the time, but more so in this case because we were committed to teaching our participants best archaeological practices. Good instruction is a methodically paced activity. Then there was the soil. Summer downpours had made it wet and sticky, especially in the humic, root-laden upper layers, and it resisted the eighth-inch mesh hardware cloth we use to capture artifacts in sifters. On top of all that, most of the people with me were simply not acclimated to South Georgia's humidity and heat, not to mention unused to steady physical labor. Archaeological excavation is hard work.

But ever so slowly the excavations progressed downward, and it soon became evident that belowground conditions in one unit were not necessarily the same as conditions in another unit. Toward the north units revealed deposits that were more or less natural; they showed no particular signs of human alteration beyond deposition of artifacts. That changed moving southward. There, just a few meters away, soils were wholly unnatural, and when exposed on the flat plane of the excavation floor, they had a kaleidoscopic appearance. We were confronted by finely swirled bands in shades of gray, resembling a sandy version of old-fashioned marbled paper. Adding to the intrigue, those strange-looking soils contained the highest numbers of artifacts.

Around this time two of the most memorable and portentous incidents of the entire project occurred. The first involved what at the time seemed to be an absurd question. It came from the late Julian Williams, one of the charter public program participants and a locally prominent amateur historian. His passion was the historical backdrop of the area we were working in, Jacksonville, Georgia, and its environs. He had even gone so far as to erect a series of homemade roadside markers in Jacksonville to commemorate various events and personalities. Much of his attention was given to the era of steamboat traffic up and down the Ocmulgee, but there was little else he had not contemplated and explored at one time or another, including the early Spanish period.

That backdrop was the impetus for the unforgettable question Julian put to me. Kneeling inside one of those first-excavated rectangles, sweating profusely and happy about it, he looked up and in all sincerity asked, "Do you think we'll find evidence of Hernando de Soto here?" My reaction was a polite but rather dismissive chuckle followed by something like, "I seriously doubt it, and here's why . . . ," at which point I proceeded to parrot the Soto narrative I had learned from Charles Hudson, Marvin Smith, and Chester DePratter.[8]

Those three had steered conventional thinking to put Soto's crossing of the Ocmulgee some eighty miles upstream from us at Macon. Their estimation revised the 1939 proposal of John Swanton's Smithsonian team that had put the crossing near Abbeville, another old river town just twenty-five miles north of Jacksonville.[9] Like most of my peers, I had the utmost respect for Hudson's work and had no basis to challenge it. And the last thing I wanted or needed to do was plunge into the ever-contentious debate about Soto and his path. I had other fish to fry. It goes without saying that Julian was disappointed by my response, especially since one of his markers celebrated the first Christian baptism in Georgia, purportedly given to one of Soto's men very nearby.

Meanwhile, the painfully slow process of soil screening was getting to everyone. In a fit of frustration, one of my assistants, Caryn Lobdell, began to lobby plaintively for using water to expedite the sifting. It's a tried-and-true method, but at that point I had not invested in the usual equipment for doing so. We were still learning the local conditions, what worked well and what didn't. One complication was my insistence on using eighth-inch mesh hardware cloth instead of the usual quarter-inch mesh. The aim was to improve our chances of capturing small glass beads in the screens. European-made "trade" beads are often a sure sign of Spanish-Indian interaction, sometimes the only one we find, and the last thing I wanted was to miss them, even at the expense of rapid progress. But that smaller mesh was also easily choked with mud and debris.

I came around to the wisdom of some kind of improvised water screening system for all kinds of reasons. It would help morale, it might accelerate our progress, and it would probably improve our ability to see things like beads during the sifting process. The simplest and quickest option was to stockpile the excavated soil in large buckets and haul it in a pickup truck to the pole barn at our headquarters, where there was running water. So all the sifting screens were moved up the road, and bucket by bucket, all the excavated soil was hosed through the fine screen. The boost to efficiency and quality of life was immediate.

The next week of the program was reserved for a group of high school students, mostly from the Atlanta area. I was especially enthusiastic about this crowd since, as I had, they were professing interest in archaeology at an early age. I liked the idea of providing them an opportunity I had never been given. Otherwise the routine they followed was no different from that of the adults.

After some basic orientation, the kids plunged headlong into excavation and, too, for the first sustained spell, the regimen of water screening. It was in the process of "washing dirt" that a second epic moment occurred.

For perspective, try to understand that there's much about fieldwork that can become a dull routine if you aren't completely into the process, which is to say fully attentive in anticipation of an important discovery. It is akin to descriptions of military service: painfully boring most of the time but in spells punctuated by total exhilaration. In archaeology, the prospect of a thrill has to carry you. Likewise, a commitment to the overall quality of results, which depends enormously on the quality of observation, has to be sustained. Otherwise it's not archaeology anymore. This holds true whether you're troweling on hands and knees in the confines of a small excavation or hovering over a sifting screen. In fact, much of my time on a site is spent roving from unit to unit and screen to screen giving pep talks to help people hold their focus—for days at a time—in sweltering conditions and aggravated by swarms of gnats.

One day, well into that high school week, we were again up at the barn-turned-lab, water-screening another truckload of excavated soil. Several people were sieving, and I was by one of the sifters when a student at another beckoned me over. She was a shy young woman named Ellen Vaughn, attending the program with her father. Behind that personality, however, was serious intent to practice all the things we had been preaching. You somehow knew she was never asleep at the screen. But for her to invite attention was out of character, so the summons alone was intriguing. As I approached, she extended a closed hand and asked, "Is this anything?" at which point the fist unfurled to reveal a beautiful sight—a multicolored, European-made glass bead, no larger than a pea (figure 3.5).

Finally, there it was: the first concrete clue of a Spanish presence, damp and glistening red, white, and blue in the palm of a student who had no idea what she had found—but somehow did just the same. My knees almost buckled at the sight. While I grinned and shouted, she smiled. Pretty soon everyone else was laughing and hooting. The realization that our quest was not folly, after three weeks of toil, made us giddy. I recall asking her in the midst of the celebration, "Can I give you a hug?" True to form, she said, very politely, "No."

Ellen's find was exciting, but from the instant the bead was revealed, I simultaneously recognized it as something problematic. It was *too old* to be

3.5 Ellen Vaughn and the first bead from the Glass Site

associated with the Mission Santa Isabel de Utinahica. In technical bead-speak, it was a type called a faceted chevron, skillfully crafted, most likely at the famous and ancient glass-making center of Murano, Italy, with seven paper-thin layers in alternating colors (figure 3.6a). Colleagues like Marvin Smith had determined that, much of the time, they occurred in archaeological contexts in the Southeast dating before 1550. And by the time Mission Santa Isabel was established in the early 1600s, they were completely out of vogue, antiques that

3.6 The first Spanish-era artifacts from the Glass Site (2006): (a) faceted chevron bead and (b) iron celt (front and back views).

had been replaced by new and different styles of beads. True mission-related beads should not look like this one. At the seventeenth-century mission of Santa Catalina de Guale on the coast, for example, no specimen of this kind was found in a total bead sample of about seventy thousand.

By the same token, a sample of one is no basis to rush to judgment. Perhaps the bead was an heirloom carried over to a mission-related site under any number of circumstances. We know from other cases it could happen. But the provocative possibility remained: could Julian Williams have been right? My mind was awhirl with competing scenarios. We simply had to keep at it and see if additional evidence would clear up the picture.

Six weeks later our first field season was nearly concluded. Five units and twenty-eight shovel tests had been completed at the Glass Site, but no additional Spanish artifacts were recovered to go with the bead and copious amounts of Indian artifacts. I won't deny some disappointment. Once again, it just didn't make sense that an incident of Spanish interaction was limited to a solitary bead that we fortuitously happened to locate. Surely we wouldn't be resigned to the same result at Coffee Bluff—another one-find wonder.

The public part of the 2006 program came to an end, but I and two assistants were scheduled to remain for a few more days to close down the excavations and our camp. This meant double-checking records to be sure essential information was all collected, and the romantic tasks of backfilling units and cleaning and loading equipment. In the midst of it all, I still couldn't shake the sense that there *must* be more Spanish artifacts on the site, and probably in the area we had been working. I decided to try one more tactic before heading home: a metal detector sweep.

We all know that metal items would have been in Spanish baggage, whether weaponry carried by a band of would-be conquerors, or crucifixes and nails in the supplies of missionaries, but archaeologists have historically been reluctant to deploy the device best suited for finding such things. People like me so closely equate metal detectors with treasure hunters that we tend to keep our distance, sometimes to our own detriment. Not only did I harbor those same misgivings, I neither had a detector nor appreciable experience with one. I concluded anyway that there might be much to gain in the face of dwindling time.

I don't recall how, but I knew Kenny Powell owned a detector and he agreed to let us borrow it. Not entirely sure of what I was doing but in reasonable archaeological fashion, I began a slow and systematic search of the area surrounding our five test units. Right away I began to get a few hits, and after ten to fifteen minutes we had flagged a half-dozen or so targets in an area of about 10 x 10 m. But the machine couldn't tell us what they were, relatively recent castoffs like shotgun shells or Spanish artifacts? Sure enough, one of the first targets turned out to be a shotgun shell "hull," one was a tin can, and another was an old nail—but not old enough. Most of these essentially modern things were hiding, not surprisingly, just below the surface in a disturbed "plow zone."

But there was one hit not at all near the surface. Once we understood it lay somewhere below the zone of mixed, plowed soil, we became more cautious with our excavation. The idea was to identify the object without compromising good archaeological deposits, and this required work in a small but formal test. Within it, not far below the bottom of the plow zone, we began to see that crazy, swirly soil that had appeared in one of the nearby test units. I didn't yet know what that soil represented, but it was pretty clear that it was an interesting and unique archaeological deposit. Finally, at about 30 cm below the surface, at the time we began to wonder if there was anything there at all, the trowel scraped against iron. With a little careful work, it became clear that this was a substantial but narrow piece of metal embedded in the puzzling soil. Everything was indicating it was an early artifact, maybe something to go with that lonesome bead.

The excavation in our cramped, mini-unit turned out to be an hours-long process because we were determined not to bungle the job. In our business the mantra is, "context is everything," and it was critical to do our utmost to document with best practices any find of early Spanish material. Inevitably, reporting the discovery would invite close scrutiny—and a jury of archaeological peers is a tough audience. So everything about it was documented with copious photographs and written records.

Once we decided that this was something important, I called my boss, Susan Neugent, who I knew was somewhere en route to her hometown not far from nearby Douglas. Fortunately she was close, and we delayed final removal until she could be there to witness it. Susan arrived with a nephew of about ten years old, and they observed the process. The suspense was nearly unbearable when at last we freed the artifact from the ground. Though it was encrusted in brownish-orange corrosion the basic shape was clear enough (see Figure 3.6b). Like the moment I saw the bead, I knew right away that this, too, was something out of place on a mission. Yet it would have been right at home among the belongings of an exploring party—like Soto's. The find was a very simply made type of iron cutting blade, usually referred to by archaeologists as a rectangular celt. It was identical to examples from other sites believed to have Soto-era metal, such as the King Site near Rome in north Georgia.[10] Now we could suddenly begin to ask out loud: *do* we have a Soto site?

It was a heady way to close the season. The implications of the discovery were nearly too much to comprehend. In short order we had two artifacts from good archaeological context that were virtually screaming "Soto!" but they were on a site far off the most accepted line of his march out of Florida. Again, maybe Julian was the wise one after all, and perhaps we were also upholding an old, Smithsonian-commission estimation of the path, at least along this section of it. Two things were obvious, regardless. The first was that these discoveries were going to be contentious. The world of Soto scholarship is fraught territory in the best of times, and to introduce evidence that challenged the received wisdom would only invite intense scrutiny and very probably skepticism. The second was that I had an obligation to try to account for these discoveries even if it meant abandoning the search for Santa Isabel. There was just too much in play, and that awareness translated into a professional obligation to get the story right. There would be no looking back for another nine years.

By way of perspective, a story about our project in the *Atlanta Journal* gives a sense of the measured stance I had decided to take in public. The reporter, Mike Toner, visited us for a firsthand look at what was going on at Coffee Bluff and Glass. We had just discovered the bead, and I cautiously laid out for him some possible explanations. Here's how he conveyed my viewpoint:

> Blanton isn't discouraged that Fernbank's initial foray into archeological field work hasn't yet turned up conclusive evidence of the missing mission. But he says it has achieved its other objective—stirring public interest in Georgia archaeology. Even without finding the mission, Blanton says the richness of artifacts in what is clearly a substantial Indian settlement in Middle Georgia warrants continued archaeological study.[11]

IV

A Temple in the Pines

Spaniards, still more spectral than real, had begun to taunt us and the proper response could be no less sober minded or methodical. It required attention to both the Native American community that, fundamentally, is what the Glass Site represents, as well as the matter of a Spanish encounter. They were closely intertwined issues, but each called for a customized strategy.

It is hardly possible to overstate the stakes surrounding our discoveries, at least from a historical perspective. Seemingly, we were about to challenge facets of widely accepted wisdom concerning Soto's route. In the first place, documentation of multiple, substantial Indian communities, dating from very late in prehistory and into the earliest historical period, in the Big Bend section of the Ocmulgee, had not been at all foretold as we began. A view had prevailed for decades that the interior Coastal Plain, that swath of territory known as the pine barrens, was a naturally impoverished region forsaken by Native people for richer locales.[1] Before us, Frankie had documented ample evidence of an Indian presence, but his sense was that the occupations were modest if not somewhat intermittent. This was what I had learned and even observed myself, to the point that Charles Hudson went so far as to cite me on the matter as he and his team argued their shift of the Soto path farther away from the lower Ocmulgee.[2] Now that sustained communities of the Lamar culture, like Coffee Bluff and Glass, had been documented in the area, an abrupt recalibration of archaeological perspectives was in the offing. We were learning that more was going on down there in the sixteenth century, solely in Native terms, than anyone had imagined.

Then there was the controversial aspect of our Spanish finds. The process of *really* explaining them was daunting. Would it be possible for me to achieve any degree of certainty about who was responsible for introducing the bead and the iron tool to the world of the Glass Site's inhabitants? Would a plausible argument about Soto be accepted even if it were to emerge? Suffice it to say, persuasive answers to those and other questions were still a long way off—if they were ever discoverable. But I was all for trying.

The balance of the summer in 2006 was spent in the Fernbank archaeology lab processing and analyzing the season's findings. The upshot was affirmation that we must return soon to try to resolve the new questions. Colleagues at Fernbank shared the sense of urgency, and with their blessing I organized a fall-season expedition back to the Glass Site. I naively envisioned it as an archaeological surgical strike, a path to instant enlightenment. Technically, the objectives were to expand on the first five units to gain clarity about the nature of the complex deposits that were producing the artifacts, both Indian and Spanish. Then, ideally, we would recover conclusive indicators of an Indian-Spanish encounter and incontrovertible evidence to explain it.

At that early stage my decision making was not based on a great deal of information, and the situation brought to mind the parable of the blind man and the elephant. But one obvious starting point was where the summertime discoveries had been made. I chose to expand eastward from there with a small excavation block consisting of six bunched, 2 x 2 m units. The thinking was that a wide-area exposure would provide a basis for assessing the origin of the unusual, swirly deposits.

I was supported that fall almost entirely by a team of volunteers. The only paid assistant was Brian Floyd. The backbone of the group was a corps of stalwart helpers who had become indispensable to what I did at Fernbank, whether in the lab or in the field. Others included my old mentor, Tim Warnock.

The coin-toss decision about where next to excavate unfortunately led in a less-instructive direction. So it goes sometimes, but the results were useful in the sense that we learned where archaeological clarity would not be achieved. Eastward of those first five units, the deposits were either largely sterile or they consisted of the thinnest of midden deposits created by incidental disposal of debris by occupants of the Indian town.

However, near the western border of our excavation block, there was a subtle but abrupt change in the soil, marking a boundary between ordinary and complicated deposits. It looked as if the "normal" kind of deposits on the east side had been replaced or buried by soils that were different and perhaps wholly artificial. This was intriguing, but the true relationship of the normal versus abnormal strata was far from clear. The extra two weeks in the field still hadn't given us enough to work with.

A couple of points relevant to the matter of archaeological clarity bear some emphasis. First, the Glass Site's soil is naturally sandy. This is good and bad. On the upside it's a dream to excavate. Shovels and trowels slice right through it. On the downside sandy soils are notoriously poor for holding signs of past human activity. Because water percolates through them relatively rapidly, and because insects, rodents, and roots also readily move through them, sandy deposits are highly dynamic. This means that the all-important soil alterations left by people, such as postholes, storage pits, and even graves, become blended into the background soil. These kinds of clues in the soil—the things we call *features*—are every bit as important as objects, but seeing them in sand requires precise excavation and a keen eye. And it is one reason it took so long to get my arms around the details of the Glass Site.

The other complicating factor is an inherent but healthy archaeological conservatism. Not all of us operate with the same degree of caution, but the majority of archaeologists are very reluctant to make hurried interpretations. Almost to a fault, we avoid concluding anything until the meaning of evidence is painfully clear. This also helps explain why it took multiple seasons of work before any real interpretive breakthroughs occurred.

Nonetheless, the second session of fieldwork had two important outcomes. One was full appreciation of just how complicated the site was. There were stark differences across it, from side to side and up and down. Also, we had gained a better sense of where we needed to go next to connect some crucial dots. The next summer season couldn't come fast enough.

Our pattern in 2007 essentially duplicated that of the first year. The Glass Site could not be ignored, but a second site was also due for investigation. Recall we were still searching for a mission at this stage, so other places on that original short list needed equal attention. The next mission candidate, located on the opposite side of the river, was known simply as 9CF46.[3] It was another of Frankie's sites that had yielded Lamar culture pottery sherds when it was prepared for pine planting. Work at both places was undertaken in the summer, and in November and December an additional, more intensive round of excavation occurred at Glass.

The summer agenda at Glass, pursued once more as a public archaeology program, called for reversing direction. It was crucial to learn what the sharply defined soil boundary was indicating, principally what it would reveal about the Indian community. Naturally, we also wanted to recover more Spanish artifacts in definitive contexts. The season's strategy specifically called for westward expansion of the original block with another nine 2 x 2 m units.

If it was complexity we wanted, it was complexity we got. From the first hour, none of the soil we were excavating was "normal." Every bit of it bore evidence of human manipulation. Otherwise, nothing about its appearance and texture made good sense. I could see that the deposits were "cultural," but I couldn't yet explain how and why people had altered that spot. The challenge was not unwelcome though because the process of making sense of soilish nuance is something I savor.

I should explain here another complicating aspect of the site, this one created by the bedding process that prepares clear-cuts for tree planting. I've described already how giant bulldozer-drawn plows are used for this work. The implements are designed to simultaneously cut two deep furrows, about 2 m apart, with blades that direct overturned soil inward to create a raised bed. Seedling pines are planted down the center of the bed, where a narrow cutting blade has ripped a slot. In the end, the former forest floor is repetitiously lined by pairs of furrows separated by a central bed. The furrow-and-bed sets are spaced, centerline to centerline, every 4 to 5 m, across hundreds of acres at a time. Fortunately, the operation leaves a vestige of unmolested soil in a series of narrow, intermediate lanes. For archaeologists, this is a hugely mixed blessing. We cannot deny that without vast clear-cutting and bedding, people like Frankie would never be able to document so many archaeological sites, so thoroughly, and in so short a span of time. But on the downside the destruction it wreaks on pristine archaeological deposits is a nightmare.

The immediate headache this presented for our Glass Site excavations, and at Coffee Bluff for that matter, was the task of distinguishing bedded from unbedded soil. I wanted, in effect, to treat the two contexts differently. The uppermost soil turned into beds and later washed into furrows would be dutifully screened, every bit of it, but if we could learn to distinguish that churned-up material from what was still intact, we could aggressively rid areas of the compromised parts. There was minimal danger of missing clues in the blended soils, and we wanted to buy time to dwell on meaningful subtleties of intact layers.

After a season or two, I had seen enough of the contrast to explain the telltale distinctions to excavators. Or so I tried. Very quickly I learned that, for less experienced people, recognizing what was disturbed and what was undisturbed was about as clear as mud. As we shall see, reading the Glass Site soils, even the intact strata, never became easy, and at times I sensed whispers that I was practicing some kind of voodoo archaeology, seeing things that others couldn't.

Learning slowly what they should remove and record, the team members advanced the excavation outward and downward, ever so carefully. I would liken their process to peeling a misshapen onion. With each hour it became clearer that this part of the site had an intriguing story to tell, but it was captured in a sequence of thin, contorted layers. Archaeologists know that every unique layer is like a book chapter, existing apart to communicate an essential segment of a larger story. As far as I was concerned, Glass Site stratigraphy—its sequence of soil layers—was akin to the Rosetta Stone. We all felt pressure not to blunder.

I want to emphasize an important point before moving on to the "thin" part of the foregoing description. There is a common belief that archaeologists shovel away in massive excavations, tens of feet deep, that involve removal of thick and crisply defined strata. Sometimes we do, but not usually. At Glass, for example, we have documented ten thousand years of human activity within an archaeological package not more than waist deep. In the upper part, where the last Indian occupation was the most intensive, the remains consist, laterally, of discontinuous accumulations. Any separate part of them seldom exceeds 15 cm in thickness, and often it is closer to four. So at the conclusion of any season, you would see us operating in a hole that most of the time might be 60 cm deep.

True to character, two weeks of the summer program and many new units later, there was still a lot of head scratching going on—at least on my part. I was seeing the sequence of deposits, but I wasn't fully understanding it. And just as predictably, an epiphany struck in the calm after the frenzy of the public program, when I and a couple of assistants were reviewing results and preparing to close down.

Because distinctions in the Glass Site's sandy soils are rarely obvious, the fieldwork required tedious rounds of surgical troweling. This is a hands-and-knees kind of activity, and in the size excavation we had at that point, it was impossible to provide full shade for excavators. My team endured numerous brain-boiling spells of the regimen, especially in the final days, indulging my quest to divine what was in the ground. Sometimes the troweling helped and sometimes it didn't, but when dots finally began to connect, we had our reward.

In the midst of one of those troweling sessions, I suddenly started to hop around and after a bit literally blurted out, "Aha!" As the startled and probably annoyed trowelers looked on, my next words were something like, "It's a mound! We're excavating a small mound." I had finally recognized evidence that, within a definable area, at least one layer of earth had been intentionally heaped on top of other man-made deposits. For some reason Glass Site residents chose to bury some of the traces of their own existence.

Purposeful mounding of earth, by the time this village was established, was an ancient practice in eastern North America, undertaken usually to create and memorialize places for burial or to create platforms for special buildings. I was, therefore, more stirred up over the implications the soil-reading breakthrough had for *this* site than simply the fact that we had discovered a mound. Mounds were almost always constructed at places of consequence. So, very shortly, I was asking new questions like, "Was this place really as special in the Indian world as it is shaping up to be?"

Let me walk through the evidence that led to that conclusion (figure 4.1). Remember first that we had encountered a thin midden when our block excavation was created, eastward of the first five units. It was exactly what one would expect at a permanently occupied town, a gradual accumulation of soil enriched by assorted waste. But at the western edge of the excavation, the midden abruptly disappeared. What was visible, instead, was a thin strip of swirly soil and a band of light-colored sand above it. When the block was extended westward, we revealed more of the fairly nondescript, light-colored sand, but with indications of vastly different deposits underneath.

At fairly regular intervals within and around our enlarged excavation, we had the benefit of other windows into the deeper stratigraphy. Some were created by initial shovel tests and test units, but most were created by the bedding plow. Because our first step involved removal of the upper, disturbed soil, even in the bottoms of the bedding furrows, the final result was scattered glimpses of the guts of the site. The revelation was that the plain vanilla mantle of sand at the top was obscuring much more interesting deposits deeper

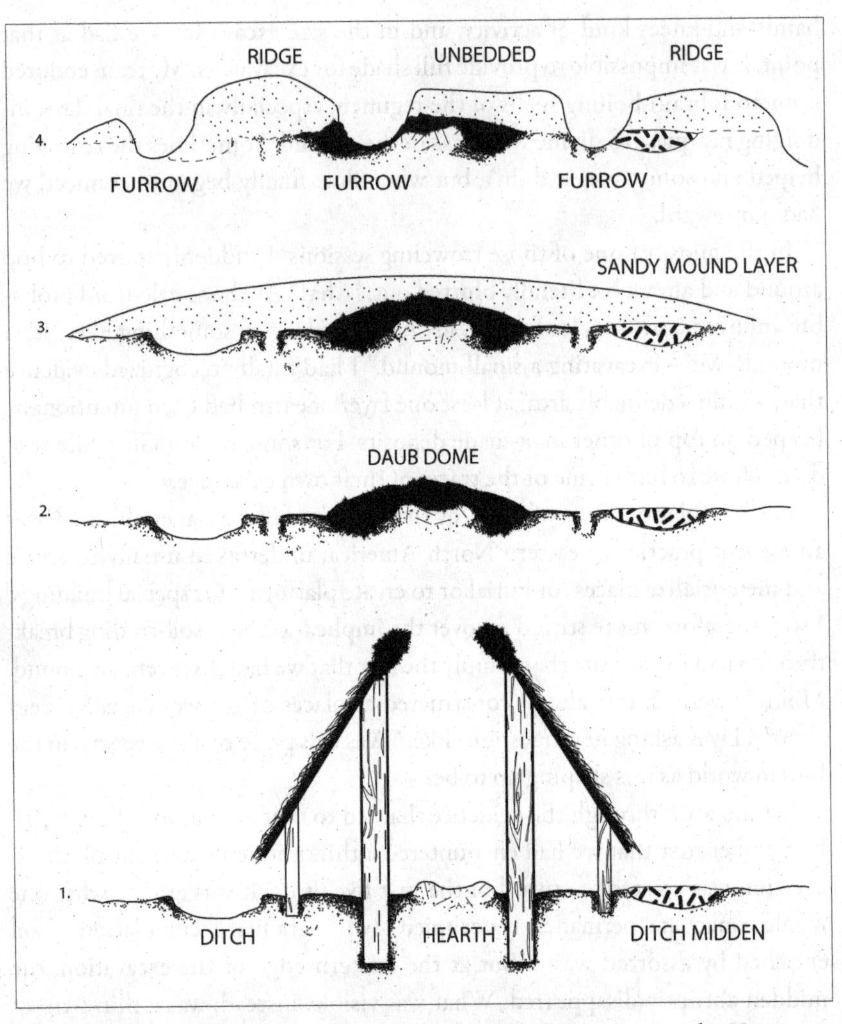

4.1 Graphical interpretation of events that explain temple-area stratigraphy. Upon its destruction by fire, the roof of the temple collapsed to leave a dome of fired daub above the central hearth (2), after which time the building ruin was ritually capped with a low mound of sand (3). Centuries later, about the year 2000, the entire site was cleared and bedded for pine planting, a process that left prominent ridges and furrows through archaeological deposits (4).

down, including some roiled grayish stuff that began to mystify us the very first season.

Moving from east to west, we could follow the thin midden until it disappeared *beneath* the layer of mounded sand. But we could also discern that the midden suddenly ended at the edge of the swirly sand. The swirly matrix, appearing very much like water-laid sediment, extended fully across the block in a wide, arcing band, running north to south. That swath was interrupted at one point by a massive slug of artifact-rich midden soil. The deposits on the other side of the swirly band were yet again different but seemed also to represent something midden-like. They were relatively dark colored, and in them artifacts were common. In effect, the clean sand had been loaded to a depth of not more than 30 cm directly above an area of peculiarly "busy" deposits. Although that much was clear, it was not yet obvious what exactly the mound was built to hide—or protect. Getting to the bottom of that, quite literally, would require another year of meticulous excavation.

The team recovered great quantities of artifacts as we disentangled the story of the soil, including two more glass beads. By this stage we were water-forcing 100 percent of the excavated soil through a proper fine-screen setup, and it was from that process that both of those new beads were found. One of them I refer to as the "Becky bead" since it was plucked out of a screen by one of the devoted local volunteers, Becky Mobley. It is an exceedingly rare type of which only a half dozen are known in the entire United States, and perhaps only double that number from the entire hemisphere. Most importantly it is a kind that has so far been found only at the earliest of Spanish-associated sites in the New World, securely pinning down events predating 1550. The other bead was a fragment of a second seven-layered, faceted chevron. It was found back at the Fernbank lab by a different volunteer who was painstakingly sorting gallons of the residual "fines" scooped from the water-washed field screens. That pair of Italian glass beauties only fed my suspicion that this was a Soto site.

Outnumbering the glass beads, by something like 4,500:1, were fragments of Indian pottery. The dominant ceramic types, far and away, were representative of the Lamar culture and especially the latter part of its known span (ca. 1450–1600). Together with the pieces of broken pots was a surprisingly large number of elaborate smoking-pipe fragments. The sheer number of these was an added indication that this part of the site was something special. In the Native world, smoking was an activity far more sacrosanct than casual. Also in the mix was a profusion of more mundane material, especially small chunks of fired clay that we refer to as "daub." In essence, daub is the plaster covering applied to the walls of Indian buildings. When those buildings burned, whether by accident or by design, the clay in the walls became brick-like and resistant to disintegration. Altogether, it was sure beginning to feel like we were working in and around a building of some sort.

By then, the complexity and uniqueness of the site required—and deserved—investigation by teams of better-trained people. It would have been irresponsible to continue the work solely with the help of less-experienced volunteers. The risk of slips with a shovel, and of not recognizing key evidence in the soil, was too great. Not to mention that volunteer progress could be slow even by archaeological standards. The solution meant committing to fully paid crews of seasoned archaeologists and to groups of university students with at least classroom training. Thus after 2008 the Fernbank public archaeology program at the Glass Site was suspended. Volunteers were still involved, especially veterans of Glass and other sites, but more selectively. In exchange, classes of field-school students from Georgia State University, directed by Jeffrey Glover, became a critical feature of the summer seasons. A dozen or more enthusiastic and disciplined students of archaeology can make things happen, and in all the right ways.

Before the public program was terminated, the 2007 and 2008 seasons brought high school–age and adult participants to two other sites on our short list. Both had been discovered by Frankie on the opposite side of the Ocmulgee, in Coffee County. The first, mentioned earlier as 9CF46, turned out to be what he expected, a small Lamar farmstead. Two concentrations of artifacts were defined by shovel testing within a confined area measuring 40 x 60 m. Excavation of three large units recovered artifacts in undisturbed deposits, but no indication of substantial features, including clear signs of structures, was found. The pottery bore classic traits of the Lamar style, but there just wasn't much of it compared to the quantities from Coffee Bluff and Glass. The best impression I could form was that this location had supported a couple of family-size groups engaged in hunting, gathering, and small-scale farming, probably housed in small but permanent structures.

Best of all, the high school students discovered a heavily oxidized fragment of flat iron deep within a unit and within a small feature. It was another European artifact in good Lamar context. But the size and condition of the piece prevented any kind of confident identification. The best we can say is that it could have been a section of a knife blade or something of the sort.

The other site, officially known as 9CF17, was also well named by Frankie as the Sand Ridge Site. It occupied a veritable island in the middle of the river's floodplain. Natural features of the kind are well known along the Ocmulgee, and all of them attracted human habitation. These huge berms are former sandbar deposits that were stranded in the swamps as the river meandered elsewhere. For humans, they became prime real estate, places where they could maximize access to the river bottom's food sources and fertile soils and still wake up with a dry backside. Better yet, they afforded the opportunity for good living in relative isolation—if the people needed it.

When this ridge was cleared and furrowed for pine trees, Frankie observed an unusual accumulation of midden in a small area. Curiosity piqued, he collected from the surface and undertook an excavation. What he discovered in the shelly midden, aside from remarkable preservation of food-related bone, was a kind of pottery foreign to the lower Ocmulgee—and it was accompanied by an unusually large number of European artifacts. What in the world was up here?

Aspects of the pottery would be right at home on the coast, in fact at places like Mission Santa Catalina de Guale. And the tiny glass beads found with it would be, too. Without doubt, this had been the home of a small Indian enclave well after the Glass Site was abandoned—but during the mission period, which was still at the forefront of our work. And by the look of the artifacts, the inhabitants were direct transplants from points east.

Obviously, this site ranked highly as a mission candidate, and we spent several weeks exploring it. With shovel tests we zeroed in on the area that had captivated Frankie and then opened seven test units of our own (figure 4.2). For all intents and purposes, our results duplicated his, with the exception of midden sampling. It appears he largely removed those deposits, and what might have been left was erased by a second-generation pine plantation. We came away with sizable quantities of the peculiar line-block, complicated

N 520
N 500
N 480
E 460 E 480 E 500 E 520 E 540 E 560
0
10 m
50x50cm TEST
EXCAVATION UNIT

4.2 Sand Ridge (9CF17) site plan

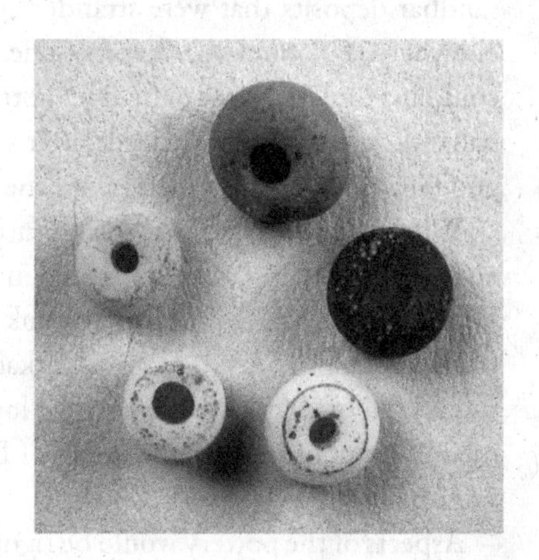

4.3 Mission-era glass "seed" beads from the Sand Ridge Site

stamped pottery; thirteen miniscule "seed" beads of turquoise, white, and blue glass; and a few scraps of bottle glass, brass, and iron (figure 4.3).[4]

As apparent as it is that this small group had immigrated inland from the coast fairly late in the seventeenth century, and that they were acquiring foreign goods from Europeans, we could document nothing at the Sand Ridge Site to say that it was a mission outpost. Indeed, the artifacts seem to be too late to jibe with the Santa Isabel mission. It seemed we were dancing all around the mission but not on it. But this site is an important indicator of how much Indian society was in flux after more than a century of European interaction and the ways in which people were moving back and forth from coast to interior as a result. As much as anything, I am left to believe that residents of the sand ridge were a desperate group of refugees.[5]

Starting in 2009 the Glass Site became the entire focus of the project. I would schedule six to eight weeks of summer fieldwork and spend the remainder of each year consumed by washing, cataloging, and analyzing artifacts and writing reports of findings. The pace of the excavation was picking up, and there was a tremendous amount of material and information to process from one field season to the next, but this cycle allowed me to digest what we were revealing in manageable bites and to thoughtfully plan each season's strategy. I didn't want to be flying blind and, instead, strove to design each field campaign around a set of clear questions and appropriate methods.

In the interest of clarity, I will compress my discussion of results between 2009 and 2010. Concentrating on the part of the site we had started with in 2006, the general strategy still amounted to progressive expansion of the original block toward the west, north, and south. And having cracked the stratigraphic code, it was a matter of taking the site apart, layer by layer, in the reverse order it had been created. Ultimately, sixty contiguous excavation units were opened, most of them measuring 2 m on a side, which created an excavated expanse of roughly 16 by 20 m (52 x 66 ft) (figure 4.4). The big payoff was confirmation that we *were* dealing with a Native-built structure, and a remarkable one at that—perhaps even the most revered building in the territory.

In large measure, headway continued to be a matter of seeing what the *soil* had to say. It was leading, and we were following. As we expanded and deepened the block, unit by unit and layer by layer, a profusion of patterns began to emerge that I could only explain as the effects of deliberate human actions.

Foremost among the signs was a large expanse of chocolate-colored soil. It would be wrong to describe it as a true midden deposit since the discoloration was just a few shades browner than the surrounding soil, but it was unmistakable. Within separate units we would always uncover the stain just below the lighter-colored sand that constituted the mound. In other words, the extent of the mound deposit and the extent of the dark soil beneath it were nearly the same, though the former extended a bit more broadly. Once we reached the darker layer it was, much of the time, also distinguished by a degree of

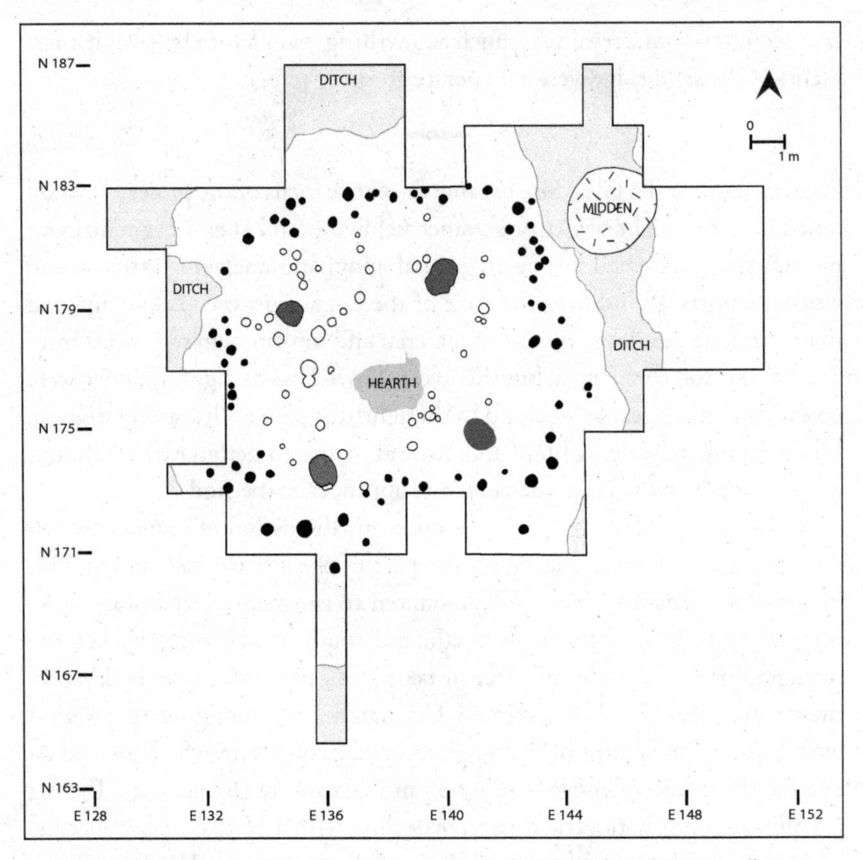

4.4 Archaeological plan view of temple area results. The large hearth is centrally located, and four large postholes surround it; smaller open and filled circles around the central area represent wall postholes; and the encircling ditch with its midden dump was exposed at several points around the perimeter.

compactness not typical of soil above, below, or beyond. This was a subtle thing, detectable as slight resistance to troweling with an audible effect. The ring of a trowel scraping against it was raised a note or two.

Encircling the limits of the darker patch was that wide band of mixed-up soil that I mentioned. On all sides we had exposed it as an arcing strip of laminated and mottled sediment. Several cross sections revealed that the swath defined a wide, shallow ditch filled mainly by natural siltation but in places by deliberate dumping. This circular trench has turned out to be one of the singular features of the entire site.

The most striking part of the ditch fill was located in its northeastern segment. We saw almost from day one that this area was yielding the greatest quantity of animal bone, and as the excavation proceeded, we discovered that it was the location of a massive disposal event. Within an area about 2 m across and to a thickness of about 20 cm, we documented a lens of greasy black midden, chock full of animal bone, broken pottery, and unusual items like shell beads—and glass beads. This load of debris had been purposefully and rapidly placed there.

Then, immediately above the very large, chocolate-colored area, within the space delineated by the ditch, we could see abundant evidence of fire. Here and there were large chunks of thoroughly burned wood, and centrally positioned was an accumulation of fired daub about 6 m across.

What we discovered beneath that heap of daub proved to be another game changer. It was a huge hearth, 2 m or more in diameter, recognizable from soil beneath and around it that had turned bright orange from intense heat, and also from alternating layers of thin white clay and ash within (figure 4.5). The interior resembled an archaeological version of an exotic, finely layered pastry. Such a feature, combined with the daub, could mean only one thing: we had definitively excavated our way to the center of a building. And judging from the size and complexity of the hearth, it was no ordinary structure.

More practically, such a hearth would be the hub in the design and use of a building. With the expectation that the floor plan was probably a symmetrical one, we had the perfect reference point for pursuing other elements of the structure. Indeed, the hearth was more or less dead center within the wider area of darkened soil and its surrounding ditch. Somewhere between their outer limits and the hearth, one would predict support posts and traces of walls.

Hearths are nice when you find them, but archaeologists more routinely identify ancient building locations by plotting arrangements of postholes. Once more we're talking about evidence observed in the soil rather than physical objects that can be removed and handled. A posthole, for example, is the filled cavity originally created to hold a wood post upright. To an archaeologist they appear as discolorations caused by either purposeful or natural filling. It is easy to imagine how burning or decay of a wooden post would discolor the soil in the hole that held it upright, as would the blending action that goes along with backfilling an old hole. Yet as true as this is, the age of

4.5 Temple hearth, exposed and partially excavated, showing fine layers of gray ash and clay mounded above super-heated soil

the hole, the nature of the local soil, and a host of other factors influence how clearly such features will show up. Much of the time they are anything but obvious, and only in the right light, and with the ideal amount of moisture in the soil, can they be discerned. When it comes down to it, identifying an arrangement of posts that defines the outline of an ancient building has been likened to another kind of archaeological voodoo. Some people are quicker to pick them out than others, just the way stars in a constellation more readily resolve into something meaningful for some than for others.

We did document postholes at the Glass Site, but it was hard-won evidence, even though we knew they were there. In the sandy soil, original staining at the site of a post fairly quickly dissipates, flushed away by the action of percolating water and other processes. But slowly I learned to recognize the unique signature of post features at the site and over multiple seasons, and with the hearth to orient the search, we were able to define the footprint of our first structure.

Most of the time, our field records described a small, phantom-like discoloration as a "possible post." The typical feature of this sort was 10–20 cm in diameter and appeared against the background soil as a mottled patch. They were occurrences, writ small, of the anomalous, "busy" soil I was forever viewing with archaeological suspicion. More and more of them were plotted on our drawings as the excavation expanded outward toward the ditch. But it was not prudent for a long time to declare any group of them a section of wall. Suggestive, yes, but definitive, no.

In time, a larger anomaly was revealed within the expansive dark zone, not far from the hearth. Though it was hardly obvious, I was satisfied it was real. But whether the blemish in the soil signified a natural tree disturbance or a building-related feature was the open question. In fact, crew members regularly balk at assignments to dig such things. A diffuse stain doesn't look like a sexy feature crammed with interesting evidence. But since each potential clue must be explained, someone always has to accept the challenge.

Rachel Hensler, one of the most dependable people on the project, eventually agreed to undertake the chore. I asked her to first section the feature by excavating only half of it. That way we would create a cross-section profile across the center from which we might glimpse details of its creation and use. At the outset I estimated the diameter of the feature to be about 80 cm, but as she began to chase the limits of the busy fill the diameter increased to just over 1 m. Before long, it had developed into a large pit that punctured the floor of the building. Even more startling was the eventual depth of the hole. By the time Rachel hit bottom, at 70 cm below the excavated surface, it had essentially swallowed her. She could fit fairly comfortably inside the excavated *half* of the feature (figure 4.6).

As the most cynical crew members predicted, the faint but massive feature contained very little beyond mixed-up soil, just a handful of broken pottery sherds and a trickle of stone flakes. Consequently, it remained uncertain whether Rachel had plumbed an old tree cavity . . . or a giant-sized *posthole.* If it was a posthole, there were no obvious companion holes to match it. For another several months, that's where things stood. We had identified a very

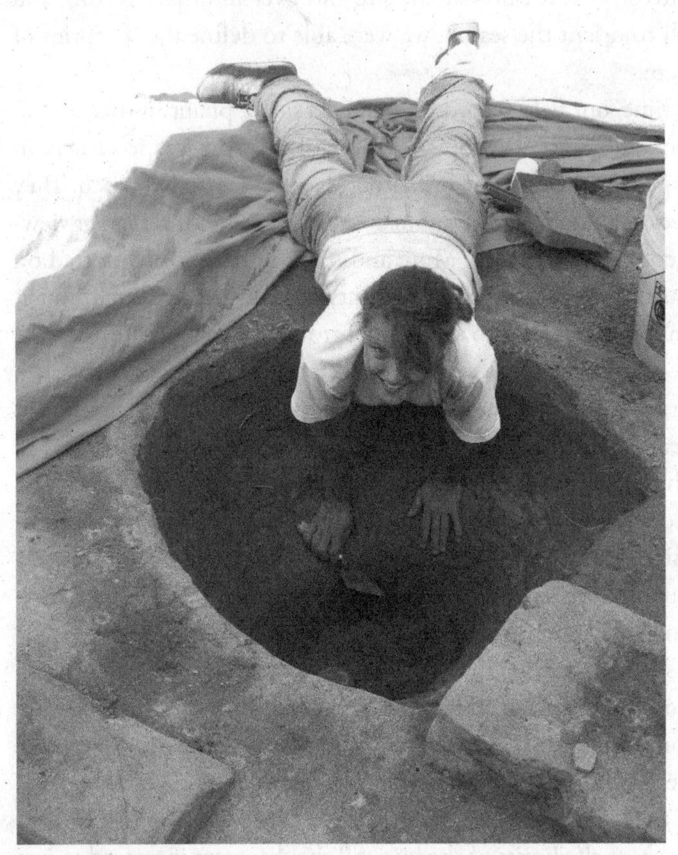

4.6 Large posthole in temple floor and its excavator, Rachel Hensler

obvious hearth at the center of a large dark patch surrounded by a ditch, and here and there within that area were numerous small, possible postholes and one gigantic, possible posthole. I was not going to persuade anyone that we had discovered a large, important building on the basis of suggestive evidence.

In theory, the 2010 season would complete our excavation in the area we had first begun to explore back in 2006. There was so much more to understand about the site that this part needed to be put to bed. Toward the end of that season, the dark area and its surrounding ditch had been more or less fully exposed, and it was time to make final records of what we had revealed. For the closing photos, I wanted to get some clear overhead shots of the entire exposure. With the advent of bucket trucks and other kinds of hydraulic lifts, archaeologists have routinely made use of them for photographic documentation. If I could arrange to get a lift of some sort down the narrow road to the site, I would have the opportunity to take those final shots and view the excavation from a new vantage point.

Fortunately the leadership at Fernbank and one of our long-time volunteers on the site had close relationships with senior people at the Georgia Power Company. The request for a bucket truck was called in, and as a public service, the utility was happy to divert one to the site for part of a day. I was not prepared for what they actually sent. By phone I had guided the truck crew to the property's gate, and pretty soon the groan of a large engine was approaching along the narrow, two-track road. The roar grew to be far louder than an ordinary truck, and soon a monstrous piece of equipment emerged, Godzilla-like, between—and above—the planted pines. It had to have been the largest bucket truck in the state, so huge I wasn't sure the driver could maneuver the thing close to the excavation without damaging it or the rest of the site. As I should have figured, the truck's crew knew its business and without a sweat positioned it perfectly for our viewing session.

The foreman then explained that the bucket could be extended way up—as in nearly one hundred feet! You would have thought that all of a sudden we were operating a carnival. Everybody—well almost everybody—wanted a ride. But pulling rank, and with architecture on my mind, the season's photographer and I took the first trip. The view was pretty spectacular—if pondering excavated surfaces gets you excited, like it does me. Plus, it was one of those coveted days perfect for taking pictures: consistently overcast so that the usual blinding sunlight and tangles of shadows were in check. At such a critical stage, the conditions were a gift. Our final preparatory touch was to lightly spray the excavation with water. With evenly moistened soil, features tend to become more discernable. It's like putting the final treatment to an artist's canvas.

With everything just right, and from our eight-story perch, color distinctions subtle at ground level became clearer than ever (figure 4.7). The central hearth and the exposed sections of the encircling ditch were the most vivid.

4.7 Overhead view of temple excavation. The perimeter ditch appears in places as a wide, light-colored band.

But some details that were not at all evident previously started to pop out. Much more discernable were alignments of small postholes. They marked sections of walls framing the darker soil of the building's floor. More surprising was the realization that a meandering network of narrow, dark-colored veins corresponded almost perfectly with the limits of the structure. We had seen their curving paths at ground level, and I suspected they were old tree root runs. But the comprehensive view we now had of their extent gave them new meaning: they were recognizable as the vestiges of a rodent community that had colonized the ruins of the building several centuries earlier.

Most of our scrutiny was, of course, given to aspects of the exposure that stubbornly eluded explanation. They tended to be the most diffuse of the variegated soil patches, but they were trying to signal to us some kind of past activity. So I lingered silently up on that lift trying to will meaning from the scene below. Clarity can come with patience, especially in this business, and I was content to scan the exposure as if I were trying to reach the sort of focal sweet spot that enlivens an impressionist painting. What your mind registers is changeable until suddenly you see "it." As truer focus is achieved, disparate swatches and lines and shapes finally become linked to form an image. What I gradually perceived was the building's system of interior support, preserved faintly as three additional mammoth postholes that, with Rachel's first one, defined a square space around the central hearth.

It was that exhilarating moment of seeing, won by hours of exertion and tedium, that led me to exclaim something like, "Good lord, there are more big posts down there! Flag 'em now!" I frantically guided placement of markers before the fleeting evidence was faded back into oblivion by the fast-drying sand. That's how indistinct they were. From the ground I would never have had confidence in what my eyes were trying to register, but with a birds-eye perspective it all made sense. Folks on the ground couldn't fully appreciate the same view I had, and I think half the crew was again murmuring, "The man's lost it entirely. Been out here on the edge of that swamp too long." But there was a solution for the deniers: excavate them and see what happens. The features will either be there or they won't.

The problem with all this, exciting to me as it was, was that we were desperately trying to walk away from this part of the site. It had been a long haul. Important new things had been learned, but the crew was weary. The temperature didn't go down, the gnats didn't take a vacation, and the soil didn't get any cleaner. What we anticipated as a final glorious act of photography and mapping had given rise to a lot of feverish new work. Three giant postholes had to be sectioned and documented. Summoning reserves after my bribe of cold beer, the team set to it, and within a couple of hours it was confirmed that those faintest of anomalies were, indeed, the filled holes for holding the massive uprights that supported the building's roof. They also demarcated what was perhaps the most sacred space in the town, the location of a sacred fire within the structure. With that, I could finally be content that we had thoroughly and persuasively documented the building, and that we could explain why it was special.

After the 2010 season, two years would pass before we returned to the Glass Site for more fieldwork. I needed time to digest the findings of the initial seasons and to write a meaty report. Doing so would position me to lay better plans for further exploration.

The usual working ratio of field to lab time is something like 1:3—or more. Thousands of artifacts must be washed, cataloged, and properly put away; records must be organized and stored; and one or more technical summaries must be written. It is slow, tedious work, but the process, if pursued systematically and thoroughly, almost always yields loads of new insights. This is not the part of archaeology foremost in the public imagination, and that is unfortunate since it happens to be the most informative stage. There are always eureka moments in the course of analysis and writing, just as there are in the field. For me, more often than not, it's the connections we make during the lab and writing phase that give the strongest virtual sense of time travel.

I will share, as an anthropological vignette, the conclusions I could reach after the first phase. Even by that point the evidence we had amassed was sufficient to conjure a pretty clear image of what once stood at the point of the excavation . . .

Imagine that you are arriving at the village by dugout canoe about five centuries ago. The roofline of a grand building—a temple—would likely have been the first sign of the community, aside perhaps from plumes of smoke and the sounds of daily chores. And because it was situated close by the riverbank, it was the first structure visitors would approach. Climbing the steep bank, you would be struck by the unmatched bulk of the sacred building against

4.8 Interpretive illustration of the temple structure's appearance (Fernbank Museum of Natural History)

the backdrop of more ordinary structures (figure 4.8). Access to it would have been impeded, however, by an encircling ditch. The shallowness of the ditch made it more a symbolic feature than an actual barrier, but the message would have been obvious. Consuming most of the space inside the ditch, the structure would be dominated by its steeply sloping, thatched roof, leaving plastered walls largely obscured by eaves. At the peak of the roof, the thatch was also slathered with clay, probably inside and out. This was a fire-suppression measure to protect the covering close around the smoke hole. The single opening in the walls, at the northeast corner of the building, was directed toward the heart of the community, precisely aimed toward the center of the town's public plaza.

Every detail of the temple was intentional. On a practical level the design ensured structural integrity and adequate shelter of interior activities. But the design was also conceived for the purpose of recording and conveying elements of a prevailing worldview. You were viewing a model of the universe.

The centrally placed fire was emblematic of the all-important sun, and the hearth that held it was a focal point of an annual world-renewal ceremony. The four massive posts surrounding the hearth, and by extension the four surrounding walls, reflected the conception of a quartered universe in which cardinal orientations carried specific meanings. The northeastward-facing doorway was aimed not only toward the center of the community but also to the sunrise on the summer solstice. And the encircling ditch, among other things, could be construed to signify the great disk on which the cosmic middle world of humans was suspended or floating.[6]

There are, of course, explicit archaeological reasons to argue that we had uncovered the single most important structure on the site and, very possibly, the most significant building in the territory. The fact of the huge hearth surrounded by proportionally large postholes was sufficient to confirm that much. At four times the size of an ordinary Indian dwelling, having an interior space that could have soared to 8 m (26 ft) above the floor, it would have been an imposing sight.[7] And because it literally housed a sacred fire, the living embodiment of the sun deity, intended to burn constantly, and additionally a sepulcher of the most revered objects, it was an imposing symbol. In it resided a concentration of power that was unmatched in the territory, so much so that its use was probably reserved for a small cohort of the highest-ranked people.

A sense of activity inside the temple is afforded by the kinds of objects we found there and by the manner in which they were distributed. Compared to other parts of the town, special objects are concentrated in and around this structure, things such as elaborate smoking pipes, marine shell, and even foreign items from Europe. Within the building, artifacts occurred most frequently toward the southwestern side of the structure, opposite and farthest from the doorway. Perhaps it was in this most secluded, private space that revered objects were stored and rituals consummated. Indeed, descriptions of temples and council houses left for us by non-Native visitors describe how special containers sequestered inside these buildings held a community's most sacred possessions.

The midden deposit in the encircling ditch and the particulars of the hearth are connected in important ways. In time it became clear that the midden was isolated at a point just outside the inferred doorway of the temple. I believe this choice of dumping location was intentional. The contents of the midden, while composed in part of seemingly ordinary debris like food scraps, also contained a collection of extraordinary objects. Only in the midden have we found high-status ornaments made of large, saltwater shells, accompanied by more than a dozen box-turtle shells and European glass beads (figures 4.9 and 4.10). Interesting, if not unusual, it also produced bones of large carnivores.

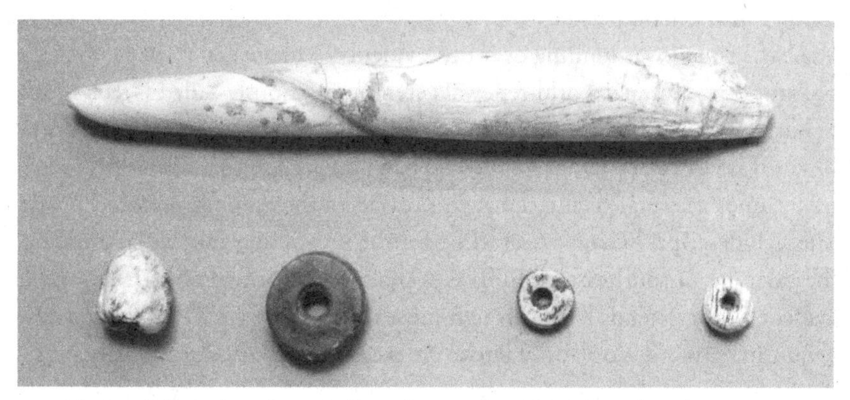

4.9 Marine shell beads and ear pin from the temple midden (max. length of ear pin fragment = 7.1 cm)

4.10 Box turtle shells from the temple midden

By removing a small section of the hearth, we could see details of its construction in cross section. They were remarkable. Before we did so, all we could recognize was clumps of ash and orangish clay altered by heat. The side-on view, however, revealed fine laminations alternating between layers of soft grayish-brown ash that we jokingly referred to as peanut butter and equally thin layers of dense white "plaster." I counted approximately four pairs of soft ash and hard plaster.

At the time I was mulling over this evidence, I happened to be reading an account of the annual world-renewal ceremony, variously called Green Corn or busk, that provided a stunning explanation of the hearth's delicate stratigraphy. It was written by James Adair, who had observed the days-long busk ceremony among several groups during his travels in the mid-eighteenth century. The rich description conveys a feeling for the most important ritual event on the calendar of southeastern Indians, a practice, according to archaeological evidence, that extends back through most if not all of the Mississippian era, beginning around AD 1000. Here is an excerpt from Adair especially pertinent to this case: "Then he [the chief] puts a few roots of the button snake root, with some green leaves of an uncommon small sort of tobacco, and a little of the new fruits [corn], at the bottom of the fireplace, which he orders to be covered up with *white marley clay* [emphasis added], and wetted over with clean water."[8] At the close of the same century, Benjamin Hawkins observed a Creek Indian busk and relates how "one pan of clay and one pan of ashes were taken to the cabin of the mico (chief), and the other two to that of the warriors, who rubbed themselves with the clay and ashes."[9]

Once again, the central fire of the square ground, and its analogs within public buildings and temples, represented nothing less than the sacred Sun, a principal deity, and they were by extension a universal centering symbol. The connotations of the fires were so great, in fact, that certain individuals were assigned to maintain them as a perpetually burning symbol.[10] All signs indicate that the hearth at the center of the Glass Site temple was treated in precisely the same manner and probably as part of the same ceremony. Once each year the sacred fire, which otherwise burned continuously in the temple, was extinguished and then relit as a sign of renewal. Those actions would help set the world right for another year.

The historical accounts raise the likely possibility that the cement-like, light-colored layers in the hearth represent a special plaster applied in conjunction with specific ritual events. Further, the ash and fired clay in the feasting dump, just outside the temple, may be residues related to hearth cleaning and refurbishment. Whether the four cycles of fire and capping that created the large dome represent four annual, busk-like events or a series of more frequently scheduled events is uncertain at this point. Neither can we know if those events represent all such cycles that occurred over the course of the history of the temple. Nonetheless, it is provocative to imagine that the plaster applications coincide with the late summer, first-fruits ceremony and thereby indicate that abandonment of the temple occurred one year in conjunction with it.

William Bartram, also a notable eighteenth-century observer, related another aspect of the busk. Describing the Choctaw version of the ceremony, he explains the process of village cleansing: "They collect all their worn out clothes and other despicable things, sweep and cleanse their houses, and the whole town, of their filth, which with all the remaining grain and other old provisions, they cast together in one common heap, and consume it with fire."[11] Thus the descriptions of Adair and Bartram effectively link layering in the hearth with the dump in the ditch. In conjunction with making new fire, the Glass Site temple—along with the entire village—was thoroughly purged of old debris, which was ceremonially heaped into the trough just outside the temple door. Not only was it a convenient location to toss the debris, but it was also a highly visible one where evidence of the ritual act was made obvious.

Evocative details are abundant in the results of our temple-area excavation, and I will conclude this section with just one more. In the course of fully exposing the hearth, we realized that below the layer of daub that entombed the feature—a layer representing the remains of the collapsed roof—there were few artifacts in the vicinity. The immediate hearth area seems to have been kept clean. One conspicuous exception was a stone tool resting directly at the edge of the fireplace. Its mere presence was a surprise, and so was its age. The artifact is among the most distinctive kinds in the region, called an Edgefield scraper (figure 4.11). The tools were skillfully flaked to create a steeply angled cutting edge, below which were fashioned opposing notches that allowed the blade to be secured to a handle. But here is the wonder: such tools are dated to between 8000–7000 BC. That is more than eight thousand years before the temple was built and used. And the context of the discovery indicates that it was not coincidentally found by the hearth. It seems to have been present,

4.11 Ancient Edgefield scraper discovered beside temple hearth (max. width = 5.2 cm)

at that spot, when the building burned. One side of it was altered by the destructive fire, smudged black and slightly reddened, while the facedown side was pristine. It would seem that this ancient, unfamiliar artifact was picked up somewhere by a resident of the Glass Site and revered as something powerful, so much so that it was included among the other unique items curated within the sanctuary.[12]

To conclude the temple-area excavation and walk away with some confidence in our understanding of it was satisfying. But it was a tiny section of what had to be a larger community. And therein was one of the major lingering questions: Exactly how large was the surrounding settlement, and how was it organized? And what about the Spanish artifacts—were we also dealing with the location of a brief encampment of Soto's full contingent, a Soto-slept-here place, or something else? Until those and other questions about the larger town were answered, our results existed in a vacuum. Context critical for a comprehensive and meaningful interpretation was lacking. It was those issues that drove subsequent seasons of work.

V

A Round Town

Today, the attention of someone standing on the Glass Site is drawn quickly to the most dramatic feature of the immediate landscape, a deeply shaded slough known locally as Lampkin Lake. It is where the level, sandy land so attractive for human habitation plunges sharply into a perennially wet world of black gum and cypress. The western limit of the archaeological site is defined by that boundary. From the air or on a map, it becomes obvious that the wetland exists on a grand scale, sweeping against the higher and drier, ancient terrace in the form of a giant horseshoe. Technically the swamp is a formerly active channel of the Ocmulgee River, one of thousands of meanders that the ever-shifting stream scoured into existence and then abandoned to become oxbows. For people living in the area, both long ago and today, the river and its surrounding wetlands are a major attraction. They are where wild foods are concentrated and where mobility is simplified by the use of boats. In our terms today, these are the places convenient to the Whole Foods market and the freeway commuter corridor. Indeed, this is precisely the kind of setting in which archaeologists expect to find abandoned habitation sites of almost any time period. Location, location, location.

Presented with this scene, I was content in the early going to imagine that the site was strung out along the margin of the slough. I was assuming that the former inhabitants would have preferred a waterfront existence, and as a result, approximately 30 m back from the old riverbank, evidence of the Lamar-era occupation would fade away. The initial archaeological results suggested as much. Our short transects of shovel tests in the area of the temple revealed a sudden drop in artifact density toward the interior. Just eastward of that important building, there seemed to be little going on. Still, I knew that the extent of our investigation at that point was painfully limited, and to declare anything more about the actual nature of the site, especially its overall size and configuration, amounted to pure speculation.

There are also tried-and-true solutions to these kinds of archaeological issues, and beginning in 2012 the project focused on resolving them. Determining the full extent of the Indian community was really a "simple" matter of thorough testing. Where artifacts like pottery fragments and stone debris occur within a large area can be efficiently determined by small, exploratory excavations about a foot in diameter; they are the shovel tests I have mentioned. The process I envisioned would involve systematic expansion of our original but limited pattern of such tests, until we were certain that they were no longer producing artifacts related to the Lamar occupation.

Questions surrounding the Spanish encounter required a somewhat different strategy. Disciplined shovel testing was not without some value, but knowing what we did about the sparsity of artifacts left by early Europeans, and what materials most of them were made from, we might best find answers by other means. The primary strategy I adopted for this purpose, as a complement to shovel testing, was wide-area metal detector survey. This was not a typical decision since archaeologists tend to have a conflicted relationship with metal detectors. As I have said, they are the tool of choice for many looters who operate with an agenda that is more mercenary than scientific. But deployed thoughtfully and carefully, the devices can be a highly effective option for data collection.

Having settled on that one-two approach, I was left with the practical matter of defining the survey universe. Would we learn what we needed with systematic inspection of one acre, five acres, or more? Spatial parameters strongly influence the amount of time, the crew size, and the eventual cost of an archaeological project. In the end, I decided an estimation of the extent of an encampment of Soto's full contingent, people, horses—all of it—would yield the most useful delineation of area and effort. The logic, drawn from knowledge of the modus operandi of explorers like Soto, was that one of their encampments would encompass an Indian community, and then some.

Fortunately, an undergraduate intern from Kennesaw State University, Andrew Carlin, was working with me in the Fernbank archaeology lab during the months preceding the 2012 season. He was keen on helping explore the question of a Soto encounter, and I gave him this assignment: based on a review of sources describing Spanish military tactics, as well as the firsthand accounts of Soto's expedition, determine the *minimum* footprint of an encampment of Soto's large party of people and animals. How much area would an overnight camp require, assuming it was organized compactly? Andrew undertook this project with gusto and by the spring of 2012 it seemed fairly clear that the group would have occupied a space of no less than six acres. But to be thorough, understanding that people and horses and gear would probably not have been packed cheek to jowl in a tight space, we designed a more liberal survey program using tight-interval shovel testing and metal detecting that would inspect eight acres.

Thanks to the involvement of Jeffrey Glover's Georgia State University archaeology field school and a gang of experienced volunteers, our predetermined study area was sampled by nearly three hundred shovel tests. Imagine an area more than eight football fields across, within which dinner-plate-sized holes were dug at a regular interval of 10 m (33 ft). From the air you would see, in the end, a pattern akin to a giant checkerboard with a hole at the corners of every square. On average a shovel test excavation would come to a stop at about 70 cm (2.3 ft) below the surface where an ancient, clayey, "subsoil" layer was encountered. Pairs of team members, steadily working for two weeks, fell into the rhythm of locate, dig, sift, bag, record; locate, dig, sift, bag, record... Throw in the little detail that moving from one test location to the next usually required bushwhacking through tick- and snake-worthy undergrowth, it is no accident that I refer to the process as "work," sometimes even hazardous duty. You don't forget occasions when a student you are responsible for is frozen in her tracks by the buzz of an eastern diamondback she can't see.

I also wanted the satisfaction of learning something from this laborious process sooner rather than later, for both operational purposes and for the sake of the crew's morale. To make that happen, an open-air field lab was organized, right on the site, where artifacts freshly removed from shovel tests were itemized. Batches of bags were regularly relayed from the excavation teams to our "lab," where artifacts were sorted and counted according to basic categories, test by test, and tallies then entered into an electronic spreadsheet. The inventory team managed to keep pace with the excavation teams so well that we succeeded in producing more or less real-time data. The synchronicity of the process was a beautiful thing to behold.

As the survey teams advanced across the project area like so many archaeological locusts, we could begin to form a crude sense of what was going on below their feet. Most everywhere there was a low-level archaeological "hum"; sterile tests were nearly unheard of. But in spots the archaeological noise rose to a high pitch. Every team had occasion to revel in tests that produced lots of artifacts. Soon enough, it became obvious that some parts of the study area had experienced a great deal more activity than other parts. Yet it took a good while to discern, in this informal way, a meaningful pattern from an ongoing chorus of sighs and celebrations. Eventually real meaning would come from the real data, and I was dying to crunch it.

Wes Patterson was one of the paid assistants that season, and he loved nothing more than information of an electronic sort. With the utmost respect, I viewed him as our project geek. Wes had earned the position by his solid work the previous year as a Georgia State field school student, and he plunged headlong into the new role, so much that he would travel to and from the field with his precious new souped-up Apple computer. Every evening, following hours of exhausting fieldwork and a pitcher of cerveza with supper, he was content to disappear into his room, fire up that computer, and play with the survey file ballooning with input from dozens of daily tests.

For a while I didn't press Wes for too much since it was premature to latch on to any apparent patterns. But before long anticipation started to get the better of me, and still Wes remained fairly circumspect about what he was seeing. By the time we were shovel testing the last acre or so, I and everyone else was clamoring for a peek at the computerized shovel test results. Wes knew it was time, too, and one evening he finally summoned me over to view the outcome.

I don't recall exactly what I expected to see on Wes's giant computer monitor, but it certainly wasn't what he revealed—with a big wide grin. There, in near-psychedelic computer graphic output, was a representation of our shovel test findings that then, and now, I can best describe as a big fat bagel (figure 5.1). The garish, hot colors on the monitor were identifying places where lots of Soto-era Indian pottery was found, and collectively, those data were forming a near-perfect ring. The warm-colored bagel was floating in a sea of cool blue, signifying the wider margins of the survey area, where only paltry numbers of artifacts were in our tests. Even writing about it now sends shivers down my back. We had learned at last, by all that effort, that the Indian village

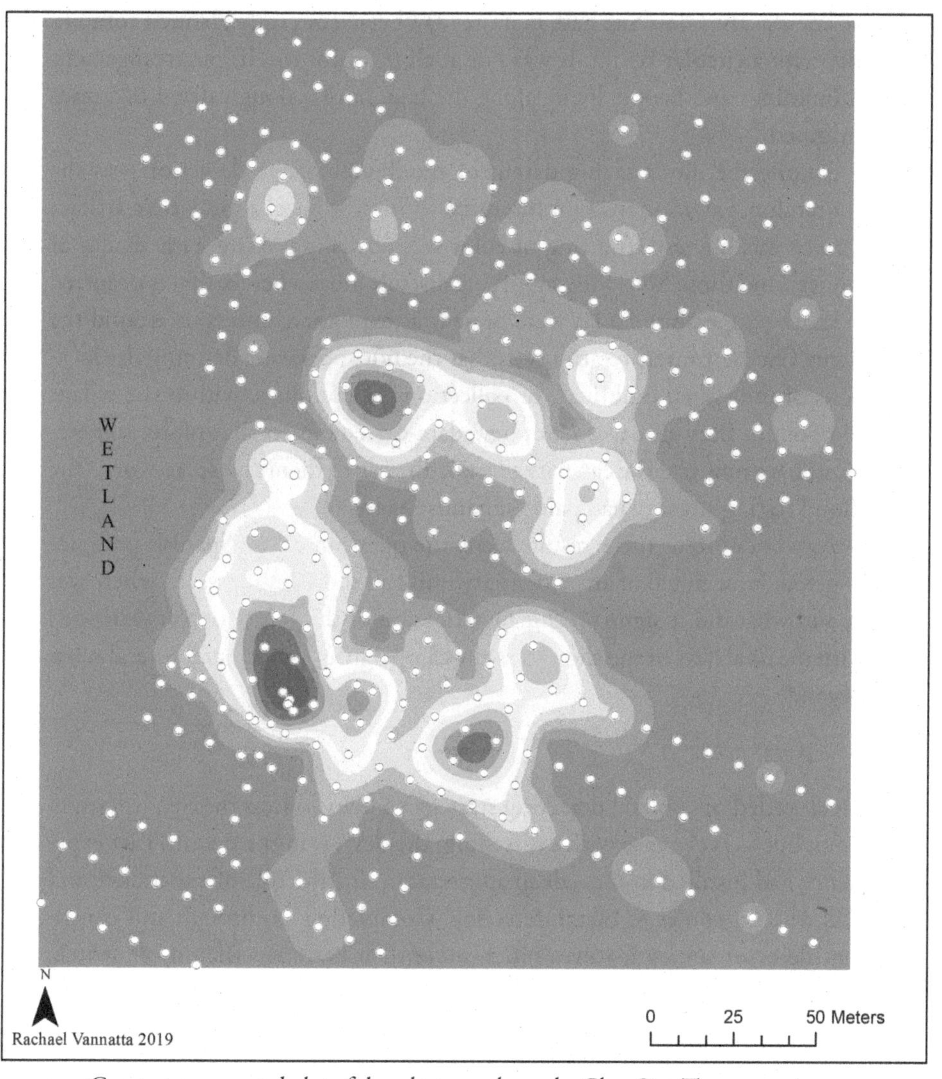

5.1 Computer-generated plot of shovel test results at the Glass Site. The circular band of warm colors identifies the area of highest Native artifact density and thus the location of the village ring. The highest density areas in the ring signify building locations.

we knew as the Glass Site had, in its heyday, been a carefully planned community with a circular layout. It was not at all the informal, linear arrangement of buildings and people living along the margin of a slough that I had once imagined.

Among the mesmerizing details of the digital village depiction was the nonrandom variation in color intensity, within the bagel zone, where artifact density was highest. The ring of color was virtually pulsing with shades of redness, and those hot spots, signifying discrete areas where artifacts occurred in relative superabundance, were present at regularized intervals around the circle. Our best interpretation was that the hot spots were defining the locations of individual buildings, or collections of buildings, within the village compound. They gave us a set of new, data-driven targets to explore, and better still, we now had the capacity to walk directly to them and set to work. The shovel testing strategy had paid off handsomely.

As wonderful as these results were, the question of the Spanish presence lingered. How much of an evidentiary trail had those invaders left, where was it, and what did it signify? Our investigation of those questions overlapped with the final days of the shovel-testing campaign and continued several more beyond.

I had settled on a metal detecting strategy to help address the Spanish questions, but as is the case with everything, the devil is in the details. Past experience had instilled in me a deep appreciation for the role of experience and skill when it comes to metal detecting. Completing a thorough and consistent detector survey involves much more than batteries, the on-off switch, and a shovel. I had once been embarrassed (shamed, really) working alongside veteran detectorists, and I had witnessed the same fate of other archaeologists. Yes, the machines are sophisticated, especially these days, but the best metal-detector operators also develop a kind of intuitive sense that makes the process as artistic as it is technical. Those were the kinds of people I wanted to lead the detector survey at Glass.

The world of metal detecting is unevenly split between hordes of hobbyist "relic collectors" and a handful of science-minded types such as archaeologists. Between them there is a strained coexistence, to put it mildly. Each faction harbors mistrust of the other since their respective motivations are, most of the time, diametrically opposed. Archaeologists abhor the thought of indiscriminate removal of artifacts from sites for the sake of personal satisfaction or, worse, to supply a market in relics. The hobbyists resent the preservation ethic that runs through archaeology, claiming that restrictions on their pastime amount to nothing more than heavy-handed government or egg-headed ivory-tower intervention.

To bypass the fray, I enlisted the help of other archaeologists who had become as skillful as the veteran hobbyists are. Many of them happen to be good friends, but it turned out that my field schedule didn't coincide with their availability, so the fallback had to be responsible amateurs. This, I'm happy to say, has become fairly commonplace, thanks largely to the pioneering work of people like Doug Scott, who made a career of metal-detecting the Little Bighorn battlefield with teams of enthusiasts.[1] The key, for me, was to figure out who the right folks were in or around Georgia.

My old colleagues in Georgia made it easy. They were very consistent in their recommendations of hobbyists, and the common refrain was hire a South Carolina man, Spencer Barker. If these guys trusted Barker so implicitly, then I knew I could too. Plus, I liked the idea of working with another native palmetto-stater. My first phone conversation with Spencer was easygoing, and our talks only got better. We shared colleagues and interests, he wanted the job, and the timing was right. He even knew my brother—small world. At the same time, Spencer was a purveyor of metal detectors, and he and his wife ran a business called Carolina Treasures. I won't deny that this gave me pause, but I had it on good faith that not only did he get archaeology, but he preferred at this stage in life to do archaeology.

What I planned to do at the Glass Site was unprecedented; never before had a potential Soto encampment been systematically surveyed this way. We recognized that a consistent level of thorough searching, over every square foot of the survey area, was necessary if we wanted any credibility. The strategy Spencer and I agreed on ran like this. He would directly coordinate the metal-detector survey according to the basic parameters I specified. Importantly, he would oversee the participation of several other amateur detectorists who had varying levels of experience. After just a few hours, he had sized up his team and skillfully delegated tasks according to his perceptions of individual ability. Nonetheless, I would find him doubling back to re-detect areas that others had covered first. He was determined to be thorough, and who could argue with that?

By the time Spencer came to the Glass Site, he had been handling metal detectors under every conceivable kind of condition for something like four decades. By virtue of that field experience, and his day job selling them, he was also the consummate technician. He embodied the ten-thousand-hour rule, that threshold of experience that can define true expertise. I was more than impressed when his van pulled up to the site, and he revealed in it an array of detecting options that I hardly knew existed. Mounted neatly on racks and shelves were several makes and models of detectors and all manner of interchangeable components and spare parts. It was a metal-detecting shop on wheels. And long before we actually got under way, Spencer quizzed me closely about conditions on the site—ground cover, soil type, soil moisture, and so on—so that he could select and tune the most appropriate equipment. When conditions changed on the site, as they did, he switched to the machine that was best for the job. Moreover, he was infinitely patient and clear-headed, attributes that translate into people skills. He was a good teacher and an effective leader.

Spencer's first experience on the site was actually during the 2010 field season when I asked him to explore a 1.4-acre area surrounding the temple block. In part, I had had it cleared of vegetation just for his purposes. I wanted to know, before we launched a massive survey, if metal detecting could be an effective option at our site at all. The answer, I pretty quickly learned, was an emphatic yes. Spencer virtually vacuumed the entire parcel, and while most of his targets turned out to be not-so-old shotgun shell hulls, an important minority of them were, definitively, sixteenth-century Spanish things. That test-run sealed the deal and led to the expansive survey in 2012.

Arguably the metal-detecting aspect of the survey project was more difficult than the shovel-testing part of it. The shovel testers had the luxury of leaping from one very specific location to another, bypassing some of the gnarly brush along the way. Not so for the detector team. They were required to swing their detectors, steadily and evenly, over the entire area. In fact, to make the point about difficulty, the first person I enlisted to cover that relatively small clearing lasted less than a day and wound up checking himself into the local hospital because he feared heat exhaustion. Walk, swing, listen, dig, over and over again for days; it is not light duty in a South Georgia summer.

For those of us engaged in other work the metal detectors could be a maddening distraction. They chirp, beep, or groan in a bizarre range of tones whenever they sense a metallic object. Larger, shallower finds elicit loud and obnoxious noises while smaller or deeper ones are registered *soto voce*. So there you are, trying to concentrate on mapping, note taking, or even shovel testing, and the soothing, ordinary sounds of the woods are pierced by electro-babble. The really hard part of it is not knowing what the detectors are announcing. Did they just detect Soto's sword or only another shotgun shell? It takes lots of self-control not to dash over and learn what every sound means.

When that part of the survey was done the results were, now rather predictably, not exactly what I would have predicted. First of all, significantly more Spanish metal was recovered than I could ever have anticipated. To learn that the number of take-it-to-the-bank, sixteenth-century artifacts numbered around thirty is probably not impressive at first. But knowing that such a large number of them had never before been recovered from a site of this kind, and by this method, should be attention getting. There will be more about these finds to come, but it will suffice now to say that they included a surprisingly diverse array of iron tools, personal items, and more specialized objects.

Equally intriguing was the way all that hardware was distributed. It was not found everywhere in the study area, which you will remember was defined around an estimation of the minimum extent of a full Soto encampment. Instead, the Spanish-related debris field was confined exclusively to the area of the bagel. There is a one-to-one correlation between the distribution of early Spanish metal artifacts and the footprint of the Indian village (figure 5.2). What was that saying about the Indian-Spanish encounter?

It was no less puzzling to realize that this unique set of European artifacts, presumably exotic and valuable in the Indian world, was coming from contexts that didn't seem so special. With only rare exceptions did we document any of them in locations that seemed out of the ordinary within the town. Several, for example, were found trailing down the steep slope of the old riverbank, a place more suited for disposal of common things than of valuable rarities.

For some it might have been a letdown to realize that all that painstaking metal detecting over such a large area was not more fruitful, unless the goal was to amass the world's largest collection of spent shotgun shells. In reality, it was beautifully productive from an archaeological standpoint. Our diligence had once again illuminated a pattern that we would have been unable to discern otherwise. And it, too, begged lots of interesting, new questions.

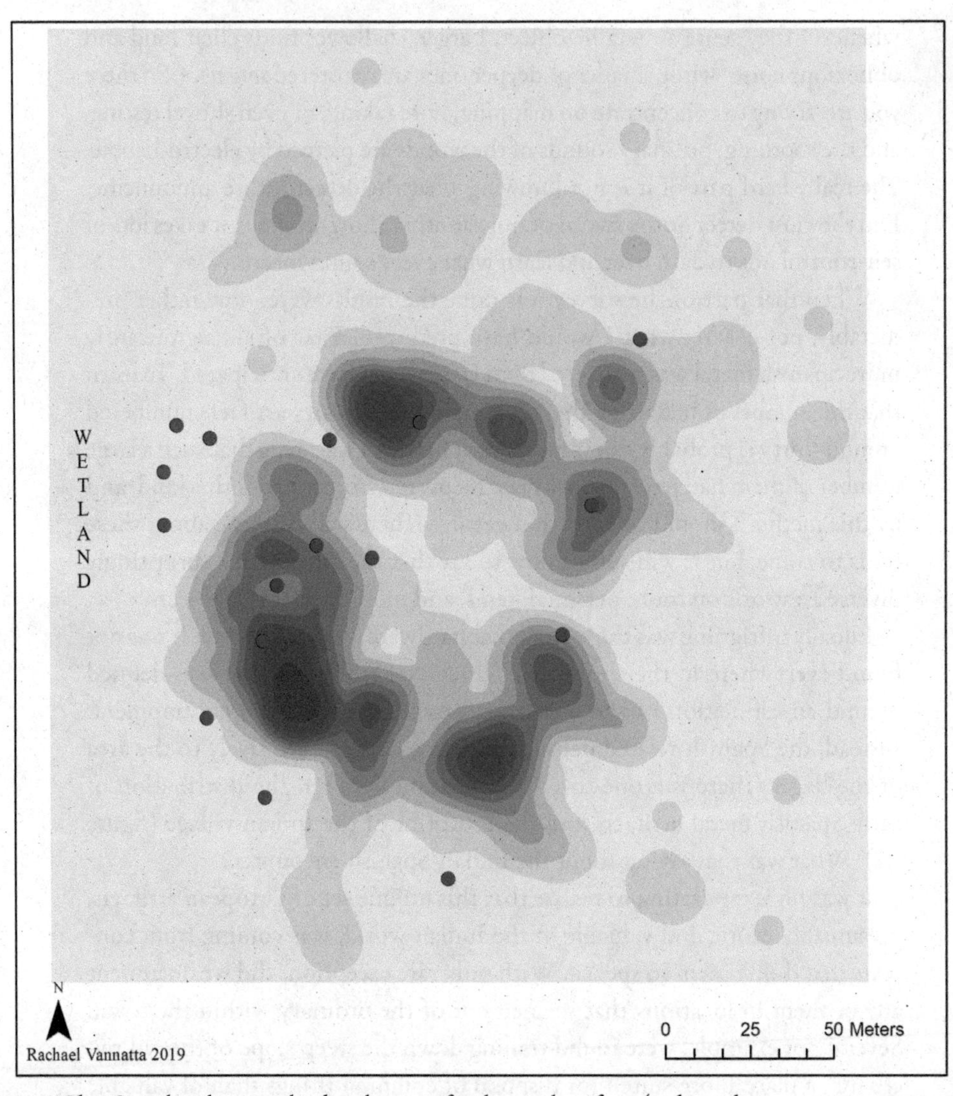

5.2 Glass Site plan showing the distribution of early metal artifacts (indicated by red circles) identified by the metal detector survey. Note that they all fall within or immediately adjacent to the Native village ring.

That archaeological fieldwork is a labor-intensive process, sometimes physical in the extreme, will be abundantly clear by now. And though it's hard for me to imagine, I can foresee a time when our shovels and machetes will be largely retired. Technology has become central to archaeology. In the same way they have revolutionized almost every discipline, high-tech tools have made our work far more efficient and precise, and the pace of change only accelerates. Today a typical project leads off with applications of sophisticated electronics, and digging tools don't make the scene until later. With the aid of instruments that give us virtual X-ray vision, an archaeological site can be sized up on a schedule far more compressed than it used to be, and by only a couple of specialists rather than a gang. Traditional approaches were necessary and prominent in our study of the Glass Site, but I was not about to ignore some of the newer and better options.

On three occasions I sought, literally, to peer beneath the surface of the site with the aid of advanced technology. In general, this brand of archaeology is called geophysics and sometimes geophysical prospecting. Much like metal detecting, but on yet another plane of sophistication, it is work best left to experts, and I'm not one of them. If you start to ask around, a person discovers, once again, that a few names percolate to the top of the practitioner list. Lots of people do geophysics these days, but some of them are especially good at it. I wanted the best I could get.

I confess, however, that the first round of geophysical prospecting at the Glass Site took advantage of opportunity more than talent. When funding is scarce, sometimes we simply do the best we can. Soon after my start at Fernbank, I made the acquaintance of an archaeologist at Georgia State University, also in Atlanta. Some friendly chats revealed that he had just acquired new magnetometer and soil-resistance equipment for his department, and he was fishing for opportunities to try them out. Why not the Glass Site, I offered? Pretty soon, he, a friend, his dog and I, all novices, were out there to test drive his new archaeological toys.

Our timing was advantageous, at least theoretically, since all this was arranged before a shovel had even made its way to the site. The idea was to see if we couldn't document some specific targets before the excavation began in just a couple of weeks. By that point Frankie Snow and I had concluded that one area was particularly promising based on surface indications—later determined to be the temple location—so I gridded it off for the first go.

Doing or watching the geophysical survey process is about as exciting as watching grass grow, just like it is for so much of archaeology. It isn't far different, in fact, from watching someone mow grass with a push mower. The surveyor traverses an area, back and forth, and over and over, on a series of parallel transects. The only difference, on the face of it, is that the geophysical tools cost substantially more than a mower, despite the fact that many of them resemble nothing more than clunky baby strollers.

Geophysical instruments like magnetometers and soil-resistance devices have been around for decades, but each generation sees incremental improvement in portability, precision, user-friendliness, and data-processing capability. My new colleague had acquired some of the latest and best on the market but . . . he had virtually no practical experience with them. This was going to be a seat-of-the-pants trial.

In simple terms here's how the instruments work. Magnetometers are designed to measure variation in the local magnetic field. The instrument senses and then records deviations, even subtle ones, from the average background field of magnetism. Relatively high or relatively low magnetic "anomalies" below the surface potentially register the presence of an archaeological feature. The presence of a foundation or a grave, for instance, will cause deviation from what is normal. The tricky part is that all manner of alterations to the soil, whether natural or cultural in origin, can create anomalous readings. And because the instruments don't yet tell us specifically whether the target is an old gopher tortoise burrow or a posthole, they must ultimately be "groundtruthed" the old fashioned way—by excavation. Ultimately the same holds true with soil resistance. The main difference is that those devices are recording the rate at which an electrical current passes through the underlying soil. Relatively rapid or relatively slower transmission potentially telegraphs the presence of an anomaly of interest.

What is exciting about geophysical survey, just like the rest of archaeology, is the anticipation of discovery. The best instruments today, coupled with a computing device, will display real-time results in graphical form. You can immediately see a virtual picture of what is being recorded beneath the surface. But those initial field images, generated from raw input, are not always clear or representative. More meaningful depictions of subsurface conditions are usually generated by post-field processing that eliminates "noise" and enhances what matters, and that was certainly true in this case. We literally dragged the devices across the furrowed site surface for hours, and then I had to wait to learn what they had detected.

As it turned out, not much. The images I received from my colleague were ambiguous at best. Imagine looking over a blurred, black-and-white X-ray or sonogram image from the obstetrician—thirty years ago. There were relatively darker and relatively lighter shades of gray on our readout, indicative of different levels of magnetism and resistance, but the distinctions did not resolve into meaningful patterns. The reaction of all of us was more or less, "Dunno."

In retrospect, I recognize that we inspected only a tiny portion of the Glass Site village over those couple of days, and that meant it was harder to see the broader contrasts that might emerge in a larger area. But I also know now that the survey area overlapped, albeit barely, with the northern edge of the temple ditch—and it's just not apparent in the images. What *is* obvious is a strong parallel pattern in the output's gray tones, as if the images were affected by some kind of extraterrestrial interference. In the final analysis, however, it's clear that the gray striping is the very real effect of that industrial-scale plowing I have described, and the imprint of it has plagued every attempt to collect useful geophysical data from the site.

Six years later, at the outset of the 2012 season, I was ready to give geophysics another go. By then we knew that the site was important and extensive, and it would have been irresponsible to dismiss the potential of further geophysical survey. I also fully appreciated that geophysics, like so many other pursuits, is a get-what-you-pay-for proposition. Perhaps an experienced technician could overcome some of the issues that got in our way previous times. That was how Chet Walker became another of the project's hired guns. Chet's reputation was exploding in all the right ways about that time, including in Georgia after his remarkable success at the great site of Etowah, north of Atlanta. He was being celebrated as "the man," and I wanted him in our corner.

Chet's debut at Glass was as impressive as Spencer Barker's. He was loaded for archaeological bear. Behind a giant pickup truck, he was towing an ATV specially rigged for geophysical survey, and the utility boxes on the rig were brimming with electronics for magnetometry and ground penetrating radar (GPR). Another full-service, mobile lab.

That year I had arranged to have more than an acre surrounding the temple thoroughly cleared of young pine trees and underbrush. This was mainly to accommodate Chet's work and, you will remember, Spencer's. The idea was to remove aboveground obstructions so that Chet could be extra thorough. In our part of the world, archaeologists simply cannot undertake a high-quality, geophysical survey unless vegetation is erased. We also did our best to rid the area of old wire flags, nails, and other metal markers we had placed here and there for mapping purposes. Magnetometers are, in some respects, fancy metal detectors and modern, near-surface ferrous metal produces bold, distracting signals.

Chet made a full sweep of the new clearing with a gradiometer-type magnetometer, encompassing the small parcel we had geophysically surveyed in 2006. He walked every bit of the area towing a custom-made "mag cart," rigged to instantaneously feed visual results to a laptop. Having now worked with Chet frequently, I know that his face will react to any really good results that appear on the screen. But in this case, there was no wide-eyed grinning. It wasn't as if the area was devoid of targets of archaeological interest; there just weren't any verifiable building outlines or the like. The anomalies that did show up were smallish and could be interpreted only with a healthy dose of equivocation. "*Maybe* this is a hearth. This one *could* be part of a ditch." And so on. The things that were most identifiable were pieces of metal that lit up the display as black-and-white dots. The other recognizable aspect of the output was, sadly, that uniform array of linear gray shadows. The legacy of the bedding plow had struck again. I was really learning to curse that infernal thing.

Later, Chet applied his GPR to a smaller area around the temple where we knew there was fairly robust archaeology, including things like a ditch. Because we were still actively excavating the temple block, the GPR coverage was limited mainly to the margins of the excavation. After Chet processed those data, we could see more compelling evidence of major features. Not surprisingly, portions of the ditch that encircled the temple showed up best.

In time, thanks to the metal detector survey, we also learned things about some of the metal targets Chet had plotted. As supposed, most of them were of modern vintage, consisting of things like nuts and bolts from logging equipment and some of our stray grid-point markers. But a few of them proved to be additional sixteenth-century Spanish artifacts, as we shall see.

As I had hoped, the combined results of shovel testing, geophysics, and metal detecting identified several discrete locations worthy of excavation. A handful of the shovel tests revealed places where an artifact-rich midden had accumulated, potentially marking the locations of buildings. Several of the metal-detector targets were deep enough, and associated with deposits complex enough, to require controlled excavation. Then there were geophysical anomalies waiting to be resolved.

Starting in 2012 fieldwork was given over to sizing up the promising parts of the site lying beyond the temple area. We had determined the dimensions of the site, but it was far from clear what exactly had occurred within those boundaries. The new objective was to gain a sense of the full history of the Indian community, together with some details of the day-to-day existence of its inhabitants. We would not, however, explore every attractive spot, or even fully excavate the ones we did choose for evaluation, but instead open them just enough to pin down what kinds of activities had occurred there and when. There was little value in doing more than necessary to answer our key questions. This sort of problem-oriented approach reflects contemporary archaeology's concern with long-term preservation. Excavate what you need to but leave the rest for future researchers.

The first of the high-value locations I'll describe involved some drama. The excavation was prompted by a discovery made by one of the more-experienced amateur detectorists on Spencer's team. This fellow, Will Andrews, represents South Georgia at its best: laconic and independent, hardy and tough, curious and bright, helpful and kind. And how could you not love a guy who shows up in the woods astride a black spray-painted motorcycle, detector strapped to the saddle? Will had long ago gotten himself a metal detector and on his own learned the better ways to operate it. Spencer was quick to recognize this, gave him lots of latitude in the survey, and grew to rely on him to cover sizable, difficult areas. That was all right by Will; he wanted to be useful, and he was happiest on his own. That's why he made more than one extraordinary find in a particularly brushy corner of the site that none of us had much hope for.

This meant I wasn't likely to see much of Will unless he had something worthwhile to report, and his instincts about what mattered were keen. The first time he emerged from his thicket, on a beeline toward me, it was to report an iron object still in the ground. Understated to a fault, Will's words require some filtering, usually to amp them up. If he said warm, I would think hot. In this instance the report was something like, "Got something over yonder you might oughta look at." My translation, "Get your ass over there and check out what might be the most important find yet." So I did, and so it sort of was.

In Will's favor, he appreciated our archaeological protocols and especially the value of context. He had carefully probed the depth of the object and, having determined it was embedded in an "interesting" deposit below the depth of modern disturbances, was not tempted to simply pry it out of the ground. He had ascertained correctly that this was not a beer can in a plow furrow. The strength of the signal the object had given him, from more than 30 cm below the surface, together with its position in a midden-like stratum, said two important things about it: it was large, and it was old.

Committing time and people to formal excavation of a 2 x 2 m unit in an area that I had never considered to be anything but marginal ran against some of my instincts, but there was also no denying that Will's mysterious artifact had to be explored according to exacting protocols. Good practice is good practice. The unit was laid out, and a team of three GSU students set to the job of peeling away soil that hid the heavy metal surprise. Once the uppermost, plowed-up layer was shoveled away, and the top of the first undisturbed level was troweled clean, it was if I was looking again into one of the first test units we had opened in 2006 over by the temple. The exposed soils were "busy" and full of Lamar culture artifacts. Large patches of gray, ashy soil, laden with charcoal bits, lay alongside equally bold patches of yellowish-orange clayey soil. It was obviously a mixed-up, unnatural deposit. But exactly what unnatural process had created it was the question hanging in the air, together with crackling anticipation over the identity of the iron thing.

The suspense surrounding this operation did anything but abate as the students cautiously continued downward. Before long, and not far above the level of the metal object, they encountered a zone of even darker, middeny soil. In it, durable Native American artifacts such as pottery fragments were common, as were other by-products of human living, like burned pieces of wood and animal bone. This was the layer that had especially got Will's attention, and we were confirming his belief that the iron object was securely cocooned within it.

Understandably, everyone on the site was distracted by the goings-on at this unit. We were all excited by the cascade of surprises, and none more than a visiting television crew. Purely coincidentally, Fernbank had worked with an Atlanta ABC affiliate to film an episode of a special series it was running called *Hidden Georgia*. The idea was to showcase important but little-known natural and historical sites in the state, and by then the Glass Site story had gained enough traction to make the station's list. We always recommend scheduling these kinds of visits late in a season since that's when we usually have the most compelling things to show and talk about, and that advice was certainly prescient this time.

At last the big day arrived. The students had done a splendid job of carrying the excavation through a complicated series of layers to reach the top of the iron object. They had used small wood picks that resembled pointy popsicle sticks and brushes to expose the top of the artifact. Pretty soon, and with cameras rolling, the object was fully revealed atop a slight pedestal of soil. There was no longer any question about what it was: a classic-style, sixteenth-century iron ax blade, obviously of European derivation. Better still, it was being thoroughly documented, by our process and the TV crew, in an undisturbed, village-related deposit.

Perhaps, "momentous" is the word that best captures the import of the find; "stupendous" might be even better. The ax is of a kind common to the Soto era, and although they have occasionally turned up in places with a history of early Spanish activity, never before had such an artifact been found in South Georgia. Once we all stopped buzzing over the ax, the bigger questions began to loom. Once more, my conception of the site was shifting radically, and for a while, it seemed to do so almost by the hour—thanks much to Will.

In a few days Will again emerged from the brush with something to report. He marched up, fist clenched, and said something to me like, "I think I found a bell." Those are highly charged words to an archaeologist working at a Spanish-related site. Different kinds of bells were carried by explorers and missionaries alike. Will's arm extended, his hand opened, and there in his palm was a jaw-dropping sight. It was the upper hemisphere of a small sheet-brass bell of a type known as Clarksdale. The name derives from a delta town in Mississippi near which several were found, and they are as diagnostic of Soto as certain kinds of glass beads. Although this rare find was lying just below the surface in the plowed soil horizon, it still impacted the way we were thinking about the Glass Site and a particular sector of it.

Will's discoveries moved new questions to the top of the agenda: What in the world was going on out there at the far eastern margin of the village? Why were these super-rare Spanish artifacts over there, and what was the meaning of the associated massive and complex deposits? The first job, quite literally, was to get to the bottom of the unit in which the ax blade had been recovered. With only days to go in the season, I innocently asked the students to wrap up the excavation by continuing down to subsoil, the ancient clay we would always eventually bump into. They were already at about 50 cm, so how hard could it be?

The answer was, it turned out, very hard. Properly coping with highly changeable stratigraphy is tedious and slow. It seemed that with every slice of the shovel or trowel a new face of the deposit cropped up. There was lots of swirly, busy stuff going on. Their unit finally reached the depth where the uniformly orangish subsoil ordinarily shows up, but it wasn't there. The clock was ticking, and the unit was not getting any easier to understand. I reduced the excavation to a quarter of the original size so that we could move more aggressively. This also meant, in the interest of time, that I would handle most of the digging.

At last, numerous strata later and nearly 1.5 m below the surface, subsoil was struck. Seldom has a bunch of archaeologists been so happy to hit soil that contains absolutely no artifacts. As satisfying as that was, we had only to glance at the complicated, multicolored cross section we had created to get sobered up again. What a deposit. Way back when, someone, or some group, had opened a massive hole, later only to be filled in both purposely and naturally. Our familiar refrain: what is going on out here?!

These surprising developments didn't enter the picture until the end of that season, in accord with a universal rule in archaeology that there will usually be a dramatic but frantic closing. Yet I wanted, and in some ways needed, fewer questions and more closure. The whole point of that year's work had been to understand the village.

I've learned over the decades that having quality time at a site is essential. To find space to think, I will frequently stay behind when the crew leaves the site for the day or maybe wander back to it in the evening. Sometimes I spend the night on a site. I also make a point to schedule a few quiet days for myself at the end of the season. Regardless, solitary meditation on the scene has proven to be, for me, an essential activity. The end of this season was no different, except my post-dig interlude was neither entirely solitary nor quiet.

Because I wanted to leave with a modicum of clarity about what was going on in the "far east" of the site, I chose to bring out the "mechanical trowel," aka a backhoe. Long ago archaeologists learned the value of heavy equipment, though it is still the common, public perception that fieldwork is strictly hands-and-knees brushing and dental-picking. However, it just ain't so. With the right questions and a respectful approach, backhoes, bulldozers, and motor graders, run by skilled operators, are a boon to archaeology. I contacted another enormously helpful local, Louie Harper, and he agreed to send over his mini-backhoe with an operator.

The scaled-down excavating equipment now available everywhere is well suited to archaeological exploration. The machines are nimble enough to work around obstacles like trees, and their smaller buckets allow for exacting, lower-impact digging. On our site, I positioned Louie's backhoe in a way that the operator could insert his small bucket into the deep and narrow end of our excavation and then extend it toward the east. The idea was "simply" to find the limits of the massive pit we had encountered. The picture afforded in the profile of the new cut left me dumbstruck. The eastern edge of the feature wasn't exposed until the skinny trench was extended more than 7 m (23 ft). For most of that length, the filled-in pit maintained a depth in excess of 1 m, and the deposits inside it were consistently complex. The scale of the deposit had me wanting to believe it was a modern intrusion made, in fact, by something like a bulldozer. But the compactness of the feature fill, and the presence in it of nothing but Lamar culture artifacts, from top to bottom, indicated that it was very much a late prehistoric or very early historic-period creation.

This bit of archaeological surgery added new facts to a growing heap of them, but genuine clarity was not exactly the result. Yes, it was apparent that the Native inhabitants of the Glass Site had made a massive excavation out on the eastern perimeter of their village, and that they had used it from time to time as a dumping area, but its real purpose was anything but obvious. My first interpretation was that we had exposed a section of a defensive perimeter, in the form of a "moat." Sharply defined, circular communities like the Glass Site often owe their final form to installation of encircling moats or palisades, and sometimes both. Plus, it was already clear that ditch-style borders, like the one that set off the temple, were part of the local landscaping repertoire.

With that, the massive feature became another of my preoccupations. Students in my 2014 James Madison University field school opened two additional units in the area and used a small-diameter soil corer to try to establish firmer limits of the "moat." A unit a few meters westward of the 2012 excavation didn't intersect it at all, giving some credence to the suggestion it was a narrow ditch. But then another unit placed a short distance northward also

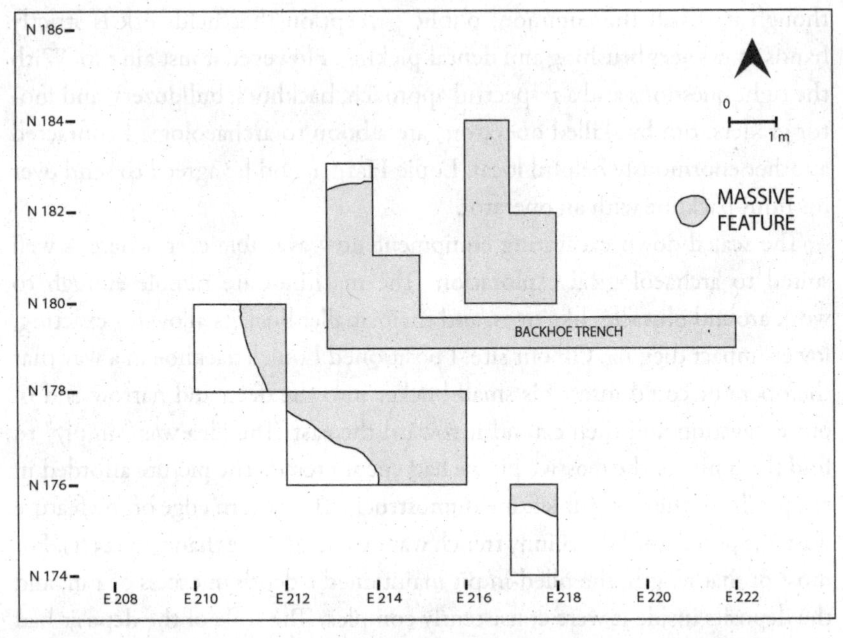

5.3 Plan of Area C excavation results. The large, ditch-like feature, consisting of large, interlinked pits, extends beyond the limits of excavation to the north and east.

failed to expose feature fill. Closer in to the 2012 excavation, the tight-interval soil cores intersected busy fill deposits at several points but not everywhere. So even when we drove away from the site that year, the additional testing had cast little light on the nature of the vexing feature.

As much as anything, it was the nagging uncertainty surrounding the big feature that required another full season at Glass. If my goal was to make meaningful interpretation of the site, then this thing had to be better understood. Under that pressure, the feature got a full-court press in the summer of 2015. Over the course of three weeks, a crew of six hard-core excavators completed excavation of eight large units, all surrounding the ax-yielding square that originally led us to the area (figure 5.3). It was not a picnic. Most of the units fell largely if not entirely within the limits of the feature, and completing them meant hand excavation to more than 1 m and, along the way, puzzling out one undulating layer after another, including some thick ones of clay that were largely devoid of artifacts (figure 5.4). Working in the deepest layers had the added challenge of transferring the soil to the sifting screens one heavy bucket at a time.

5.4 Cross-section view of complex deposits filling the ditch-like feature in Area C

At last, however, the results started to mean something. Based on artifacts, there was no longer any question that the feature was a Lamar culture creation. It became clearer, as well, that the "ditch" was actually a series of large, deep pits, averaging more than 2 m in diameter, dug somewhat haphazardly on a north-south axis. Each pit had been incrementally filled by alternating spells of natural siltation and human dumping. But the question of why they had been dug and filled where they were was not entirely resolved. The best I can offer at this stage is that, fundamentally, they represent clay mines, places where the orangish clay subsoil was obtained for wall daub and perhaps for pottery clay. In satisfying this practical need, the site's residents may have decided to give the pits the added value of defining the community's limits, perhaps in a manner that would deter intruders. Then, over time and out of convenience, the village-edge cavities became convenient dumping places. In effect, mining pits were linked to form a perimeter ditch that eventually served as a landfill.

Other priority locations in the village were not ignored. It was easy to imagine how the regularly spaced concentrations of artifacts within the village ring were announcing the locations of domiciles. Assuming this inference was valid, samples from those areas would provide critical perspective on the day-to-day existence of ordinary residents, giving balance to the glimpse of privileged activity we had stumbled onto at the temple. Two of the hot spots on the north side of the village were fairly intensively investigated in 2014 and 2015, and a third was lightly sampled in 2012 (see figure 3.4).

In each of those places, our excavations documented unequivocal evidence of a structure. Beyond a relatively high density of artifacts, what that evidence consisted of varied from place to place based on the parts of the buildings our units managed to intersect. What we saw also hinged on the life history of the structures themselves. Within the nine test units we opened across a hot spot poetically designated as Area A, structural evidence was limited mainly to posthole features. As I described in the temple discussion, alignments of the filled sockets for wall uprights are the standard archaeological signature of a building in our region. The mixed and usually darkened soil filling the posthole cavities allows them to stand out against the homogeneous native soil. The arrangement of excavation units in Area A was such that we could not plot the full outline of a structure, but in the aggregate, the extent of posthole features, artifacts, small pit features, and midden define a building-related activity area of around 140 m^2 (figure 5.5). The very small quantity of wall daub that turned up here is taken to indicate that this building did not burn, unlike most of the other structures we've discovered at Glass.

Even before our testing of Area A was completed, it had earned the name "Pipemaker's House." This is the other location on the site, outside the special confines of the temple, that has produced unusual numbers of elaborate ceramic smoking pipes. And among the objects that turned up with them was an elongated "squeegee" of clay, bearing fingerprints, that potentially is cast-off pipe-making clay. Otherwise, there is nothing to suggest that this building was not a basic dwelling.

The quest to make sense of the building in nearby Area B, in no small measure because two unusual glass beads surfaced in 2014, involved two seasons of investigation. The beads expanded the pool of evidence for an Indian-European encounter at the beginning of the colonizing era, but they seemed to be announcing a second round of interaction post-Soto. Suffice it to say, the sizable, trench-like excavation we made in Area B in 2015 was designed to give those small beads more meaningful context.

The 2 x 14 m trench, consisting of five contiguous and one outlying units, opened a window on a structure's floor from beyond its south wall to the central hearth, and then a bit beyond the north wall (figure 5.6). Respectable

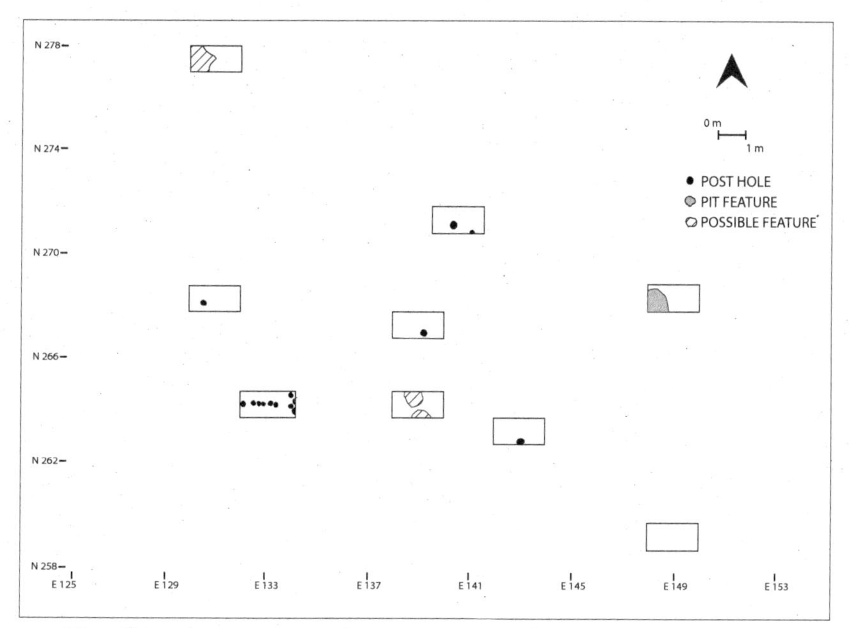

5.5 Plan of Area A excavation results

quantities of daub in the three 2014 units had clued us to the presence of the building, and chunks of it in the new trench confirmed not only that it was there but that it had succumbed to fire. The location of the central fireplace was plainly evident, first of all, from the same kind of localized daub layer that covered the temple hearth. The clay plaster that had been applied to protect roof thatch around the smoke hole had fallen straight down onto the fireplace. Once we removed the daub layer, a telltale patch of intensely heated soil was exposed at the point of the actual fireplace. Evidence of substantial postholes was documented 5 m south of the hearth, indicating that the structure fully measured twice that distance across.

The modest numbers of Lamar potsherds and other artifacts in and around this building indicate, perhaps, that its abandonment and destruction by fire were planned. It seemed as if it had been emptied of valuables in advance. At the same time, the large size of the building leaves us to ask if it was not also built for some special purpose. It is common at Mississippian sites to discover at least one larger-than-average dwelling, usually interpreted as that of a chief and his family.[2]

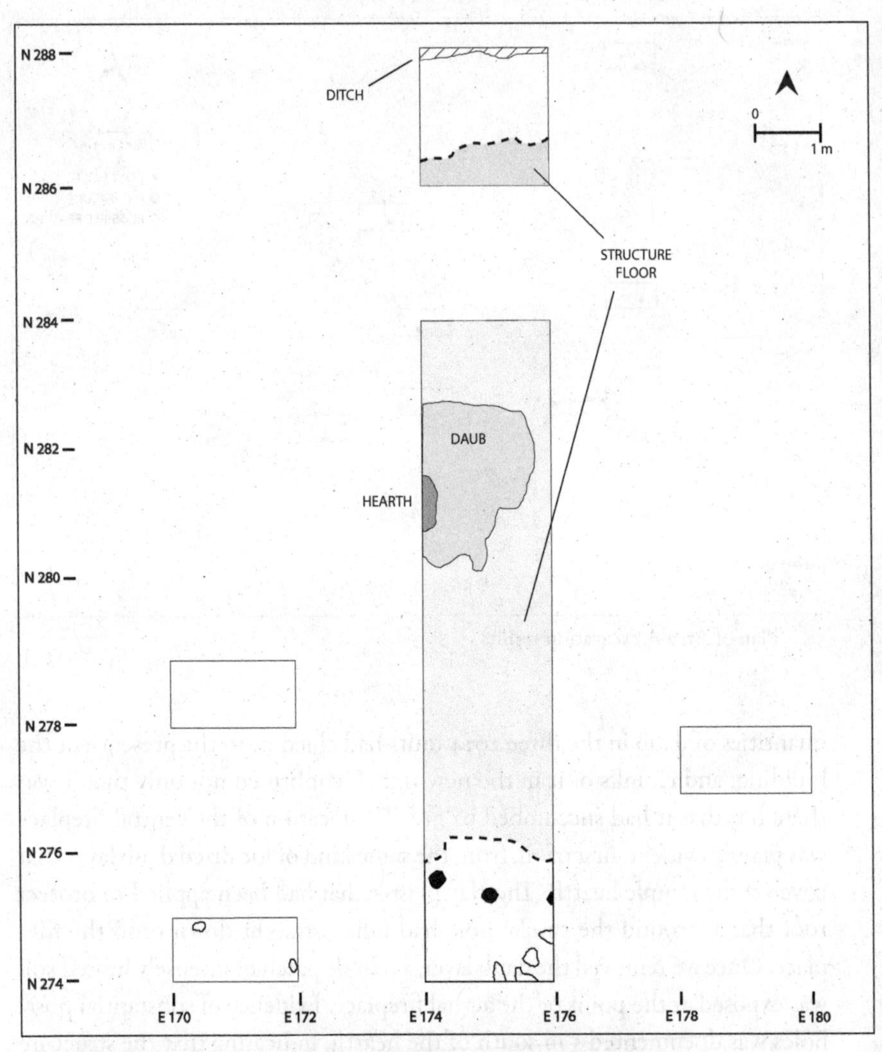

5.6 Plan of Area B excavation results. Posthole features and clumps of fired daub mark the southern wall; the central hearth was smothered and surrounded by a dome of fired daub; and a glimpse of what might be the perimeter ditch is exposed in the northernmost unit.

A third village-area structure was located in 2012 by a single 2 x 2 m unit, not far east of the temple. One of our shovel tests had turned up a bagful of large Lamar pottery fragments, and the unit was placed directly on top of it. Excavation led to exposure of a section of a structure floor, indicated by a thin accumulation of dark-colored midden and a hint of compaction. Equally indicative of the floor level was a "pot bust" lying on the compacted surface. This is what the shovel test had struck, and in the end, we plotted and removed large sections of two Lamar bowls (figure 5.7). Together with a relative

5.7 Reconstructed sections of Lamar pottery bowls excavated on the floor of a village structure

abundance of burned roof supports, the evidence from this unit pointed to the site of another structure that had caught fire without warning.

It took a decade, but I believe, at last, that we have the archaeological basis for a reasonable description of the late prehistoric Native American community we know as the Glass Site. Yes, it is a place where rare evidence of Spanish exploration has been discovered, but it was founded and occupied in an Indian world and not in a European one. The decisions and actions of Native people made it what it was, and it is from that essential aspect of the place that a sound interpretation must begin and end. This is to say not that our understanding of that Indian world is comprehensive but only that we have accumulated sufficient evidence to set down, in outline form, the site's story. It is a scaffold onto which I will later drape the equally incomplete body of evidence for European encounters.

In my mind's eye, I can see that the village established on that sandy terrace, at least by the year 1450, was developed under a formal and perhaps ambitious plan (figure 5.8). Its layout and the features of some of the buildings within it, in addition to some possessions of the inhabitants, point to a community of prominence in the region, as opposed to the small, backwater hamlet that I and others at first believed it to be. There is far more reason to believe, in other words, that it was a place of consequence and that we should no longer be surprised that someone like Soto viewed it as a sensible destination. More about the community and the complicated evidence of those encounters are our next topics.

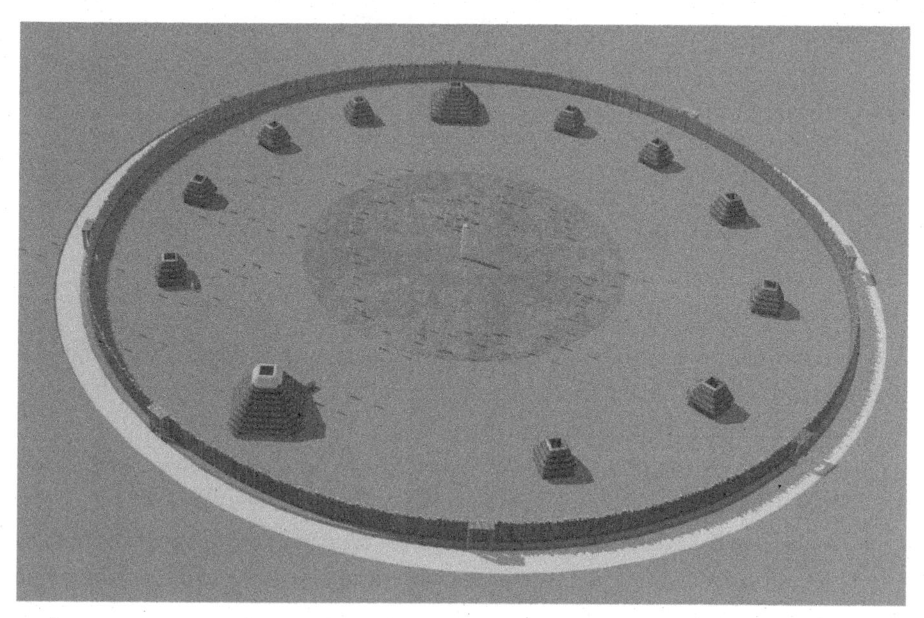

5.8 Interpretive illustration of Glass Site village
(Fernbank Museum of Natural History)

VI

Calling Cards of a Conquistador

The Glass Site, the place of a former Native American Indian town, has produced an unusual number of European-made artifacts dating from the sixteenth century, many of them probably manufactured before 1550. It is true that the entire collection of them would fit inside a shoebox, but it is just as true that the total number of similar artifacts from almost any other site outside Florida would fit into an even smaller container. The unusual diversity of objects in the Glass Site collection is just as curious as the quantity. Both facts would seem to mean that there was something out of the ordinary about the place and about the encounter, or encounters, that brought them to the town. If nothing else, it all speaks to the extreme rarity of tangible evidence linking us to Soto and other of the earliest European visitors to the region. And make no mistake, the bulk of it also says we are not dealing with the Catholic mission I set out to find.

It is for those reasons that I devote a full chapter to the least-common artifacts. Call it desperation if you will, but it is the hard truth that unless archaeologists learn to wring every drop of meaning from these meager leavings, we have little to nothing to work from. Just a little bit of scrutiny will almost always demonstrate that there is more to the objects than meets the eye. Even the homeliest of these things are bridges to people and events that would go unrecognized in their absence. And sometimes the tailings of humanity are powerfully evocative. With little to no imagination on our part, they can give a glimpse of another time, and with just a little more they will conjure sounds, smells, and even emotions.

Still, merely reporting discovery of a tiny glass bead or a relatively shapeless piece of iron is prone to elicit little or no excitement from the average person, especially in a vacuum of other information. In fact, I sometimes get the sense that people feel just a little sorry for me when I jump up and down over such a find. Our society has for so long been awash in sophisticated manufactured goods that glass and iron are taken for granted. But we must be reminded that what is commonplace now, and what was familiar even in sixteenth-century Europe, had no precedent whatsoever in the Native world of the Southeast. Sure, the Indians were making beads of shell and metal things of copper. But for them, multicolored glass beads and shiny, hard, and sharp iron tools might as well have been smartphones. Both the goods and the know-how to produce them were completely alien. Thus, these seemingly mundane objects were, in that context, sufficiently enchanting to have at times a head-spinning influence over the affairs of fully lucid people. Indeed, glass and iron were the counterparts in the Indian world to gold and silver in the Spanish mind. They could make people a little crazy, just as they do archaeologists sometimes.

The Beads

Believe it or not, for some archaeologists glass beads are the raison d'être, the alpha and the omega, of their professional lives. They work to know beads inside and out—how and when they were made, where they came from, and how they were used. And we love them for this kind of deep knowledge, eccentric though it might be. On many occasions I've carried to such authorities the glass beads I've found in different places, feeling every bit the supplicant before the oracle. We can chuckle about it, and why not? But don't be mistaken about the archaeological importance. The interpretation of entire archaeological sites—or entrada routes—sometimes hangs on the meaning of just a few beads. They have certainly loomed large in the Glass Site story.

Glass beads are fairly prominent, numerically, among all the early European artifacts we've found at the Glass Site. Even so, it is a mighty rare event to find one, and they always seem to turn up when and where we least expect them. I would not describe their distribution on the site as random, but where they do occur, they seem just to be sprinkled around. We've found them in disturbed and undisturbed deposits, and around the temple and elsewhere. The finders have been students, volunteers, paid crew, and even me. All told, we've recovered fourteen of them, and every single one has been cause for an after-hours champagne celebration. Let us now look more closely at what they might mean.

6.1 Chevron beads. The largest bead, lower right, has black rather than the usual blue glass layers.

The majority of the site's glass beads, eight by count, are of the same type as the first one found by Ellen Vaughn. They are known as chevron beads for the distinctive starburst pattern visible on the ends that is created by V-shaped folds in separate glass layers. The colors of their ultrathin glass layers alternate, most often between shades of red, white, and blue (figure 6.1). The makers of the beads were purposely creating this look, and to enhance it, they abraded facets onto the ends, lending them a quality of gaudy gemstones.

There is good reason to believe most of the glass beads used for trade by the Spanish in the sixteenth century were manufactured in the ancient glassmaking center of Venice, Italy, and specifically on the tiny island of Murano. Historical documents give the strongest clues of this origin.[1] Because beads evolved into a kind of currency in the encounters between Natives of the Americas and the Europeans flowing there, bead production grew into a lucrative enterprise. Indeed, details of the manufacturing process for complex bead types like chevrons were fiercely guarded pieces of proprietary information, as were glassmaking secrets in general. Quality control over the production of such intricate and small things, and on such a grand industrial scale, was an impressive feat to say the least.

The competitive nature of the glassmaking industry at the time turns out to have advantages for archaeologists. In that kind of business environment, there was a tendency to alter the features of beads frequently, as a means of holding consumer interest. Fashion sense back then was as fickle as it is for us. What counts as stylish today is sure to succumb to something new and different tomorrow. When that tendency exists, archaeologists can rely on the stylistic attributes of things like beads as virtual clocks. We now know, for instance, that one style of chevron bead dates earlier than another. So, consistent discovery of a single kind at the Glass Site says a great deal about the timing and duration of the Indian-Spanish encounter.

Getting into the weeds of beads, every one of the chevrons from the Glass Site has these attributes: small size, seven layers, and faceted ends. By and large, bead people agree that it is a type manufactured almost exclusively in Venice between 1500 and 1570. The attributes of this particular variety contrast with the style of chevron beads prevalent at late sixteenth- to seventeenth-century sites like Mission Santa Catalina de Guale. There they have only five layers of colored glass and were finished by tumbling to be round and smooth rather than faceted by grinding.[2]

From these well-established patterns, one would be very hard pressed to believe the Glass Site encounter did not occur outside the sixteenth century, and likely in the earlier decades of it. In practice, the correlation between seven-layered, faceted chevrons and Soto-era sites is pretty firmly ingrained among archaeologists in the region. Not only do they date to the right time; they're seldom found terribly far from the earliest paths and habitations of Spaniards.[3] That is why they are on a kind of checklist of Soto site indicators. And that is why that first bead found by Ellen was so arresting.

About 2009, after reports of our discoveries of some chevron beads had filtered out, there was still strong pushback from certain archaeologists over the suggestion we were dealing with a Soto site. Among the reactions, I heard second-hand that a senior colleague refused to believe the claim unless Nueva Cádiz beads also turned up. Well, right on cue, our next season produced two of them, both in the temple-area excavation.

So what exactly is this kind of seemingly obligatory bead? They are scarcer in general than faceted chevron beads, and they are even more firmly linked with the early part of the sixteenth century. They can be a solid indicator of Soto's wanderings and also of his predecessor's. In appearance, they are as distinctive as beads come. All Nueva Cádiz types are tubular in form, and some are as long as 6 cm, although the more common type in our region is much shorter, averaging something like 1.2 cm long (figure 6.2). Also, some

6.2 Other early glass beads. *Left to right*: "Becky Bead," faceted Nueva Cadíz, and twisted Nueva Cadíz (twisted Nueva Cadíz = 1.3 cm long).

of the types were formed by twisting the still-malleable glass "canes" so that they cooled to look like licorice sticks. Beads of this kind were almost always made to have three layers of glass, usually two in shades of blue, ranging from turquoise to navy, and one of white. And like the early-style chevrons, the ends of many Nueva Cádiz are faceted as a way of showing off the separate glass layers. Nueva Cádiz beads, incidentally, are named for the first Spanish town in South America, on a small island off the coast of Venezuela, where they were first found by archaeologists in sizable numbers.[4] Most importantly, even more so than with chevron beads, there is an almost spooky correlation in our region between the places Nueva Cádiz beads have been found and the projected path of Soto, especially in the interior.[5]

In the spirit of full disclosure, the archaeological waters have been muddied by discovery of Nueva Cádiz–style beads at later, seventeenth-century sites in the Middle Atlantic and Northeast regions. For example, at Jamestown in Virginia they turn up in copious numbers in association with the 1607–10 fort. Most assuredly, lively debate surrounds the quest to explain this competing pattern, but by and large the trail leads to the Dutch. On one hand, it seems that leftover trading stock held by the East India Company was acquired by the budget-conscious London Company, and on the other, it was a matter of disenfranchised Italian glassmakers relocating to Amsterdam, where they resumed production of an old-style bead.[6]

Perhaps related to the two Nueva Cádiz beads at the Glass Site is a solitary example of a third bead type. It seems to be not only the earliest of the early but also the rarest of the rare. I referred to it in another chapter as the "Becky Bead," after the local volunteer who found it. This one looks in form like a tiny football, but true bead people prefer to compare its shape and size to an olive pit. Against a cobalt blue field are three relatively wide, spiraling white stripes (see figure 6.2). Because they turn up so infrequently, they don't even have a catchy popular name ("Becky Bead" notwithstanding), only a classificatory one: "Type 24."[7]

The Glass Site specimen is the only one of these that exists in the United States outside Florida, where, so far as I can determine, around six others are known. Elsewhere in the Americas, they are known from places such as Hispaniola and Peru.[8] What the numbers and the contexts of discovery suggest is that this kind of bead is especially diagnostic of the earliest phase of Spanish expansion into the hemisphere, comfortably before 1550.

One is pressed to ask the question, in fact, of whether this bead type is more indicative of expeditions that predated Soto's, such as that of Pánfilo de Narváez in 1528.[9] Certainly in Florida the find spots for them coincide fairly neatly with Narváez's projected track. And the Glass Site's location is not so far away that it could not have later been moved inland.

The key is that as a collection, the majority of the beads from the Glass Site—the faceted chevrons, the Nueva Cádiz, and the Becky Bead—are very much aligned with expectations of Soto-era events, if not earlier ones. By the 1970s, archaeologists in the region had observed the co-occurrence of particular artifacts on and near Soto sites often enough to hazard a definition of a "kit" of telltale things. Then and still now, the so-called kit includes chevron and Nueva Cádiz beads. The kit concept is not far-fetched at all since more or less the same suite of objects signifies—and even predicts—the earliest Spanish sites throughout the Americas, whether linked with Soto, Pizarro, or Coronado, among others.[10]

And then there are three glass beads that exemplify the messiness built into archaeological findings. Almost always, exceptions to the prevailing pattern will turn up, especially if you explore a site long enough. To the point, while it is true that 80 percent of the Glass Site beads conform to expectations of a pre-1550 episode of contact, the remainder of them—these three—aren't so tidily dated. They might be outliers in the collection, but that doesn't mean they're any less important to our story.

Two of this triad are literally the most plain-vanilla kind of bead one can find. They are small, spherical, opaque white beads, with the size and look of

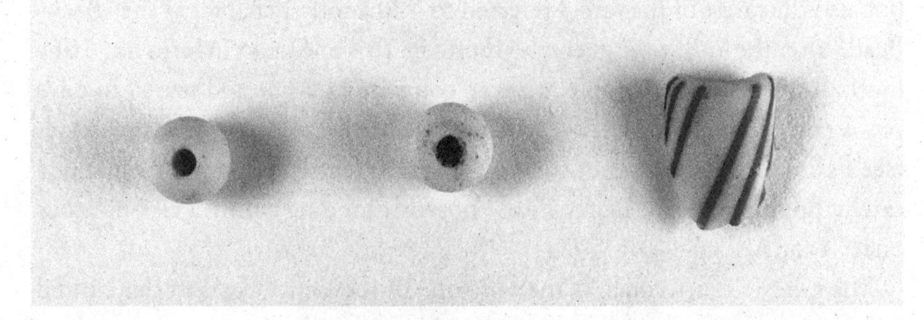

6.3 Additional glass beads, all from Area B. *Left to right*: two spherical, opaque white beads and tubular white bead with thin, spiraling stripes.

an artificial pearl (figure 6.3). Their plainness robs them of the kind of distinguishing features that permit narrow dating. They are among a handful of types that enjoyed extremely long popularity, very likely because they were so easy and inexpensive to produce.

Until recently we were pretty stuck with a wide date range for this category of bead. As useful as the stylistic interpretations may be, analysis of beads on those terms always entails a bit of shrugging shiftiness. Most problematic for me is the license the ambiguity in dating can give to doubters. Where I see Soto in the beads alone, I can't deny that others have grounds to challenge my narrow-gauge argument. Happily, advances in archaeological science have created avenues to disperse the haze. Super-precise, laser-driven instruments allow nondestructive identification of chemical fingerprints in glass beads. Elliot Blair is making a career of this approach, and he has determined that all those plain white beads in our area are really not the same after all. Beginning with the huge Santa Catalina sample, he has determined that chemically they neatly break out into two groups: an early variety with high levels of tin, and a later one with less tin and more antimony.[11] Working together, he and I have determined that the pair from the Glass Site are of the early kind, generally predating 1625.

Last, there is one truly oddball bead. In reality we recovered only about a quarter of the original mass of this bead, but that is enough to identify the type. Whole examples from other places are shaped like a short tube. Inlaid into an opaque white background are at least two sets of three thin, parallel blue stripes that spiral around the tube. Ours is one of the two beads found in 2014 in Area B, in the vicinity of a Native-built structure, the function of which we're still debating.

So why is this bead so unusual? First of all, it seems to be the only one of its type reported from the region north of Florida and east of Tallahassee. In that area these beads are rarer than Nueva Cádiz types. It is relatively familiar in post-1550 French colonial contexts, hundreds of miles west or north of Georgia.[12] So surprising was the discovery of this aberrant bead at Glass that it contributed to the shredding of my plan to end the work in 2014. It simply didn't make sense, and in some ways it still doesn't. Why would we be finding a later-dating "French" bead on a site that otherwise seemed to be producing only early sixteenth-century Spanish artifacts? But recall that the second bead from this area, one of the spherical white beads, would also be at home in a later context. Alas, considerably more excavation at the site of that structure produced not a single additional bead, or any other European artifacts for that matter. Even so, we can surmise that these two beads, in a building on the opposite side of the plaza from the council house, are divulging a second episode of Indian-European contact.

The Bell

Also on the checklist Soto-hunters carry around in their heads, of signature objects that would have been on Soto's own packing list, is a small type of bell archaeologists call Clarksdale. Most of us would describe them as medium-sized sleigh bells, and indeed, they were originally designed to be attached to horse harnesses and the like.[13] Day to day, their jangling must have contributed to the general racket that accompanied an entrada's advance from one Indian town to another. But we also know that they were repurposed by early explorers as items for the Indian trade. Apparently, newfangled noisemakers became another object of local desire.

Generations of archaeologists have recognized the solid connection between Soto-related sites and Clarksdale bells. The bells do frequently occur at Indian towns along the explorer's projected path. In fact, after a time, I had to wonder whether one of those bells would turn up at the Glass Site. It only stood to reason in the face of other evidence we were turning up. Then, right on cue, thanks to Will, there it was.

6.4 Clarksdale bell (diameter = 2.8 cm). Only the upper hemisphere was recovered.

An inspection of a Clarksdale bell reveals that it consists of four parts. The three parts made from thin sheet brass were assembled to contain the fourth, a small sphere of iron. Separate upper and lower hemispheres were connected around the middle by crimping together flanges created for the purpose. But the two halves were joined only after a suspension loop was secured through a hole in the upper part and then soldered on the inside, after the iron tinkler was dropped in. The finished products averaged 1 in (2.5 cm) in diameter. In the world of bells, the characteristics of the type are quite unique.[14]

The example that turned up on the eastern edge of the Glass Site consists only of the upper hemisphere and its suspension loop (figure 6.4). Nonetheless, it is demonstrably a portion of a Clarksdale bell and, in turn, a powerful suggestion of a Soto encounter. The known sample of the bells from the region consists of at least two dozen specimens, scattered from peninsular Florida to the delta lands of Mississippi and Arkansas. And while the correlation is not perfect, that distribution conforms fairly well with Soto's route and sometimes with the sites of other early Spanish expeditions.[15]

The Silver Pendant

A silver pendant might be the very last thing anyone would have predicted at the Glass Site, even knowing there was a Spanish connection. It is not among the items basic to the gift kit, and like some other European objects at the site, it is without exact precedent in the region. What that means is, of course, the question.

The pendant was fashioned by perforating a wafer-thin, water drop–shaped piece of silver at its apex (figure 6.5). If one didn't know better, one would think that it was a modern-day quarter flattened by the wheel of a train and later punched through. Indeed, I initially believed the pendant was a pounded-flat Spanish coin, especially since there is some intriguing topography consisting of narrow ridges and grooves on its surfaces. I imagined them to be the distorted vestiges of an original coin stamp. Not to mention, an assay of the metal reveals that it is "coin silver" alloyed with tiny amounts of copper and lead.

The pendant came from inside the temple like several other Spanish objects, specifically adjacent to a burned post forming part of the south wall of the building. I'll never forget the incredulous reaction of the excavator who discovered it. So shiny was the metal, even after centuries in the ground, that

6.5 Silver pendant (*left*, front; *right*, back; max. length = 3.9 cm)

she first asked, almost apologetically, if it wasn't a piece of modern foil. That would have been a problem, as she was implying, but we quickly determined it was anything but a bit of stray trash.

Not long following discovery of the pendant, I had conveniently planned a trip to New York City for other purposes. My new research into early Spanish coins reminded me that the American Numismatic Society was headquartered there, so I made an appointment for a consultation. I just knew my hunch about a modified coin was going to be confirmed. But it wasn't. The curator who inspected the pendant simply couldn't be persuaded that it had been fashioned from a coin, Spanish or otherwise. Nothing about the network of markings made any sense to him. Plus, the weight of the pendant, something I had recorded prior to the visit, didn't match known weights of any standard currency of the era.

In the final analysis, we're left only to speculate about the precise origin of the pendant. Alloyed silver made its way to the region from Europe and from South America or Mexico.[16] Silver extracted by the Spanish from New World mines was sometimes cut with additives before it was formed and shipped to the treasury in Spain, just as it was in Europe. While it is true that Indians could have obtained silver and gold relatively directly from exploring Spaniards, they also seem to have been scavenging precious metal from shipwreck sites on a fairly routine basis.

Regardless, the alloyed silver pendant was very likely crafted by an Indian, perhaps from a portion of a sectioned coin. The metal was hammered flat, to about the thickness of a dime, and formed into the squat, oval shape. Opposite the narrow end punched through for suspension or attachment purposes, the lower margin bears several regularly spaced, very small notches, maybe for decoration. Everywhere the pendant's surface features and edges are softened from long and steady wear.

It remains a possibility, though far less certain, that this piece was a gift from Soto to a local leader. There is an account in the entrada chronicles that describes just such an exchange reasonably close to, if not at, the Glass Site. The story was passed down by Ranjel in describing the peaceful interaction with the leader of the province of Altamaha. In return, the chief was rewarded with gifts, including a feather decorated with silver.[17]

The Ax

Many of the early European artifacts fall into the heavy metal category. Consisting of one kind of iron tool or another, most are not much to look at because the shapes they were given are so simple. That can make their functions hard to determine, but there is no mistaking the purpose of one iron tool, the hefty ax blade discovered hardly more than 10 m from the Clarksdale bell (figure 6.6).

The broad, downturned cutting edge of this ax is typical of sixteenth-century types, and so distinctive is the form that it has earned its own appellation, the Biscayan ax. The name refers to a territory in Spain where iron for tools was mined and forged.[18] The Glass Site example is missing the eye that would have allowed attachment to a handle. But this is actually a fairly typical, if not predictable, modification, since the Indians were prone to maximize their tool-getting opportunities by removing and repurposing the band forming the eye into a separate yet lighter and simpler cutting blade. Exactly

6.6 Biscayan ax, from which hafting eye has been removed (max. length = 11.7 cm)

how the iron axes were taken apart in Native hands is not exactly clear, but it had to have mainly been a matter of time, energy, and determination—and perhaps also abrasives.

If one looks around the Southeast, it is possible to discover only six other places where identifiable Biscayan axes come from good, Spanish-related archaeological context.[19] Infrequent discovery of true ax blades, compared to more common and less sophisticated types of iron tools, probably has something to say about the circumstances of their introduction. Both historical accounts and archaeological settings indicate that gift items were ranked and distributed according to a prestige scale. Under this hierarchy an ax would most likely be reserved for high-level exchange, such as from leader to leader. If this is true, it signifies the prominence of both the Glass Site and some of its residents.

Soto and company actually made reference to the distinctive axes in recounting one unsettling discovery. They had arrived at the fabled province of Cofitachequi and set to ransacking holy places in search of treasure. In one temple, at a place called Ilapi, they rifled through bundled burials only to happen upon European things. Quoting the secretary, Ranjel, "they took out that emerald and it was made of glass, and after that one, more and more beads of glass and rosaries with their crosses. They also found Biscayan axes of iron, by which they recognized that they were in the district of land where the licenciado Lucas Vázquez de Ayllón was lost."[20]

The Glass Site ax is the artifact Will Andrews located during the metal-detector survey and later exposed by students within the fill of the large pit-like feature that might have been a defensive ditch. Alongside it were large numbers of Lamar pottery sherds, among other Native artifacts. But further excavation of the feature produced no additional European items. Why an artifact of presumed value to either a Spaniard or an Indian was discarded in the ditch defies easy explanation. The best I can offer is that it was a deliberate act aligned with the sort of ritualized dumping we observed in the shallower ditch surrounding the temple. Many of the layers filling the outer ditch also included lenses of midden, occasionally with large sections of pottery vessels. Perhaps both locations were designated for annual, busk-related dumping, one for temple debris and the other for village castoffs.

The Celts

Rest assured, I'm not suggesting that we also turned up hints of transatlantic exploration by Celtic kin. My reference to "celts" describes the simplest of all the iron tool types from the site, of which we now have the largest collection in the Southeast (figure 6.7). Not only are celts the most numerous sort of iron artifact at the Glass Site; they are rather ubiquitous across the village—they seem to turn up everywhere. And unlike some of the other artifacts, these are of a type quite familiar to researchers of Soto and his ilk. They were unquestionably a basic item on the packing list of more than one expedition.[21]

A celt, in archaeological lingo, refers to a no-nonsense woodworking tool of very simple form, essentially a small hatchet blade without any obvious modification for hafting. But hafted they were, by simple insertion into a socketed handle, and secured by lashing or by friction. Native people of North America had been making their own celts for some two thousand years before European arrivals, but they were produced mainly from stone. Then, starting about a thousand years ago, less functional celts were also fashioned from high-quality, native copper as objects of display.

The iron celts from the Glass Site, and elsewhere, look very much like those special copper celts displayed by elites in late prehistoric southeastern Indian cultures. In outline they are narrow rectangles, sometimes with slightly flared

6.7 Iron celts (max. length of longest celt = 11.8 cm)

cutting edges on one end. The extent to which their shared form is coincidental or purposeful is tough to say. The main point is that there was precedent in the Indian world for tools and status items of just this kind, making the local Natives somewhat predisposed to value them.

The very first metal tool we found at the Glass Site was such a celt, and after five years the count rose to seven. As the photograph reveals, this kind of tool was made in a highly standardized manner (see figure 3.6b; figure 6.8). They're about the size and shape of a granola bar but thinner. With only a minor range of variation, they average 10.7 cm long, 2.5 cm wide, and just shy of 5 mm thick. All were finished by beveling one of the ends to create a cutting edge. These tools could undoubtedly have been used by members of an exploring Spanish party, but there is also reason to believe that they mainly were manufactured and carried for the purpose of the Indian trade.

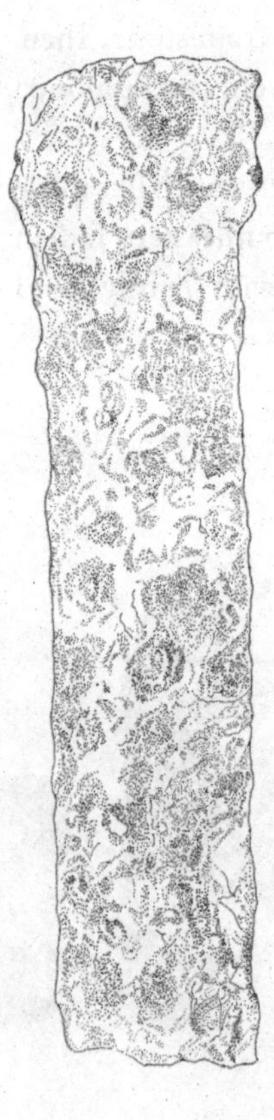

6.8 Illustration of representative iron celt

"Standardized" describes overall size and shape, but one discovers on close examination that the celts are unrefined. Compared to Biscayan axes and certain kinds of large chisels, for instance, these celts can only be described as crudely finished. Surfaces and lateral edges are uneven, and thickness can shift abruptly. I will argue that the cavalier attitude toward quality control is exactly what one would expect of a process focused on efficient mass production of trade items. In other words, it aligns with the manufacture of cheap giveaways during preparation for an expedition. Indeed, many of the irregularities these pieces display leads me to suggest they were made from scrap metal. Everything about them implies a hasty process of heating, cutting, hammering to shape, and beveling, one after the other.

This scenario finds support in the fact that celts are one of the most common, if not the most common, kind of iron tool on early contact sites. It would seem every would-be explorer in the New World had learned that chests of low-cost chisels would get him what he wanted in Indian territory, especially if they were accompanied by bags of beautiful beads.

As I have also described, indigenous craftsmen were fashioning the same kinds of tools from broken-apart ax blades or any other suitable scrap of iron. Plenty of evidence also indicates that Spanish craftsmen were resourcefully fashioning celt-like tools from old barrel hoops, especially at forges set up at later outposts.[22]

The Awl

Awls occur with some regularity on potential Soto-era sites and also on many others tied to early exploration and colonization. They are another kind of exceedingly simple tool, but they served the purposes of both European trekkers and indigenous people. The Indians had been making awls for thousands of years using bone, wood, and other perishable material, as they had celts of stone, so they would have readily found uses for imported counterparts fashioned of metal. It was just that the metallic nature of the European ones radically raised their appeal. Something that seemed the very definition of mundane suddenly assumed properties never imagined by the original makers.

The exalted status of imported iron objects is signified by our discovery of the Glass Site awl on the floor of the most important building in the community. It turned up during one of our painstaking troweling operations, when

6.9 Iron awl exposed on temple floor

the temple was just coming into focus. With the stroke of a trowel one of the crew members exposed a mere trace of rust-colored soil. But that was enough to alert everyone to the possible presence of something special, especially since just a day or two before we had discovered one of the chevron beads very nearby. Soon, using sharpened river-cane picks and small brushes, the excavator fully exposed a pointy-looking mass of rust on the building's trampled floor (figure 6.9).

It was quite something to figure out what the artifact actually was. Lively banter surrounded the question. On the flimsiest of terms, members of the crew staked out positions right away. It was the hilt of a dagger, the business end of some kind of weapon, or maybe "just" an awl. There was even the prediction that it bore the monogram "HDS." The encrustation allowed lots of room to speculate.

Fortunately, none of the fuss distracted us from proper handling. Back in Atlanta I arranged for preconservation imaging at the Emory University School of Medicine. The results, viewable in a dynamic 3-D format, revealed very clearly that a fully intact, bipointed object was at the core of the crusty, oxidized mass. "Awlish" became part of my lexicon. With that piece of high-tech intelligence, I next placed the artifact in the hands of Fernbank's consulting conservator. As she did with all the Glass Site metal, she used a multistep cleaning process to remove the oxidation down to the original and still-sturdy iron.

After a time what we were presented with was an extraordinarily well-preserved object, 12.5 cm long, with a finely sharpened point on one end and a somewhat blunter point at the other (figures 6.10–6.11). At the midsection the tool widened significantly, at which point, to our great surprise, the cleaning exposed a decorative cartouche in raised relief, on just one side. "Well-preserved" and pristine are different things, and it remains for the beholder to decide if the decorative emblem is an eye or some kind of abstracted floral motif. Regardless, this piece was crafted with a dose of care not given to things like the celts.

Determining the meaning of this object led to some enlightening investigation of Renaissance-era metalsmithing. I learned that Spanish ironworkers

6.10 Iron awl (max. length = 12.5 cm). Note raised, decorative cartouche at center.

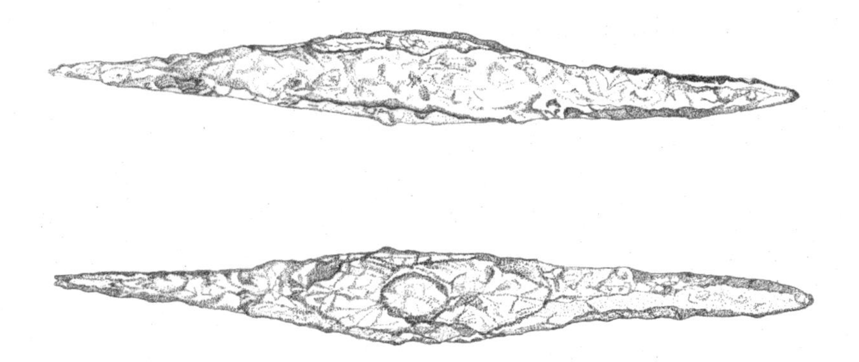

6.11 Illustration of awl. Note raised, decorative cartouche at center.

had by then attained the pinnacle of skill, and their achievements were celebrated throughout Europe.[23] Plenty of finely crafted iron objects of even a household nature abound in museum collections, but the real masterpieces are found on grillwork that adorns the windows, doors, fences, and gates of churches and palatial homes. Suffice it to say, applying a simple raised decoration to an awl was fully within the realm of possibilities. By stamping the heated metal with a preformed die, an ironsmith gave a stylish finishing touch to our awl.

In the world of exploration and conquest in the Southeast, and even the hemisphere, this last act of a metalworker moves the Glass Site awl from mundane to unusual. None of the awls documented at sixteenth-century sites in the region bear anything remotely like this design, or really any decoration at all. The closest example might be from Puerto Real in Haiti, on the island of Hispaniola, where Christopher Columbus established a settlement. Marginally similar examples are also known from contemporary sites in England.[24]

To the question of actual function, nothing indicates that our embellished awl was not made and used as others were for punching holes and so forth. The slightly longer and sharper end was the working part, and it stands to reason that the shorter, blunter end was inserted into a wood, bone, or horn handle. One of the regular volunteers in the Fernbank archaeology lab, an avid sailor, suggested it could have been a marlinespike. Marlinespikes are essential items in any traditional sailor's kit, used for working rope and lots of other things. I have always been intrigued by that possibility and can't see any reason to abandon it altogether.

The Large Chisel

My attention was drawn, in one instance, by the fact that Spencer's metal detector and Chet Walker's magnetometer pinpointed the same subsurface target, though they had not worked on the site at the same time. In completely independent sweeps of the large clearing we had made around the temple for their purposes, the existence of an artifact had registered as an obvious anomaly. Their instruments couldn't divine the object's true nature, only that it was probably sizable and potentially deeply buried. Until then, all the Spanish metal we had located was relatively close to the surface. Regardless, I had learned to resist the temptation to run down every intriguing lead as it presented itself, so I postponed further investigation of the target until we had met the goals I had laid out for the season.

Because there was really no telling what this target was, I elected to investigate it one weekend when the larger crew was away. With the help of Frankie Snow and the crew chief, James Stewart, we laid out an excavation unit over the point specified by both Spencer and Chet and set out to determine in the old-fashioned way what was catching the attention of their instruments. Anticipation was running fairly high, I won't deny, but as we progressed deeper, the giddiness eventually turned into tension. By the time we reached 50 cm below surface, our mind-set had become extra curious since nowhere on the site had we yet located Soto-era material below that depth. Then we were at 60 cm and nothing, 70 cm and nothing. Something like dismay took hold. Chatter melted into quizzical looks that all but said, "Are we digging in the right place?" or "Did those guys just get our goat?"

A particularly deceptive factor was the qualities of the soil. Usually, deeply buried objects are located in fairly obvious features, such as pits, that were opened and then filled by one means or another. As we've seen, these actions create suspicious indications in the form of discolored and mixed deposits. Here there was nothing so apparent, only fairly homogenous light-colored sand. Then somewhere around 60 cm down, with a thunderstorm threatening and daylight dimming, I could discern oh-so-subtle changes in the soil. Slightly darker patches appeared within the light yellow sand. Spying that irregularity restored a degree of archaeological normalcy. Maybe we were onto something after all.

Moments later one of those unmistakable smears of rust-stained soil appeared. We backed off on the pace of excavation and substituted for the trowel our wood picks and brushes. Slowly, slowly the rusty patch grew into a long and narrow mass, stark against the much lighter sand. We documented the object in place by drawings and photographs, and finally the time came for lifting it free. As we did, in spite of the oxidation, there was no mistaking what this artifact was—and we were awestruck yet again.

The stout piece of metal was a chisel that measures 22.9 cm long and 2.2 by 1.4 cm in section (figure 6.12). It weighs in at a hefty 456 g (1 lb), some seven times the weight of things like the celts and the awl and also a bit heavier than the ax blade. While large chisels have emerged as signs of Soto elsewhere, the

6.12 Large iron chisel (side view; max. length = 22.9 cm)

more usual form is round in cross section and not as long as the piece we recovered. That variety is best known from the Tatham mound in Florida.[25] Square-form chisels like the one we found are a bit problematic because not a one like it has turned up elsewhere. That these differences might eventually prove to have significance has become a question.

We also have not fully resolved the matter of the artifact's context. This object is the most deeply documented of all the early European artifacts from the site. For perspective, we pass through the Lamar/Soto-era stratum almost everywhere on the site by the time our excavations reach 50 cm below the surface. At depths of 75 cm or more, we have penetrated deposits containing artifacts no younger than seven thousand years. What was it that brought the chisel to this unheard of level?

I have to believe that the large chisel was present within a purposely created feature, namely, some kind of filled-in pit, and probably the tool was very intentionally buried within it. The feature, found so unexpectedly in the course of excavating the chisel, might, in fact, have been created originally as a grave. The Glass Site's soil is unkind to bone, and there would be no reason to anticipate preserved skeletal remains, but burial pits should still hold durable funerary objects, including things like iron chisels. Indeed, most of the heavy chisels found on Native sites elsewhere in the Southeast are from mortuary context because they became highly valued symbols of status.[26]

The Brass "Badge"

Ellen Vaughn's magic must run in the family. Ellen is the student who found the first Glass Site bead and her brother, Andrew, working in the temple area a couple of years after she did, excavated an equally decisive artifact. By his time, the presence of a large building was obvious, and we were taking a delicate look at the firmly packed floor and features within it. The day of the discovery, he was assigned to a rather nondescript oval of dark soil just over a meter north of the large central hearth. It was also a day we were hosting a group of Fernbank VIPs. The crew was on orders to look sharp and to be good hosts, but I was also wishing for something exciting to happen since these were some of the folks who were underwriting the project. Plus, when visitors get revved up about what we're seeing and doing it brings to everybody a sense of accomplishment that can get lost in the day-to-day grind.

The stars were in alignment. The guests from Atlanta had gotten my fifty-cent tour and had gathered around the large excavation, taking in the scene and quizzing excavators. Meanwhile, with Frankie observing, Andrew was hunched over his feature, troweling away at the deep brown soil within it, sweating gallons in the sweltering heat—and probably also from the unwanted attention. The show-and-tell had had the right effect, and I was off to the side chatting with onlookers. Suddenly, Frankie snapped to high alert and called me over. It's not his style to interrupt anything, so I had to gather he wanted to share news of something really good, or really bad. Andrew, looking slightly dazed and hoping he hadn't messed up, pointed to a swatch of green showing against the dark soil of the feature. I cut my eyes to Frankie, then to Andrew, then to the green thing, and back to Frankie, "Copper?" He smiled, and bated silence fell over the scene.

What young Mr. Vaughn had exposed is another of those Glass Site firsts. Akin to the single olive-shaped bead, it is an indicator of the early Spanish era but of a kind just once documented outside Florida.[27] The piece he had found was only a portion, not more than a quarter section, of a particular kind of square sheet-metal "badge." It had been decorated by forming a raised central dome, surrounded by closely spaced dots along the perimeter, in the repoussé method (figure 6.13). Later analysis told us that the metal was actually a copper alloy, brass, and therefore material of certain European origin.

Precedent in Florida has given archaeologists reasons to assign these kinds of artifacts to the general category of prestige items in the Native world.[28] They are not common, and when they are found, it is almost always in a nonordinary context like a grave or a mound. They correlate strongly with the early Spanish era since the vast majority of them are known to be made by the Indians from imported metal, sometimes scavenged from shipwrecks, including silver and gold in addition to brass. The standard shapes are square, like

6.13 Brass badge (max. length = 3.8 cm). Note remnant of raised central "boss" and perimeter decoration consisting of small, punched dots.

the one we found, or they can be round. The other defining attribute is the pattern of protrusions at the center and along the edges. In size and depending on shape, they compare to a playing card or a small jar lid.

In view of that background knowledge, a badge in the temple area makes perfect sense. The structure was an exclusive space, and other objects signifying special status, of both local and European origin, have been found within it. And like all the other special things from the site, it serves as an indicator of the unusual rank of the village itself.

It goes without saying that this was another in a string of electrifying Glass Site discoveries. Moreover, it was exciting for our visitors to witness. The timing did seem almost too remarkable to be true. But there it was, and in the course of explaining to them what the object was and what it meant, I was nearly overcome with genuine emotion. Those are the occasions when a release of the fatigue and tension surrounding this kind of project is welcome and needed.

The Brass Bead

A small metal bead was excavated very close to the large structure in Area B, around which two of the anomalous glass beads were found. Discovery of this diminutive artifact is, among other things, a testament to the skill of the project's lead metal detectorist, Spencer Barker. I've already praised Spencer's ability with a detector and his wise strategy for completing the survey. He pretty much double-checked every bit of the site himself, and it was in that mode that he discovered the brass bead. The tiny target issued the faintest of signals, a quick, tremulous squeak that any other hot and weary searcher might have ignored altogether, since so many of the faint sounds generated by

6.14 Rolled brass bead (max. length = 0.7 cm)

the machines are false reads from ferrous stone and the like. But not Spencer. He ignored nothing.

The bead had been made by rolling a small cutout of sheet brass into a short tube. Beads like it are familiar on early contact sites, beginning in the era of Soto and continuing thereafter for some two hundred years (figure 6.14). They were easy for Europeans to produce, and a good thing since they proved to be so popular among Natives for adornment. Their production, however, was not limited to the European side. An argument can be made that the majority of rolled metal beads, whether brass, copper, silver, or gold, were actually the work of Indians. Ample evidence shows how Native Americans extended the life of introduced utilitarian goods, such as brass kettles, by cutting them into pieces for ornaments, among other things. And as with the celts, the beads had counterparts made prehistorically but out of copper.

The Brass Handle

On the final day of the metal detector survey, on a part of the site we had neglected to examine until that point, Spencer's team extracted what I first thought must be the broken clutch lever from a four-wheeler ATV or a dirt bike. "Meh," was my initial reaction, a response colored by the location of the find, on the steep bank leading down to the swampy slough, alongside the two-track road that ran across the edge of the site. We had not ignored the slope out of any belief that it would not produce information of value. Being what it was—an uninhabitable stretch of former riverbank—our assumption was that it might have been a place suitable for general dumping and thus formation of a village midden. What I least expected to find there was precious European goods. There were enough stray beer cans and bottles up and down

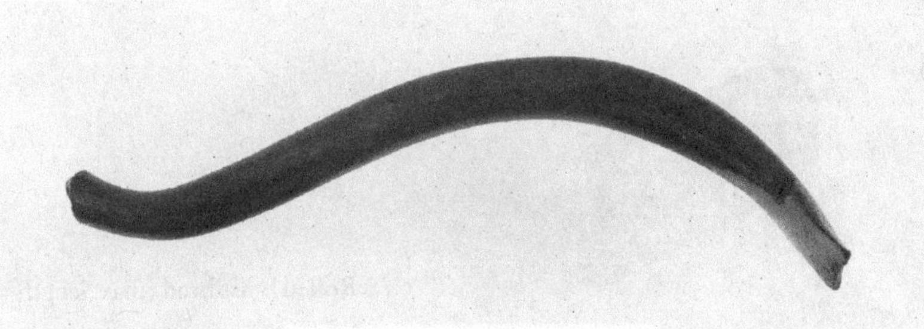

6.15 Brass ewer handle (max. length = 11.1 cm)

the bank to indicate that any "European" artifacts would mostly signify the thriving, local hog-hunter culture.

Right away, though, my cynicism turned to deep curiosity since there were aspects of the "clutch lever" that just didn't make sense. First, the material didn't square with that interpretation: the object was made of brass, as indicated by a greenish patina (figure 6.15). The elegant, serpentine lines of the artifact were also more pronounced than would be practical for an ATV lever.

I don't recall exactly when my mind began to catch up to the meaning of this artifact, but it was well after we closed down the field season and I had the opportunity to spend time in the lab with the things we had found. Archaeologists are prone to obsess over artifacts, as you know by now, especially when they aren't understanding them, and that kind of fixation began to define my relationship with the "lever." I could not convince myself it *wasn't* another kind of sixteenth-century Spanish artifact, but I was otherwise clueless. The weapon-part possibility was my leading hunch, and I pored over books and websites with photographs and illustrations of period arms. Crossbows and arquebuses, for example, are operated with simple handles and levers that, at a glance, are similar looking, but they just aren't the same as the piece we had found. Neither could I convince myself that it was part of a sword hilt, though many hilts were designed as elaborate baskets of curving metal, including brass.

Then I began a more general search, scouring for anything else of the period that might be a match. That led me into the world of decorative arts, at least so far as many museums and private collectors define it. A prominent subcategory of this domain is objects of religious art, and that is where I began to find the closest analogues to our piece. Especially in earlier periods, certain Catholic religious rites required containers for water and other liquids, and prominent among them were vessels known as ewers, essentially a pitcher in today's vernacular. Most of them were made of metal, ranging from brass to silver and gold. I discovered seemingly countless images of sixteenth- and seventeenth-century ewers with gracefully curving handles. Eureka! And on another fortuitously timed New York trip to visit our son, I forced my family to endure a search of the Metropolitan Museum of Art's exhibitions of ewers—where I came across even closer matches (figure 6.16). Numerous depictions of ewers in Renaissance paintings also reinforced my confidence.

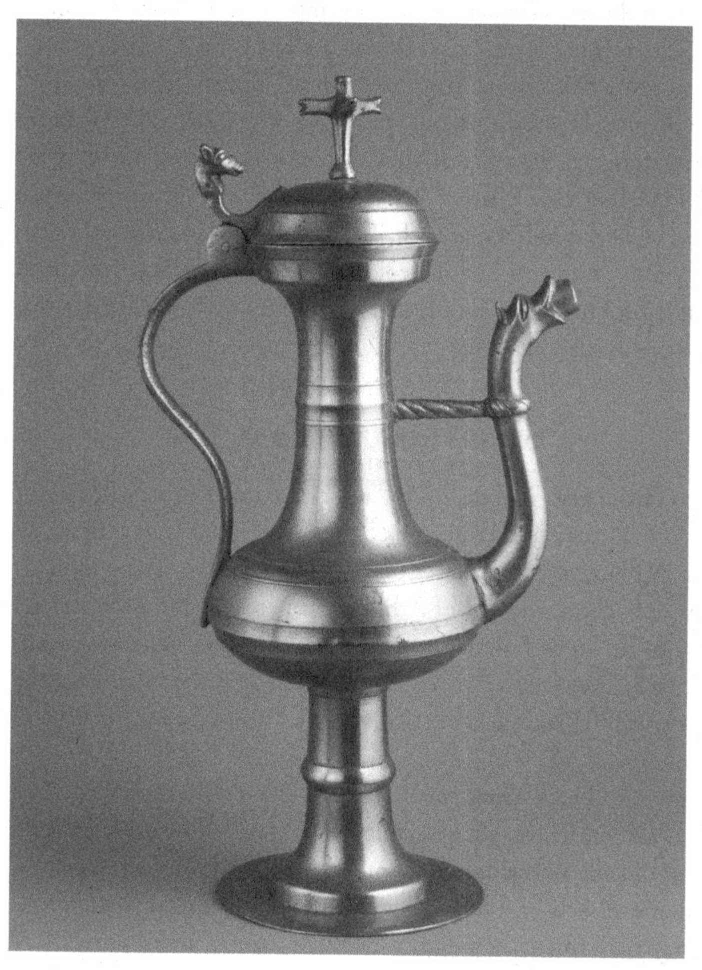

6.16 Brass ewer in collection of Metropolitan Museum of Art

The best part was the fact that all this made sense. We are told Soto's party included at least seven Catholic churchmen. And in fact, there actually seems never to have been a major expedition or colonizing attempt, under any European flag, unaccompanied by religious functionaries. The prevailing view around the conquest and settlement of the New World was that it was the work of God. Demonstrating the vital role at the time of church-based rites are descriptions of the deep pall that fell over the Soto expedition in the fall of 1540 after an Indian attack led to destruction of several items of religious paraphernalia. Ranjel describes it this way, "[Burned were] all the . . . clothes and ornaments and chalices and moulds for wafers, and the wine for saying mass, and they were left like Arabs, empty-handed and with great hardship."[29] As far as those Spaniards were concerned, it was a dark portent.

Not surprisingly, a few objects basic to Catholic liturgy have turned up in the region previously, including on Native American sites like Glass. In Alabama, for instance, a brass candlestick holder and a brass bucket were found at the Pine Log Creek Site.[30] What is far less clear is exactly *which* party the Glass Site ewer originated with. The possibilities include Soto's entrada, but they also extend to Ayllón's colony, an early French venture, and the Spanish mission I had wanted to find. I will more fully consider all these alternative sources in a later chapter.

Additional Brass Artifacts

Within meters of the ewer handle, on the old riverbank, the metal detector squad turned up another mysterious object. I've described it as a finial, or decorative cap, for lack of better understanding (figure 6.17). It, too, is made of brass but is only about the size of a thimble. In cross section the artifact is triangular and cast to be hollow through the body rather than solid, as if it were meant to fit over another piece. At the top of it is the small stub of a broken-off protrusion. Precisely what this artifact was used for is unclear, as is its age.

In the temple-area block, three small pieces of brass were excavated. Two are thin sheets smaller than a postage stamp (figure 6.18). One has a tiny perforation that would allow attachment to something. The other is a segment of a curved band, most likely part of a finger ring. Especially during the mission period, Indian gift allotments commonly included rings of various sorts.[31]

6.17 Brass finial (max. length = 1.3 cm)

6.18 Other small brass artifacts. *Top left to right*: Two sheet brass scraps, one perforated, and a finger ring fragment; *bottom*: finger ring fragment (max. length of bottom ring fragment = 2.2 cm).

In the village, near the large structure in Area B, a larger, more obvious fragment of a finger ring was found by the metal detector survey (see figure 6.18).

Additional Iron Artifacts

Five other iron artifacts are important to describe. What appears to be the butt end of a heavy wedge was excavated from secure context in the temple area (figure 6.19). Tools of the general type are rather common on early Spanish sites. A small chisel was found in the metal-detector survey in the northern part of the village (see figure 6.20). On the old riverbank, the metal detector team also found a "rattail" knife of iron. It is a form typical of sixteenth-century tableware, designed for slipping a bone or wood handle onto the narrow end opposite the blade (figure 6.21).

6.19 Iron wedge fragment (max. length = 7.3 cm)

6.20 Small iron chisel (max. length = 5.8 cm)

6.21 Rattail knife (max. length = 14.2 cm)

6.22 Weapon tip of iron (max. length = 6.0 cm). Note solid, pyramidal tip is bent double toward the center.

6.23 Reworked iron blade fragment (max. length = 8.1 cm)

In the northeastern quadrant of the village ring, a somewhat problematic iron artifact was recovered (figure 6.22). I believe it is the business end of a weapon, designed to be crimped onto a shaft, though the lower socket had been pried open at some point. The size suggests that it was attached to something heavier than the average crossbow quarrel. But the opposite end, though bent double, is fashioned into a solid, four-sided tip—exactly the way armor-piercing quarrel tips were designed in Soto's day.[32] Regrettably, the condition of this artifact doesn't allow easy resolution.

Another possible military artifact was found at the western edge of the village (figure 6.23). It is a section of a heavy blade bearing an obvious, original bevel on one edge. After it was broken, the ends appear to have been crudely modified by grinding, and the upper edge was hammered. The best we can offer is that this is a portion of a repurposed sword or drawknife blade.

Nails and Lead Shot

A largish number of nails and pieces of round, ball-type ammunition, or shot, are also part of the collection of metal artifacts. I am featuring them partly for the purpose of describing some of the artifactual noise we have to contend with, and the lengths to which one goes to distinguish "good" from "bad."

It would be fair to wonder what nails have to do with this kind of site at all, and the short answer is perhaps nothing. But "perhaps" leaves certain possibilities open, and mainly in this case, I have to consider the original mission question and the possibility it introduces of a church, if not other buildings. But tacks, nails, and spikes are not unheard of on expedition-related sites either. Carts, crates, and shod horses are among the things that would have depended on them. We must also be alert to the whys and hows of intrusive, modern debris. Pristine, single-occupation sites are rarer than you might think, and it is always necessary to figure out what goes with what, if for no other reason than to defend against skeptics who would be happy to pounce on misinterpretations resulting from contamination.

By the time our excavations were ended, 106 nails had been recovered. Two things establish that the vast majority of them are by-products of late nineteenth- to early twentieth-century activity during the heyday of logging and naval stores extraction. First, the larger share of nails was mass-produced by industrial-age processes developed for making square, machine-cut fasteners or, in lesser numbers, round wire nails. In this region, nails of both types would not predate the first decades of the 1800s. Furthermore, the vast majority of the "modern" nails were concentrated, most helpfully, in a limited area of the site where few of the earlier, Spanish items were found. The aggregate facts led us to conclude that a short-lived, special-purpose work camp was set up on the edge of the slough at the turn of the nineteenth-twentieth centuries.[33] Nails were, in fact, the greater part of the evidence supporting this interpretation since ceramics, glass, and other metal of the same age were exceedingly rare. The important outcome is that we documented things from the work camp well enough to isolate them from metal left three or more centuries earlier.

There remains, however, a small subset of nails that might have something to do with either a sixteenth- or a seventeenth-century Spanish presence. These few fasteners bear traits indicative of hand crafting at the forge of a blacksmith and not in a factory. The problem is that hand-wrought nails continued to be produced as late as the mid-nineteenth century in areas like South Georgia that were remote from industrial centers and major markets. Candidly, the ambiguity surrounding the age of the wrought nails plagues interpretation of their significance. In spite of considerable scrutiny, the best I could offer on the question of Spanish affiliation is "maybe," and if pressed I would have to admit "doubtful."

Nails are not among the items on the traditional Soto-hunter's list, but that view is changing. In the last decade or so, consensus has grown around the link between one very unique kind of nail and exploration-period sites associated with Soto and Coronado.[34] They are called carat-headed nails, literally because the heads of them look like the punctuation mark. The sharply downturned, narrow heads sit atop a relatively short shank, and it is commonly believed that they were farrier's nails. Regardless, it is now true that finding one of these is tantamount to finding a faceted chevron bead or a Clarksdale bell. But so far no such object has turned up at Glass.

Dealing with the twenty-eight pieces of round-shot ammunition involved the same kind of close examination, and the same uncertain result. Simple round shot was the first kind of ammunition used in firearms, beginning perhaps by the end of the fifteenth century. Though shot's popularity waned, it never fell completely out of use. Today, for example, there are "black powder" hunters in South Georgia who make use of round shot, and there has never been much decline in the use of good old buckshot. So the trick is to find a way to cull the new from the old, and there are a couple of ways to do so.

One option is to identify the mode of manufacture from telltale features left on the piece of shot itself, providing it survives in reasonable condition. The earliest kind was handmade in a simple mold, of which there were different types. The common characteristic of them all is a slightly protruding, flattened disk left when the ball was clipped free of excess metal in the mold. On the same handmade shot, it is also sometimes possible to find a fine, raised mold seam. Modern, industrially made shot was not formed the same way and thus lacks those features, leaving its surface relatively unblemished.

Another way of distinguishing relatively old from relatively new is chemistry. An assay of the chemical composition of "old" lead shot, dating from around the mid-nineteenth century or before, will reveal a content of nearly pure lead. Shot manufactured industrially, beginning in the twentieth century, will be alloyed, usually with tin, or sometimes contain only other metals to the total exclusion of lead.

At Glass we have determined that eighteen of the round bullets show marks of hand molding and that they were produced from nearly pure lead. The remainder bear signs indicative of later production. Even with those categorizations, it is hardly possible to determine with confidence that any of the "early" ones have anything to do with sixteenth-century happenings. It only lingers as a possibility, as it does with that handful of wrought nails. Plenty of deer hunters have roamed across the site over the last two hundred years.

Fretting over the traits of round shot is not merely archaeological indulgence. Soto-related accounts specifically mention arquebusiers, men who carried primitive firearms called arquebuses. The crossbow was unquestionably the weapon of choice on the expedition, aside from bladed weapons, but the accounts indicate that there were also a good many gun-toting members of the party.[35] They would have loaded those virtual hand-cannons with small round shot, and indications are, they were ever eager to demonstrate them for the benefit of the Indians.

Few archaeologists, I included, wouldn't want to have a collection of artifacts like this to work with. But I've learned how true the saying is, "Be careful what you wish for." It would be so much easier if all the early European artifacts were classic elements of the imagined gift kit, but as in this case, that's seldom the way it works. What we wind up with more often is a highly suggestive but still mongrelized assortment of things. If we imagined it as a statistical distribution, we would describe a hefty quotient of classical, sixteenth-century artifacts peaking at the center, but it is flanked by tails accounting for not-so-classic and later-dating things.

The centered majority of things in the Glass collection, I will maintain, powerfully evokes Soto—and perhaps earlier ventures, as well. Either most of the artifact types I have described are strongly linkable to the earliest European incursions, as so many have so often argued, or they are not. We can't have it both ways. Then there are a few items from the site that are out on one tail of the distribution, such as a few of the beads. They strongly imply a second phase of contact. We can judge from this that the proverbial sky did not fall with Soto's coming and going. The people of the Glass community endured to witness a second wave of the invasion.

Then there are some objects that are plain old enigmatic, at least as we understand the world of material culture today. Lead shot and wrought nails top the list. But neither are brass rings and ewer handles isolatable to one neat decade or two. Necessarily, I don't try to force them into one set of events or another. I can live with the uncertainty. And total lack of clarity shouldn't paralyze the process. There is still a coherent story to be told even if it doesn't center on Mission Santa Isabel de Utinahica.

VII

A Big Bend Province

The Glass Site's assortment of unusual European artifacts deserves the attention it has attracted, but those foreign objects must not be allowed to overshadow the facts of the indigenous Indian community they come from. For most of the sixteenth century, the Spanish were operating in the Southeast more as visitors than as residents, and at any point their numbers were miniscule compared to those of the Natives. In every sense, the region remained the dominion of Indians each minute of the two centuries through which it endured the competing claims of Spain and France. Day in and day out the decisions of Old World interlopers concerned, in some manner, their relations with indigenous people. To the extent a relationship of dependency existed, it was tilted more toward the Europeans, whose policies hinged on an expectation of Indian food, labor, and souls. The Spanish colonial story and the remains of it found by archaeologists mean nothing outside a Native context.

Even conservatively speaking, Native Americans can lay claim to a history in the Southeast that reaches fifteen thousand years back, and the outlines of that long story are captured in our results from the Glass Site. Many of the types of stone tools we found there are testament to the comings and goings of ancient foragers over the course of eleven millennia. Those earlier people surely appreciated the setting of the site for most of the same reasons it attracted the village-dwelling farmers who were witness to European incursions. Well-drained high ground, surrounded by productive wetlands, would meet all the basic needs of small hunting and gathering groups.

The subject of this chapter, however, will be the final era of Native occupation. With aspects of it described already, my goal here is to braid the evidential strands together to evoke a meaningful sense of the living Glass Site, the bustling and pivotal human community it was between about AD 1450 and 1560. After all, the mere presence of this town, and the supporting settlements around it, forces adjustment of older views about Native American history in this part of Georgia. What we've found in that regard wasn't supposed to be there either.

As often as not, a society develops within a fixed territory over an extended period. We can see the archaeological precedents and can track in-place evolution. Differently, the people affiliated with the Glass Site seem to have come out of nowhere to secure a territory on the lower Ocmulgee. Nothing in the archaeological record indicates that local Lamar communities could lay immediate historical claim to the Big Bend area. If any Lamar culture precursors inhabited the immediate area, they remain invisible. Because archaeology also says no groups were frequenting the area for a hundred or more years prior, Lamar or otherwise, the migration to the Glass Site and places like it was probably uncontested. That opportunity in itself must have been an attraction.

Not far up the Ocmulgee, in the Macon area, and also up its sister river, the Oconee, the Lamar story played out more typically. Archaeology has demonstrated the in situ emergence of late Mississippian societies over a larger interval, from about AD 1300 to 1700 (figure 7.1).[1] In time, they grew into separate sociopolitical provinces, within which activity was coordinated from a capital town boasting one or more large temple mounds. They are places that hew closely to the classic model of Mississippian cultural development. And it is for those reasons that the favored projection of the Soto route passes through their territories and not the Big Bend. The logic of that argument is not necessarily flawed, but as I shall argue, it is not infallible.

Our Big Bend Lamar population quite likely had its origin in those upstream territories. Scholars have come to recognize worldwide that "chiefly" societies, organized as the Mississippians were, are inherently fragile. A range of stresses, not least of which might be population pressure, were resolved by different responses. Outright collapse, perhaps better described as dissolution and dispersal, was not unheard of. Indeed, David Hally and David Anderson, among others, have shown that regional Mississippian polities were subject to cycling between periods of expansion and contraction.[2] They estimate their

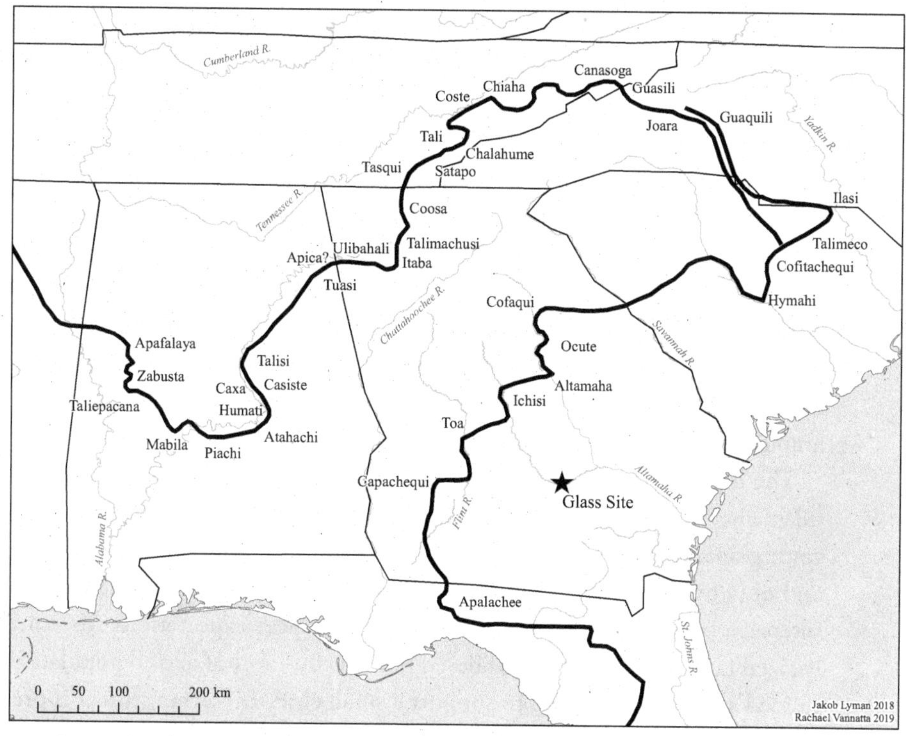

7.1. Locations of Native provinces along Soto's route (after Hudson 1997)

usual lifespan, from one ruinous downturn to another, would not exceed seventy-five to one hundred years. It is reasonable to suggest that the population centered on the Glass Site had voted with its feet sometime after AD 1400 and moved to the Coastal Plain from a no-longer-inviting homeland in or near the Piedmont. Buttressing the argument is the nature of the pottery from places like Glass and Coffee Bluff. Their sherds are dead ringers for pieces excavated in those fall line and Piedmont polities, far more than they are for other contemporary locales.

Whatever its origin, an immigrant Lamar population chose to situate itself on the lower part of the Ocmulgee River a few generations before its existence was disrupted by Europeans. Frankie Snow had begun to detect evidence of these events, and our Fernbank-sponsored research has verified them. Whereas two decades and more earlier archaeologists dismissed the area as a vacant sector, they must now acknowledge the existence of another

Lamar polity in Georgian space. The absence of ancestral settlements and large mounds in our project area speak to the brevity of its existence, but even in nascent form, it was present and probably enjoying reasonable prosperity into the early sixteenth century.

Importantly, the Glass Site bears all the hallmarks of a provincial capital, as we shall see. But looking more widely, the other Lamar sites we tested as part of the mission search, together with others identified by Frankie's surveys, serve to define the extent of the province (figure 7.2). They are plotted on both sides of the river within a 700 km^2 (270 mi^2) area, extending from near The Forks to Jacksonville. This falls well within earlier determinations of the average, 1500 km^2 territory for Lamar provinces, and it also indicates that an ample buffer stood between it and the nearest rival territory.

The majority of the sites within this space are far smaller in size than the Glass Site. This we know best from Frankie's notes but also from some of our testing operations. They lack evidence for more than one or two structures, and only on rare occasion do they include middens indicative of lengthy or intensive occupation. All these characteristics meet expectations for family-sized farmsteads where, considered holistically, most of a local population resided and generated food to support a small elite. This arrangement is precisely what has been documented in the Piedmont provinces and throughout the Mississippian sphere.[3] Presently we know of many potential farmsteads relatively close to the Glass Site that merit exploration.

One or two settlements within the Big Bend province, other than the Glass Site, might also have risen, at different times, to capital status. They approach the same size, and they include relatively well-developed middens within which artifact density is high. This is a sign that the new province, short-lived as it was, had begun to accumulate its own history and to experience the same old challenges that demanded occasional spells of reconfiguration. To the extent we can judge the chain of events from available evidence, Glass was neither the first nor the final territorial capital. Ceramic analysis results point to Coffee Bluff as the earliest of them. Yet another of the local Lamar sites yields pottery made slightly differently, and it is also where a very late type of glass bead and a piece of metal were found on the surface.[4] That site, in fact, emerges as the best candidate for the seventeenth-century mission that was the beginning thrust of the project.

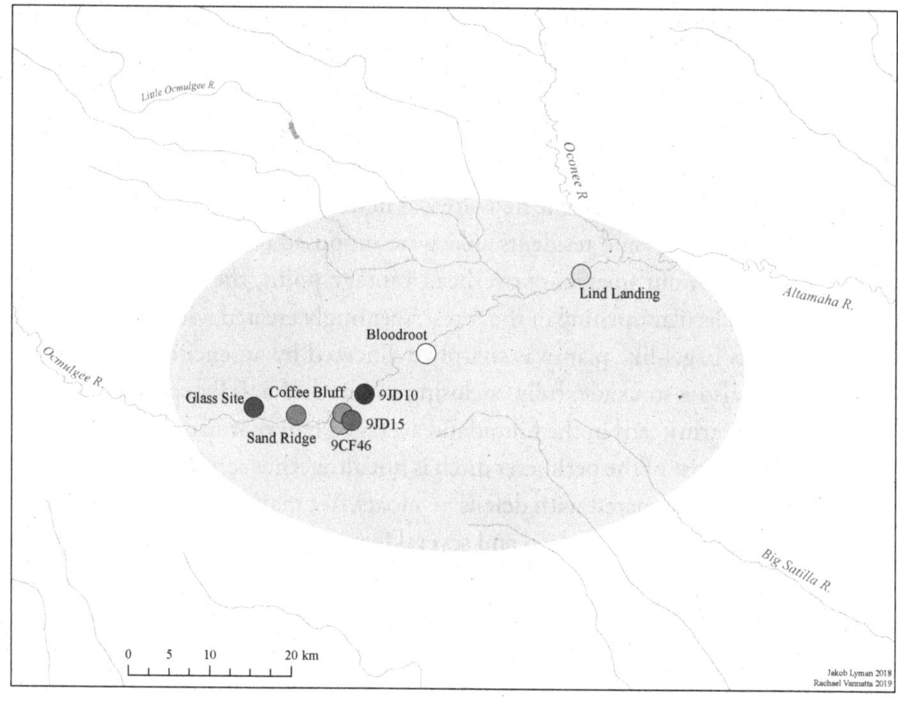

7.2 The Big Bend province and major archaeological sites within it

Capital towns in Mississippian provinces were strategic contrivances, as most any capital is. Locations for them would have been chosen by weighing issues like food potential, soil quality, accessibility, security, and visibility. As far as the Glass Site is concerned, the process worked well. The local ecology alone, featuring the river, fringing wetlands, and nearby uplands, ensured ready sources of sustenance and raw material. Underfoot, the sandy ground would drain, and it was also loamy enough to be a superior soil for mixed patches of corn, beans, squash, and tobacco.[5] Connectivity was also good. For Native people using dugout canoes, the Ocmulgee would link the site to far-flung places, eastward as far as the Atlantic coast and northwestward into the heart of the Piedmont. A web of overland connections was enabled by the site's proximity to established foot trails.[6]

Had we by some means an opportunity to hover above the Big Bend province five hundred years ago at ten thousand feet, the Glass Site would stand out as the obvious exception among settlements. Its larger size and formal layout would have instantly attracted attention, and that was the point. The Glass community was exceptional because it was designed to be so. Relative to surrounding farmsteads, the new site was bestowed with certain monumental qualities. Visitors and residents alike were supposed to be moved by it.

Seen from our imaginary overhead vantage point, the capital site would occupy a circular opening in the forest, seemingly created with a giant cookie cutter. Its bagel-like plan was sharply delineated by an encircling ditch and perhaps also a stockade, fully enclosing 1.13 ha (2.8 ac). By contrast, the unbounded farmsteads in the hinterland averaged half that size.

The purpose of the perimeter ditch is not altogether certain. Often features of the sort are equated with defensive moats. Yet many, like the one at Glass, measure only a few feet deep and several feet wide and, therefore, would not present an especially challenging obstacle. Had a palisade been positioned at the inner edge of such a trough, its effective height would have increased but only marginally. From a defensive standpoint, then, the ditch would have been more a deterrent than safeguard. More usefully perhaps, the ditch made an important symbolic statement, visually setting a privileged realm apart from ordinary space. And in that capacity it needn't have been a gaping cut.

Elsewhere I have described the Glass Site as compact because, compared with the most powerful and long-lived Mississippian centers on the continent, it can't compete in terms of overall size or in number of mounds. Take, for example, the state's premier Mississippian capital of Etowah, located in a broad valley outside Cartersville, Georgia.[7] Three enormous mounds tower above a village defined by a massive moat that encloses tens of acres. Yet the comparison is not an entirely fair one since Etowah boasted a much longer history, having been established as early as AD 1100 and then occupied on and off at least until Soto chose to visit it in 1540. Had it been left alone, the younger Glass capital might have developed on a similar trajectory. But speculation aside, the main point to remember is that the Big Bend province had begun, fundamentally, to function like any number of other Mississippian polities.

Let's now bring ourselves to ground level and imagine a stroll through the town. Entry alone would have had a moving effect on visitors. The perimeter ditch and perhaps a palisade separated, physically and visually, an orderly and sanctified realm of power from space that was subordinate and subject to disorder. The imposition of boundaries effectively defined a compound that was exclusive and shielded, forcing attention on crucial elements of the enclosed space.

The circular plan would have guided attention toward the center. There, an open area about 70 m (230 ft) across defined a public plaza. In my meditations, I imagine it as a manicured expanse of packed sand. As our shovel tests demonstrated, common activities and disposal of debris were prohibited within its confines. Mississippian town plazas tended to be reserved for special events, often of a ritualized nature. A host of sources report that a common focal point of plazas was a centrally placed "trophy pole," festooned with scalps among other things, that most of all served as the target in a ritualized ball game.[8]

In the zone between the outer edge of the plaza and the inside of the ditch, an array of structures was arranged. Their positioning, like the other features of the compound, was almost certainly a matter of some calculation. Probably the first decision concerned the location of the elemental, public buildings crucial to the functioning of a capital enclave. The one of these we may be most confident about is the temple. It was strategically sited southwest of the plaza. From that position a doorway could open toward the center of the plaza, creating a northeasterly line of sight from the interior that linked the sacred fire to the center of the village, and then to the point of the summer solstice sunrise (see figure 3.4). This building was also symbolically isolated by its own encircling ditch.

We cannot yet tally the actual number of buildings within the village ring, but there are ways to reach an estimate. One of the clues is the presence of hot spots in the distribution of pottery fragments (see figure 5.1). Excavations confirm that many if not all of them mark the locations of buildings, and on that basis, we can treat the seven obvious concentrations in the ring as a minimum building count. Because population estimates are vital for archaeological interpretations, our profession has also devised clever formulas to generate a sense of human numbers. Following the lead of the King Site analysis, a calculation based on village area gives a liberal population estimate for the Glass Site of 113–257.[9]

The majority of the village structures were residential, a fact born out by the nature of most of the site's artifacts. By the same token it would be shortsighted to believe that domestic spaces within the capital were akin to household spaces at a farmstead. For example, the structure we have looked at most closely beyond the temple, in Area B, stands apart from the average Lamar dwelling at least in terms of size. It is spacious by comparison, measuring 10 m square, rivaling the temple across the plaza. Because it is also the only other place where we've recovered glass beads, there is reason to think it might have carried some special significance. Because the temple was not a dwelling, we must wonder where the chief, priests, and other of the highest-ranking people would have resided with family members. At other Mississippian villages archaeologists have discovered one or two houses that are bigger than most.[10] In fact, it has become an expectation to find a grander dwelling, and almost universally they are interpreted as chiefly residences. Perhaps that is what we are seeing in Area B at Glass.

In the same vein, I have described how traces of a structure in Area A were dubbed "the Pipemaker's House." We know very little about it right now, but the many smoking pipes around it beg interesting questions. Purely speculatively, we might ask whether it housed a religious practitioner.

In time I would not be surprised to learn that nearly all the buildings within the village compound were exceptional in some manner. Bigger, better, and special were, by definition, what a capital town was about.

The ground at the Glass Site is saturated with artifacts, mostly of kinds left by the Lamar compound's residents. Our scientifically extracted sample of them, removed from only a small portion of the total area, is tens of thousands of items large. They've all been scrubbed and sorted, counted and weighed, poked and prodded, discussed and debated, and compared with other samples. The yield of information from that rather clerical process, one consuming far more time than the fieldwork, lies at the heart of the stories we can tell.

The vast majority of the artifacts are fairly mundane—sherds of broken pots, by-products of toolmaking from stone, and scraps from meals. In fact, the average person doesn't even recognize these leavings for what they are, especially if they spy them outdoors on the ground. But in the hands of people determined to jolt life back into them, they are like strands of DNA. Having successfully reconstituted a great many of those strands, we realize that the Glass Site's Native artifacts are not always as ordinary as one might assume. In many respects they are qualitatively different from what we've encountered in the satellite settlements, in the same way the site's buildings and their layout are different.

Archaeologists have become especially good at coaxing stories from "potsherds," the fragments of ceramic vessels we find by the bagful. That success is partly explained as analytical opportunism. Because pottery, even fragments of it, is about as durable as stone, virtually every bit survives to be found. In addition, potsherds are often as prevalent, if not more so, than any other trace of people on a site. It only makes sense to take advantage of such a ubiquitous information source.

Ceramic analysis has also succeeded because the behaviors of people are recorded within pots. Their makers operated according to some ingrained and relatively fixed patterns. Members of a culture, including potters, learn rules about what is and isn't an appropriate way of doing things. As one archaeologist put it, "pots are tools," and their production is constrained by understood principles of engineering.[11] Containers also become convenient "billboards," intentionally embellished to convey messages about beliefs and belonging (see figure 5.7).

In the right hands, the secret life of pottery is reborn, and how pottery-aided insights have been generated for the Glass Site is a particularly happy story. Lots of people have been involved in the project, and the experience has sometimes inspired careers and original research. Rachel Hensler is one of those people. Convinced after four years of field and lab work on the project that archaeology was the life for her, she completed studies for the PhD at the University of Kentucky and has written a dissertation based on a wide-ranging analysis of pottery from Glass and several related sites.[12] The question that launched her research involved tracking the effects of Indian-European interactions via the medium of pottery. Might it be possible, she asked, that the ways ceramic containers were made and used underwent alterations, consciously or not, to accommodate a cascade of new social alignments, territorial upheavals, and the like, especially in the wake of European intrusions?

There is a lot to what Rachel has accomplished, but what I find most fascinating is the way Big Bend Lamar pottery is proven to track the evolution of the province, even before the likes of Soto came on the scene. Cultures are constantly changing, and Rachel's study elegantly demonstrates how that process can be discovered in the most unlikely places. Archaeologists are responsible for charting the course of human events, but none of that would be possible if the things we make and use, like pots, were not permeated with hints of intention and values. Today we are sometimes rattled by the ways personal devices capture intimate details, but in a way, that's really what our possessions have always done.

Rachel's findings reinforce the emerging sense of how communities making up the Big Bend province were culturally and historically linked, and how they changed. The insights are based on analysis of a sample of over three thousand potsherds from five different sites located within 25 km (15.5 mi) of the Glass Site, all dating between about AD 1400 and 1700. Four of the sites were evaluated as part of the Fernbank project, and one of them was collected and tested only by Frankie Snow.

Multiple attributes of the sherds indicate that potters at nearly all the sites were the product of a single cultural tradition. They had learned to make ceramic containers according to a common code. No surprise, their pots were almost always fashioned from local clays. Suitable sources had been discovered, and they were mined for generations. This Rachel determined by microscopic inspection of the broken pieces. Under magnification tiny particles of quartz, mica, and other minerals become visible, and the relative proportion of one to another serves as a virtual fingerprint for a clay deposit.

The common tradition also exerted influence over function and style. Pots were produced in a standard set of sizes and forms, amounting to a series of graduated bowls and jars designed for cooking, serving, and storage. Then, each category of vessel was universally finished with a particular combination of "decorative" treatments. It is because the pressure to conform to those customs was so powerful that we, as archaeologists, have the luxury of talking about what it meant, in one sense, to be Lamar.

Still, the Lamar tradition, like any set of cultural norms, was not entirely fixed, and Rachel convincingly charts how pottery-making practices evolved at the local level. Incremental shifts occurred across the board. We continually witness this through our own lifetimes. A late-model Ford Mustang doesn't look anything like the classic '67 edition, but I can still recognize it as a Ford Mustang. And the really interesting questions, of the kind Rachel was probing, is why things change that way.

In the Big Bend province, variations occurred in even the most basic aspects of the pottery production process. It was not necessarily as simple as digging and using clay from one of the local sources. Rachel's study of pottery "pastes" indicates that mica-rich clays were favored for making serving bowls, while another mixture of grittier texture was preferred for cooking and storage jars. Most likely these Lamar-culture choices were informed and sophisticated, related ultimately to purpose and performance. Cooking jars would have been subjected to extremes of heating and cooling that most bowls were not.

Also in the functional sphere, the shapes of pots were subject to variation across space and time. In the first respect, Rachel confirmed the suspicion that the diversity of pot types was greater at the few larger sites than at the many smaller sites. This fact sustains the capital versus farmstead dichotomy. At the Glass Site, for example, commonplace storage containers and cooking pots were accompanied by several kinds of serving vessels absent or extremely rare on smaller sites. One was a shallow, wide-brimmed dish resembling a pasta bowl, and the other was a kind of cup, likely reserved for privileged usage.

Shifts in pot shape, over the two-or-more-centuries history of the province, are indicative of a realignment of cultural influence. Across most of its history, potters in the Big Bend province, produced ceramics that adhered closely to the tradition inherited from Piedmont forebearers. It would have been easy, for a time, to lose a Big Bend pot on a Piedmont Lamar site, whether in terms of form or decoration. By the seventeenth century, however, certain types of vessels began to adopt the lines of pots associated with coastal communities, specifically the mission-related towns at places like St. Catherines Island. The best example is the replacement of the old-style *cazuela* bowl having sharply in-turned shoulders, with a bowl featuring a narrow upright neck, giving it the shape of a church bell. In tandem with this change was a gradual, overall reduction in the use of ceremonial serving vessels, like those so common at the earlier Glass Site.

The more stylish details of the pottery were, of course, also subject to change. Indeed, they followed the pattern of diminishing diversity that was charted for vessel shapes. Generally speaking, the three larger sites feature a wider range of decorative treatments than smaller sites, but the Glass Site more so than any. This is true in terms of the number of motifs either incised (etched) or stamped onto vessel surfaces as they were made.

Rachel shows us how even the most minute aspects of pottery decoration evolved, probably as an unconscious response to deeper cultural change. In her well-dated samples, the width of folded lips on jars increased, the spacing between incised lines decreased, and additions of dots and dashes to etched

7.3 Examples of incised motifs on Lamar pottery from the Glass Site. The motifs in the central column are unique to a vessel form called a brimmed bowl.

patterns became more common (figure 7.3). Having recognized those trends, archaeologists are supplied with a new proxy for age. It now becomes more feasible to know when a pot was made and when a site was occupied without an expensive radiocarbon date.

Similarly, the analysis documents a shift in the nature of the designs applied with carved wooden paddles. At the outset, pottery in the province was commonly marked by paddles carved with curving-line motifs, including bull's-eyes and interconnected *P*'s. But by the mission period, in the seventeenth century, flowing lines were largely replaced by sharply angular ones, very often arranged in a cruciform pattern (figure 7.4). Many years ago, in fact, Frankie was drawing attention to the newer, angular stamp pattern, calling it "square ground."[13] It may be another indicator of the unprecedented cultural forces that began to emanate from the coastal zone where related motifs are commonplace.

All these pottery-centric observations suggest quite strongly that a population of Native people successfully established and sustained a separate territory in the Big Bend portion of the Ocmulgee River. It emerged by AD 1400

a

b

7.4 Examples of complicated stamped motifs on Lamar pottery from the Glass Site: (a) curvilinear motif and (b) rectilinear motif.

and flourished for two hundred or more years before dissolving, to some degree under the effects of European-induced strains. Incrementally, the effects of Spanish missionizing and Native responses to them broadened to affect the affairs of interior groups like the people of the Big Bend province.

Rachel's analysis also documents how, at any given time, the sites within the local territory were not complete clones of one another. Especially relevant is her discovery that, throughout its history, the Glass Site was exceptional from the standpoint of pottery. In a word, pottery from the site was unusually diverse in every way. The crux of this tendency is that the Glass Site was not simply exceptional, but exceptional in the singular ways expected of a principal town, one recognized as the seat of power and the place of exalted activity. The range of variation in clay mixtures, vessel forms, and pottery decoration tell us that it was the local hub for regional commerce and the focal point of large and mixed gatherings.

The sites that may be its successor capitals exhibit similar patterns but not to the degree that Glass does. Still, the pottery is emitting strong signals of the whereabouts of that elusive mission site. At one of those later sites, rivaling Glass in size and artifact density, Frankie had previously found a glass bead reminiscent of types common at mission sites on the coast. Now we know pottery at the same site bears traits reminiscent of the same places.

Smoking pipes. Intermingled with pieces of pottery containers, in surprising numbers, are pieces of ceramic smoking pipes. There is no place at the Glass Site without them, other than the plaza, but we have seen already how they are uniquely concentrated around some buildings. The way they are made also sets them apart, and "bizarre" is probably the best word to begin a description.[14]

Like most pipes they were fashioned to include a bowl to contain burning tobacco and a stem through which smoke could be inhaled, but they were also embellished by skilled artisans in astonishing ways. Very often the clay was modeled in raised relief and to form various appendages, for the purpose of creating visages of otherworldly creatures.

Many of them are avian depictions, but they are not the birds we know. Careful inspection of the few that seem, at first, to portray a familiar bird reveals that the figures are actually composite representations of features specific to a range of species. The parrot-like beak might be combined with the crest of a woodpecker and so on. One especially prevalent type is highly

a

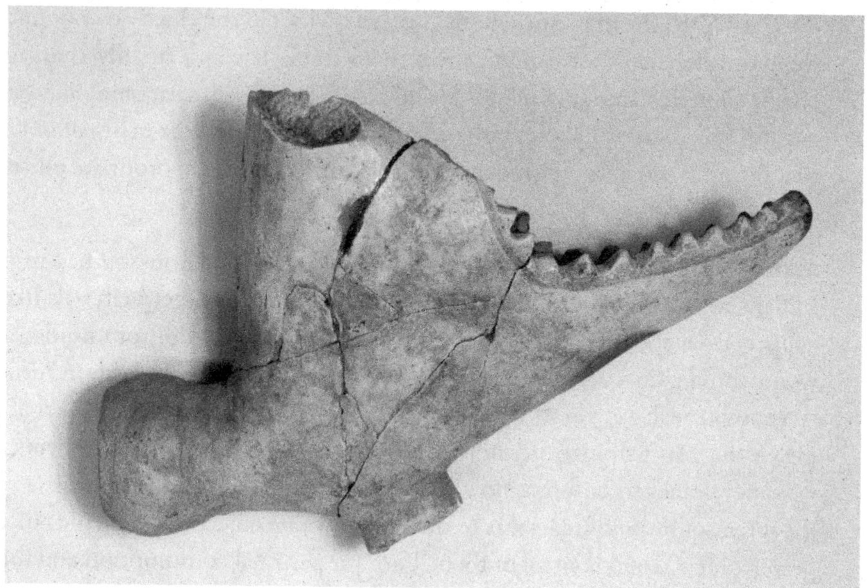
b

7.5 Ceramic smoking pipes: (a) typical trumpet-style pipe and (b) unusual "possum-gator" pipe (max. length of pipe b = 11.6 cm).

abstracted, but it still emphasizes attributes of birds. Protruding from the top of a large bowl, on opposite sides, are long, slender, beak-like appendages. The composition is suggestive of a young bird, head thrown back and mouth wide open to receive a morsel of food. A unique example combines nonavian features such that the final rendering is accentuated by a grotesquely gaping and toothy maw. We just had to dub it the "possum-gator" (figure 7.5b).

Reinforcing a sense of exclusivity, smoking pipes were made from a particular kind of clay, different from the kind chosen for most pottery vessels. It is very high in kaolin and when fired is lighter in color than most cooking or storage pots, which tend to be dark gray or even black. Firing the pipes often imparted a muted orange or salmon color, but many were further enhanced with bright red paint, particularly where birdlike eyes are depicted.

We can infer at least two things from the unusual abundance of pipes at the Glass Site. The first, once more, is that activities in the chiefly compound were as different as we would expect them to be. It was a ritually charged setting in which smoking played a vital role. The other is that smoking was not, for members of Lamar communities, a common social or habitual practice. Burning and imbibing tobacco smoke were sacred acts appropriate under only certain conditions.

Marine shell. Long before Europeans introduced glass and iron, southeastern Indians were assigning value to things made from hard-to-get materials like copper. Even spear points and other essential tools, if made from nonlocal stone, could gain a certain cachet. Possession of such exotica might, in turn, serve to burnish a reputation or convey prestige. From time to time, including in the Mississippian period, expansive and highly controlled networks were developed to ensure a flow of status-linked goods. Make no mistake; the intent of those systems was to direct high-value objects to the hands of a powerful few. Their control of them, both for personal consumption and for gift-giving purposes, was all about maintaining a privileged rank. For a while, our discovery at the Glass Site of Native-made, status-linked artifacts was a surprise, but in retrospect it is not. If it is the capital town that I am arguing it is, it would be more surprising not to find such things.

Fairly early in the temple-area excavation we began to turn up beads and other adornments made from shell. Locals will tell you that the Ocmulgee River is full of shell, and I myself have enjoyed combing sandbars for large mussel valves, hoping to luck onto one containing a knobby pearl. The same freshwater shells are a regular occurrence on the site, too, since mussels were always on the local menu. The shell beads at the temple were something else, however. They had been shaped and drilled from pieces of much larger, single-valve shellfish called whelks—and they live only in the ocean.

Our final count of marine shell beads was only four, but it is telling that they came exclusively from the temple area. With them, and of the same material, was an artifact called an ear pin. The one we recovered had lost the characteristic knob fashioned at one end and consisted only of the long, pointed part designed to be inserted into a pierced earlobe (see figure 4.9). Throughout the region fancy ear-gear exactly like this pin became standard insignia of higher-than-average status, and saltwater shell was a virtual coin of the realm. Marine-shell artifacts tend not to be scattered randomly across Mississippian sites but are consigned to exclusive contexts like graves or special buildings, just as they are at Glass.

With these few things we are presented again with a sign of exception. A chief and his retinue who called a site like this home would surely have broadcast their standing by a code of dress that required display of marine shell. We can deduce further that they were participating in a system of exchange that reached as far away as the coast, and perhaps to both the Atlantic and the Gulf shores. By maintaining that tradition, Lamar leaders were poised to incorporate new kinds of preciosities, including foreign products from Europe.

Arrow points. As with pottery fragments, the site is littered with thin, sharp slivers of stone—artifacts we refer to as flakes, or more elegantly by the French term *debitage*. They are the by-product of eons of toolmaking by people who took up residence there, even if for only a night or two. For every forty or so pieces of this debris, our excavations produce a finished piece, sculpted into a useful shape by controlled removal of unwanted material. The overwhelming kind of flaked stone material we see is one variety or another of chert, a relative of flint that was naturally accessible here and there on Georgia's Coastal Plain.

Indigenous groups replaced atlatls and spears with bows and arrows at least by twelve hundred years ago. Smaller and lighter arrows were tipped with smaller and lighter stone points. Throughout the region the favored shape for arrow points was a simple triangle, and this was the prevailing pattern for about as long as bows and arrows were in use (figure 7.6).

It is difficult if not impossible to distinguish a triangular point made before the Lamar village was established from one that was made during its

7.6 Typical stone arrow points (max. length of longest point = 3.6 cm)

time. In any event, these expendable tools were usually fashioned according to a least-effort practice. A local but poor-quality type of chert, available just across the river, was sometimes chosen for the purpose, but only if larger pieces of higher quality, coastal plain debitage left over from earlier occupations were not collected and put to use first.

Pottery disks. A signature but perplexing type of artifact on Lamar sites everywhere is pottery disks. At the Glass Site we have found nearly one hundred of them. They average about the size of a poker chip and were made by abrading potsherds into the desired round shape. Their production amounted to another form of recycling, and because their origin is so pedestrian, the disks are not one of those things concentrated in particular settings. They show up everywhere, and if anything, they may be less abundant in exclusive contexts.

The mystery is what they were used for. Whatever their purpose, it was either commonplace or popular. Some have suggested they were caps or stoppers for containers. But I am inclined to put stock in the more common view that they were pieces for playing some kind of game.

Animal bone. Across most of Georgia, soils naturally tend to be on the acidic side. Acids break bones down, even quicker if conditions are damp. Outside unusual circumstances, ancient bone will have deteriorated to the consistency of cornmeal, frustrating attempts to recover and identify it. That explains why archaeologists working in the state are surprised when they find bone at all, and more so when it has survived in a condition that makes it recognizable as something other than merely "bone." The Glass Site is no different in those respects, and it was essentially unheard of for us to log species-specific bone.

One small area, however, retained just the right conditions for maintaining bone in good condition: the lens of midden inside the temple ditch. We can thank a relative abundance of mussel shells dumped alongside the bone for the preservative effect. The calcium carbonate in them neutralized the soil's natural acidity. Believe it or not, I witnessed the attitude of excavators in the midden swing from excitement to irritation. Yes, it was an important trove of information, but even in good condition, the bone was still old and subject to damage. Intense concentration was necessary and exhausting to maintain.

Back in the Fernbank lab, we dutifully washed and inventoried the bone, but a full and accurate appraisal required the help of a specialist, called a zooarchaeologist.[15] These are people who know as much or more about biology as archaeology. Some of us knew enough to distinguish mammals from reptiles or birds, but that wasn't sufficient. We had a rare opportunity to gain a sense of dietary patterns and local ecology, with a sample from a unique location, so I found a person qualified to do the job properly.

A few things stood out after the analysis, but visually, none more than the box turtles (see figure 4.10). All told, there were eleven complete box turtle shells in the mix. I affectionately refer to them as our herd of turtles. We can only speculate about the reason for their presence, but the practice of using turtle shells for dance rattles and as dippers is well known. And as a food item, some believe that box turtles reflect a pattern of garden hunting. Women and children, in particular, could have handily collected these sorts of slow, terrestrial critters in the course of tending fields, foraging, or simply playing.

The bone sample was also unusual because it was not dominated by large mammals. Whitetail deer routinely outstrip most other animals in terms of their contribution to the Native meat diet, but here that was less true. Deer were present, but so too were lots of smaller mammals such as opossums, raccoons, squirrels, and rabbits. Aquatic and terrestrial turtles, for instance, account for over 30 percent of the total. Other bones further testify to the extreme breadth of the diet. It was not below the Glass Site's residents to collect and dine on a variety of reptiles, fish like catfish and gar, large and small birds, and mussels. Especially curious is the presence of a few bones of brackish water fish such as hard-head catfish and drum, indicative of food gathering in the tidal zone or perhaps trade with people living there.

Some bones are those of species either fully extinct or extremely rare today. Two from the passenger pigeon (*Ectopistes migratorius*) is an example. Though wiped out from overhunting by the early twentieth century, endless flocks once darkened the sky. Nighttime roosts, we are told, made for easy pickings.[16] The anklebone of a black bear was also identified, as was the canine of a "large carnivore."

Sadly, this assemblage of animal bone is a tease. There are things we have learned from it, but they aren't a sufficient basis to decipher site-wide patterns of subsistence. Always, we inherit gaps in our evidence, and this is a big one at the Glass Site. Still, it is worthwhile on its own merits as the likely remainder of a busk-related dump, the result of ritualized feasting and cleansing. What surprises me most is not the midden's existence just outside the temple door but the unseemly character of it. Studies of Mississippian diet often contrast the quality of foods consumed by elites and everyone else, and, predictably, the few percent at the top tended to eat pretty high off the hog—or the deer, as it were. They enjoyed more of the finer cuts from large mammals and other game.[17]

So why are we seeing in this sample equal parts mammal and swimming or squirming creatures? The ready answer is the immediate environs. The site was surrounded by aquatic habitats. I can imagine that some of the remains are tribute items ultimately passed up by the elites. It is also possible that the mixed assortment is a sign of stress, a possibility deserving more study.

All the evidence I have shared, from artifacts to discolored soil, our archaeological stock in trade as it were, bears veiled witness to human existence at the Glass Site. Those imperfect clues stand, in fact, as the sole reflection of its founding people and the culture that defined them. There is no alternative portal through which we might view them. From our study of their residues, I can try to articulate a perspective on the place and the time they were a part of, one that is meaningful at least to us in the present.

Having parted with an ancestral territory upstream and in or near the Piedmont, a group of newly independent pioneers settled on this stretch of the Ocmulgee to make a new beginning.[18] It was understood, by force of tradition and long experience, that the viability of the endeavor depended in part on a functioning and secure capital. It would be the place where the highest functions of the province were concentrated, namely, command, control, and communion.

It is not a reach to conclude that, for a time, the Glass Site was the principal community within the young province, and until we have evidence to the contrary, I will also propose that it was one of the first of its capitals. A multitude of indicators support this notion. The five dates we have obtained from carbon dating bracket the period AD 1425–1625, and on the whole, the site's artifacts, whether Native or European, are of earlier types than occur at the other larger sites. The one exception seems to be Coffee Bluff.

The site was the residence and base of operation for the provincial chief and a cadre of official subordinates, plus their close relatives. In this sense it represented a chiefly compound where leadership and high-level functionaries found sanctuary. Affairs of state would transpire there, whether routine or ceremonial in nature. It would be the place from which strategic decisions would flow, as well as the place to which distinguished guests would gravitate.

Because matters of both governance and religion were inextricably bound in the society, the capital elites were responsible for reinforcing the order of the cosmos. Many sources tell us that priests and shamans were among the high officials and had great influence. Their essential functions would require a private space, a holy of holies, where a perpetual fire was maintained, proprietary ritualizing could occur, and sacred paraphernalia kept safe.

The entire social system, built on a caste-like hierarchy and an agricultural economy and in need of mutual defense from competing groups, would have required regular reinforcement. One essential underpinning would be a ritual calendar that prescribed a series of outright or quasi-religious observances. The capital would host the more important of them, at which times the majority of the populace would be in attendance. Our archaeological indicators say they included, at least, the occasions of astronomical events like the solstices and renewal and harvest ceremonies like the busk, or Green Corn.

The vitality and centrality of the social order, and maintenance of it, were so ingrained that it was purposely captured by the layout of the town and the buildings within it. At every turn, a resident or visitor would confront symbolic representations of the ethos and, more powerfully, the cosmology behind it. In effect, the Glass Site and many things in it can be read through archaeology as a microcosm of the Lamar worldview. It was a conception of the universe that situated the earthly realm between an upper and a lower world. The model encapsulated tension between good and evil, peace and war, and life and death. Humans, in their middle world, struggled to balance the relatively benign forces of the upper domain with the dangerous ones below. Addressing those concerns would have been a preoccupation at capital compounds.

The plan of the Glass Site can be read in terms of those preoccupations. The bagel becomes the disk of the middle world where balance was crucial. Eyes would be drawn to an obvious center point around which cardinal directions were enshrined with special buildings. By entering the temple, and perhaps any of the structures, one would confront the same model again. Its floor plan and orientation adhered to the same strictures, all very tangibly represented by the arrangement of major posts, walls, and the door relative to a central hearth. And if somehow the message still wasn't clear, one would discover portrayals of the same worldview at mealtime. Pottery was inscribed and stamped with elegant abstractions of an ordered cosmos. And on and on.

We do not yet know what it was that spelled the end of the Glass Site occupation. Recall that elsewhere archaeologists have calculated the lifespan of a typical Mississippian province at no more than a century. We also understand that the functional lives of provincial capitals were even more delicate. The competence of individual chiefs, the popularity of ruling dynasties, the ravages of external conflicts, and climate change have all been implicated in one case or another.[19] In any event, the post-Glass society appears, in time, to have rejected aspects of traditional ceremonialism, so far as this can be ascertained from patterns in pottery, and it was in concert with orientation toward coastal missions.

Whatever the circumstances, aspects of the abandonment appear to have been orderly. Deliberate burial of the temple was apparently one of the final acts. But before the temple site was ritually put to rest, it would seem the building was first destroyed by fire. An abundance of daub and some burned timbers tell us this. Here again, we cannot determine whether the burning was intentional or accidental, but controlled retirement of the sacred edifice would not be out of the question. Considerable power had been concentrated there, and managing it, even in "death," was vital. Organized abandonment might also explain some of the layers in the ditch feature. Analysis of the soil column verifies low-level filling for a while by natural siltation and occasional dumping. However, the bulk of the ditch fill is coarser and highly varied, as if the rate of intentional disposal increased late in the life of the feature.

To know Mississippian archaeology and, by extension Mississippian culture, is to know the Glass Site village and the province it governed. There is nothing about their arrangement or history that is unusual. These many elements of the Big Bend realm capture the essence of a cultural pattern that was long in tooth by Soto's time. Lamar culture evolved in Georgia as a later version of the extraordinary Native mode that took the Southeast by storm by the twelfth century.[20]

That consistency is one of the important points of this book. We have documented a quintessential example of an evolving Mississippian polity and its capital town where it was not anticipated. Doing so forces new thinking about the geography of the Native world late in prehistory. That was the central theme of Charles Hudson's intense interest in the Soto story. It also opens new possibilities for evaluators of the Soto venture. Suddenly we are forced to consider a new enticement for such an explorer of the Southeast. The Big Bend province is exactly the kind of place he would beat a path to.

VIII

Elusive Closure

Some serious explaining is still left to do. The existence of an Indian province and its encounters with alien invaders are now beyond dispute, but these facts raise several irksome, newer questions. Exactly what happened to bring European things to the Glass Site? Can we put a name to the people who introduced them? What was the nature of their encounters with Natives? Did the interactions have a lasting effect? The answers constitute the climax of our archaeological whodunit.

But let's first confront the more vital question: why does any of this matter? My own response has three parts. First, and harking to Charles Hudson again, an accurate track of the earliest explorers and colonizers is our entrée to Native American cultural geography. It penetrates the gauzy veil separating historical time and prehistory. Quoting Hudson's own justification, "If a sufficiently accurate [Soto] route could be worked out, it would become possible to put together a picture of the social geography of the sixteenth-century Southeast—a map of who lived where. From this point of reckoning, it would then become possible to recede back into the past to examine how the sixteenth-century native societies had evolved from earlier Mississippian antecedents and to proceed forward in time to show how this 1539–43 Southeastern world gave way, fell apart, and reorganized itself into the peoples of the eighteenth-century South."[1]

Historical precision is another benefit. If we agree that the events are important, then there is an obligation to portray them accurately—or as thoroughly and objectively as we can. The events our shovels have roused to mind are emblematic of a period of radical change, not merely in southern

Georgia, or the region, but throughout the hemisphere. They are expressions of the emergence of the modern world order, a legacy we are still grappling to comprehend.

Last, research of this nature stands to bring some meaning to the perennial issue of cultural "clashes." It is unlikely there will ever be a time or place immune from the anxiety and tension that can permeate cross-cultural encounters, particularly first contacts. The ambition is to glean meaning from historical cases of foreign interventions in the Southeast and, short of that, comprehension of their intricate complexity.

All along, however, the main driver is a desire to get the essence of the Glass Site story right. Only then would it be sensible to explore its wider implications. That seminal goal is about settling on the most plausible explanation for the evidence, the best-fit scenario that accounts for the archaeological residues in terms of actual human events and behaviors. The preceding chapters have laid out a fact pattern, our exhibits A, B, and C so to speak, defined by the dispassionate, thorough, and systematic process I have tried to follow. What ensues now amounts to my closing argument, starting with the Soto possibility.

Yes, I have concluded from available facts that a significant portion of the Glass Site evidence is best attributed to an encounter with Soto's entrada, and this book is not the first place I have argued for it.[2] I cannot validate the claim beyond a shadow of doubt, but I can mount a fulsome argument that makes a great deal of circumstantial sense. Many of my colleagues see the strength of the case, but some also reject the assertion. To understand the resistance to my interpretation, we must review a bit of scholarly backstory. It helps to know something more about the leading reconstructions of Soto's path, the received wisdom as it were, and why they have or have not carried his route through the territory of the Big Bend province.

Fortunately, there are details drawn from the original relations of the entrada that are largely immune from debate. It makes sense to begin with them as I sketch out the entrada's itinerary during the spring of 1540, when it first progressed through Georgia territory. This bit of stage setting establishes basic parameters of time and place and imparts a sense of the atmosphere that surrounded the events. Consider it a summary of Soto's relevant whistle-stops.

Soto and his followers did not exactly enjoy a vacation in the Sunshine State. The going was hard, even beyond sniping by the Indians.[3] Rumors notwithstanding, nothing that they had endured in the first eight months promised a big payoff. Soto wanted—and needed—to change that, and the plan of action, come spring, was to make haste for richer towns and ore-laden mountains. He had hundreds of armed personnel to mollify and to motivate.

The litany of tribulations since his first landing called for a gut check. By November 1539 the troopers had finally reached a powerful and prosperous Indian province in Panhandle Florida, at today's Tallahassee, where food was in relatively good supply. This, Soto decided, was an opportune location for an extended time-out. Having failed to make a rendezvous on the Gulf Coast for resupply, he faced the weighty decision of whether to fall back or plunge ahead. More than three months of fireside deliberation, affected by local intelligence gathering, culminated in the decision to decamp and go for broke.

The path forward was to be charted by two teenaged Indian guides, Marcos and Perico.[4] Described as Native traders from points north, the two young men had embarked on what, for them, were essentially work trips. They bumped into Soto in the process and were swept up by the proceedings. The language of their homeland, Yupaha, differed from that of Natives in Florida, but they were fluent enough to do business. This enabled a chain of translation between the traders, the once-captive Spaniard Ortiz, and Soto, amounting to a tricky telephone game of communication.[5] But enough was understood to reckon that the two Indians knew how to navigate the system of trails northward, and that they had knowledge of a rich territory called Cofitachequi in possession of metal from the mountains beyond. The Spanish reaction . . . what are we waiting for?

On the third of March 1540, the Spanish army, augmented by chained-together, corn-carrying Indian porters, broke camp and began its lurching advance northward. The entrada resumed its pattern of connecting the Indian dots, finding sustenance, gathering information, and, ideally, learning of places to plunder. Soto knew he would not find what he was looking for right away. Cofitachequi lay weeks ahead, past lesser provinces and stretches of deserted territory. In sequence, the first provinces they intersected, from southwest to northeast, were Capachequi, Toa, Ichisi, Altamaha, Ocute, and Cofaqui, beyond which was a forbidding no-man's-land ahead of Cofitachequi (see figure 7.1 for approximate locations).

We are led to believe that their pace was quick and even forced at times. From present-day Tallahassee to the Savannah River at the Georgia–South Carolina border, the entrada covered a distance of at least 450 km (280 mi). It was a stretch requiring some forty-six days to traverse. Through Georgia they were most of the time barging into a different Indian province every couple of days. Only twice did the group linger anywhere longer than four days and between stops they were averaging about 20 km (12.5 mi). It is generally agreed that most of the way they were observing the sights and sounds of the Coastal Plain, and only toward the end did the company enter the Piedmont uplands.

The chronicles are reasonably consistent about a few other details of this segment. The starting point is safely fixed at Tallahassee, where archaeology and historical records conjoin to identify the Anhaica province and the entrada's winter headquarters in it.[6] Mention of large spring-fed lakes within days of departing Anhaica squares well with what we know about the landscape of southwestern Georgia just above the Panhandle. The Dougherty Plain in the area of Albany is an archetypal karstic landscape featuring countless sinkholes, some of which form spring-fed, natural lakes.[7]

Crossings of four major streams were coordinated, most of them full and fast as they are prone to be in springtime. In the Flint River basin, the rivers they called Capachequi and Toa drained the provinces of the same names. Two others flowed through the provinces lying between Ichisi and Cofaqui, and the orientation of the first in this pair was cause for remark. It distinctly followed an easterly course, a powerful indication to the trekkers that they had advanced beyond Gulf-oriented basins into Atlantic-draining ones. Even then the Spanish had enough sense of geography to infer that they were then upstream of the territory chosen by Ayllón in 1526.[8]

At Capachequi the reception they received was unfriendly, spillover from their strained interactions in Florida. An ugly reputation had begun to precede them.[9] Right away a guerilla strike left one Spaniard dead and three others wounded. At the same time they were seeing signs of a cultural transition. The Indian houses of Capachequi and Toa were described as substantial and cave-like, very unlike the lighter, thatch- or mat-covered dwellings they had seen and sheltered in farther south.[10] Simultaneously, Muskogean dialects, the languages of Marcos and Perico, became lingua franca and replaced the Timucuan language of Florida.[11]

From Toa, Soto made a dramatic nighttime dash that was to lead them across the Gulf-Atlantic divide and close to that east-flowing river.[12] He had slipped away from the main column under cover of darkness, with a phalanx of mounted men, no doubt eager to demonstrate meaningful progress. About then, and perhaps not coincidentally, Indian receptions became relatively gracious. It was apparently a new stratagem adopted on the Native side to cut losses. Call it a self-preserving charm offensive. This was especially true beginning in Ichisi territory, and the tone held fast through several successive provinces. Stores of Indian food were shared, and in return Soto was moved to bestow gifts and erect Christian crosses.[13]

Whether the next provinces, of Altamaha, Ocute, and Cofaqui, were located along the third or the fourth river is disputed, but everyone agrees they were closely spaced. Each was no more than a day's travel from the other. Cofaqui, however, was poised at the edge of the "desert," the buffer zone separating those lands from the realm of Cofitachequi. That point also marked the apparent limit of Perico's working knowledge. We are told by the chroniclers, with no small measure of frustration, that this is where Perico lost his nerve. Displaying or at least feigning distress—maybe even madness—he would only point rather than continue in the direction of the intimidating, rival chiefdom.[14]

Lots of quibbling results when scholars try to become more specific about the path, but it will pay to examine less agreed-upon but still salient details of the classic path reconstructions, maintaining our focus on the first Georgia traverse. Their differences embody the essence of the debates that linger.

In terms of basic research, the investigations of both Swanton and Hudson were exhaustive and, for their eras, state of the art. Authoritative translations of period accounts underwent point-by-point comparative analysis, and details like measures of distance were deliberated. Likewise, available archaeological information was considered, as was scholarship concerning Indian trails, place-names, and languages. Legions of experts and local informants were interviewed. Both also suffer from the same, unavoidable limitations. Entries in the original sources are usually vague in their terseness and, frequently enough, inconsistent. Never has supportive archaeological information been complete. Effectively, then, every attempt to reconstruct the path of an explorer constitutes a working hypothesis, something to be put to the test, and not a statement of certainty.

The eldest of the respected route studies is the work of a federal commission formed in advance of the nation's 1939 quadricentennial observance of Soto's landing. John R. Swanton, one of the nation's most famous anthropologists, led the effort. The final report published by the Smithsonian Institution remains a critical resource.[15]

Most notably for us, John Swanton's team had the entrada marching quite close to the Glass Site (see figure 1.2). They decided that Soto first intersected the Ocmulgee River near Abbeville in Wilcox County. Their argument inspired an official historical marker on the town's courthouse lawn, and later it impelled Julian Williams to erect his own signage in Jacksonville and to pop the question he put to me back in 2006. Swanton's team placed great stock in the description by one commentator of the easterly flowing river, and Abbeville is at the upper part of the Ocmulgee's great, east-sweeping bend. They were also influenced by the name and location of the Altamaha River in estimating placement of the Altamaha province. Linguistically it was only natural to associate Altamaha, the place, with the modern-day river into which the Ocmulgee flows some sixty miles below Abbeville.

Swanton found independent support for Altamaha's position in documents that described post-Soto events. With time, the coastal missions had become staging points for briefer, interior expeditions, and more than one of them followed the course of the Altamaha. The best known was led by Gaspar de Salas in 1597 for the purpose of introducing Fray Pedro de Chozas to inland provinces. In his official report, "Tama" was described by Salas as eight days upstream from St. Catherines Island, located near the Altamaha's mouth.[16] Using these separate sources, the Swanton team was able to triangulate Tama's approximate location "into the neighborhood of Abbeville . . . [and] parts of Dodge and Telfair counties."[17]

Swanton and his team placed the first of the provinces we're concerned with, Capachequi, Toa, and Ichisi, in the Flint River basin. Then, the provinces of Ocute, Cofaqui, and Patofa were situated on the Ocmulgee just above the Altamaha. The report acknowledges that the "section of the journey, through the province of Ichisi, namely between Toa and

Altamaha, is somewhat difficult to trace owing to obscurities in the original narratives."[18]

One possible remedy for those ambiguities was recourse to archaeological knowledge. But what Swanton and company could garner was woefully lacking, and certainly no one had yet filed a report of early Spanish artifacts anywhere along this stretch. The mound site of Pine Island, not far from Albany, they identified with Capachequi, but it is now understood to have been abandoned by Soto's time.[19] The presence of another mound site near Hartford, across from Hawkinsville, led them to assume it was "an important crossing place" and, therefore, the point where the entrada had left Cofaqui by crossing the Ocmulgee. However, this site, too, has since been determined to predate Soto, and by centuries.[20] They dismissed the relevance of the tremendous complex of mound sites in the Macon area because, "the failure of [the] chroniclers to mention these mound groups, supposing they were encamped at any time near one of them, would be as marvelous as are the mounds themselves."[21] Significantly for us, the Swanton team ultimately placed the Oconee River crossing at a place called Carr's Bluff, not far above Dublin, a point to be explained later.[22]

Forty years along, in 1980, Charles Hudson, allied with Chester DePratter and Marvin Smith, set out to take another look at the route (see Figure 1.2). Theirs is the reconstruction that enjoys the most favor today. The timing was right from a scholarly standpoint because, at their disposal, was the yield of considerably more and considerably better archaeology. Likewise, breakthroughs in historical research had occurred.[23] Their work was further inspired by anticipation of an international observance of the Columbian quincentenary in 1992. Worldwide, historians and archaeologists were awakened to bring a more accurate and more honest appraisal to events surrounding first "discovery" of the New World.

Four years into their project, the Hudson team published the first fruit of its analysis. The article addressed Soto's initial pass across Georgia.[24] As they were for Swanton, keystones of the proposal were estimated locations of the Native provinces that the Soto accounts consistently identified between Panhandle Florida and the Appalachian range. The researchers believed they could recognize them from archaeologically plotted constellations of Indian settlements arranged around at least one capital town. More often than not, the capitals were signified by prominent earthen mounds. They also took into account the presence or absence of telltale European artifacts like glass beads and iron tools. And, finally, they applied their own interpretation of standard distance and geographical clues.

The Hudson route diverges considerably from Swanton's under heavy influence from a ballooning archaeological record. For all intents and purposes, his team gravitated to the most prominent concentrations of Lamar culture sites. The Ocmulgee crossing, for example, was determined by where such agglomerations were and weren't documented. They rejected Swanton's intersection at Abbeville because no one, including Frankie Snow, had observed Lamar sites of any consequence in that area. They also learned from Frankie and from me that the same was true of the areas downstream and southward.[25] At the same time, they were aware of quite different conditions in the other direction. The Lamar site is in Bibb County, just below Macon, and it is surrounded by related, smaller sites.[26]

Not long before, Smith and DePratter had also been principle figures in a major University of Georgia effort to document archaeology along the upper Oconee River, in advance of flooding by a new hydroelectric project.[27] The upshot was unprecedented investigation of an entire Lamar province, later argued to represent Ocute.[28] In the meantime, a different Hudson student, John Worth, was dispatched to the upper Flint to survey for Lamar sites.[29] He promptly identified another Lamar province in the vicinity of some prominent mounds. This one, they surmised, represented Toa territory. It only made sense, then, to situate Soto's Ichisi between their projection for Toa and Ocute, conveniently in the vicinity of Macon.

In addition, Hudson, Smith, and DePratter differently interpreted two major stream crossings. Swanton believed the "great river" to be the Flint, but Hudson argued it was the Ocmulgee, an attribution that seems sound in light of Soto's midnight run from Toa. Then the Hudson group decided that the next "considerable stream," flowing "eastward to the sea," must be the Oconee.[30] That is where they located Altamaha.

The archaeological foundation of this reconstruction was far superior to what Swanton could build on, but once again, we're learning that it had its limits. Above all, the incompleteness of knowledge concerning Lamar settlement in the Big Bend region was a handicap. It is abundantly clear—today—that perceptions of sixteenth-century Indian occupation in that area were gravely flawed, mine included. Where once there was no Lamar province, there now is. The Hudson route is also quite mound-centric or, more precisely, big mound-centric. Large, late-dating mounds emerged as a common denominator among the principle provincial towns they thought they could identify. It is not fair to severely take this association to task, but especially in retrospect, it may prove fallacious if applied too rigidly.

Also, concrete evidence of Soto's passage, in the form of imported artifacts, was entirely absent in their day in the stretch between Tallahassee and the Appalachian front of North Carolina. Nowhere had objects reasonably linkable to Soto been documented. Thanks to the Glass Site investigation, that is no longer true. But the beads and other items found elsewhere on this stretch of the Hudson line are universally of styles that are decades or more too young.[31]

Summarizing, a comparison of the Swanton and Hudson reconstructions gives assurance in the initial direction of the march and in the general whereabouts of the Capachequi province. In the same way, the two teams agree that Toa was located in the Flint basin. Farther along, their estimations of the path are not at all complementary, and the door is left wide open for interpretation. This is especially true of the position of the Ichisi province. The researchers all bemoaned the lack of clarity about this territory in the original chronicles. Swanton argues it lay upstream of Toa on the Flint, and the Hudson team situates it on the Ocmulgee near Macon. Problematically, the first of those rivers falls within a Gulf-draining basin and the other within an Atlantic basin. This also means that the Swanton reconstruction puts Soto's encounter with the Ocmulgee River downstream near the Big Bend, and that the other puts it upstream at Macon. They both agree that Altamaha must have been somewhere in the Altamaha basin, a vast area, but the decisions as to where are quite different. So while neither group was working with the benefit of our Glass Site findings, a retrospective evaluation of the work indicates each, in different ways, was successfully putting supporting pieces into place.

Our appraisal of the Glass Site evidence will also benefit from advance review of archaeological criteria applied to the crucial question, how would we know a Soto site even if we saw one? The Glass Site is obviously not the first place to provoke the issue, nor am I the first archaeologist to suffer hypertension over the prospect. In the historical realm the stakes are high, and that is what accounts for inordinate effort to establish a calculus that culminates in the right call. To be wrong might be difficult, but to be reckless is the kiss of death. Over the decades, so many false claims of Soto discoveries have been put to rest that a colleague once quipped that they're now greeted the same way pronouncements of cold fusion are.

I previously addressed the question, in a technical report about Glass Site findings, using criteria set down by predecessors. I knew my own work would be judged accordingly, but I also went on to propose some refinements that give more emphasis to acquisition processes and the factor of human agency.[32] Doing so doesn't raise the bar of acceptance a great deal higher, but it forces more explicit acknowledgment of the complexity of the events. Before we evaluate the Glass Site findings against that model, it will help us to be clear about the terms of assessment.

Is it the right stuff? First, we must find some consensus about the artifacts uniquely indicative of our period. No one denies that definition of diagnostic "kits" or "complexes" of sixteenth-century artifacts is an imprecise business, but because of recurrent associations between things and places, confidence is growing. The pioneering work of Charles Fairbanks (1968), Jeffrey Brain (1975), Ian Brown (1977, 1979, 1980), Marvin Smith (1987; Smith and Good 1982), and Kathleen Deagan (1987, 2002), continued by researchers like Jeffrey Mitchem (1991; Mitchem and McEwan 1988), Keith Little (2008), and Greg Waselkov (2009), allows us to better distinguish collections dating from the time of initial Spanish exploration from those more likely connected to subsequent periods.[33] Nonetheless, about the best resolution we can achieve, temporally, is measured in decades.

For our purposes, then, the distinction between artifacts representative of the 1500–1565 interval and the following 1565–1600 interval is most pertinent.[34] Traditionally, it was the relative frequency of particular types of glass beads and bells that resolved this coarse distinction, but increasingly, unique types of nails, military hardware, and tools are also understood to be sensitive markers of time. All such things, for example, were central to identification of the Martin Site as the first winter encampment of the Soto entrada.[35] In that case, beads like seven-layer chevrons, military items such as a crossbow quarrel and chain mail, nails, and coins were most persuasive.

Is it the right place? We know that the modus operandi of the Soto entrada involved exploitation of Indian communities. It is likewise understood that Soto and others utilized existing paths, not only for the sake of efficiency but also because they were chosen by the Indian guides who led them. Thus it stands to reason that entrada-related sites will occur proximate to established Indian trails.

Charles Ewen and John Hann also specified how winter encampments of the Soto entrada would always occur in association with large Indian towns.[36] The same would be true, I believe, of most multi-night encampments during periods of the march. However, single-night encampments would not necessarily carry the same expectation, nor would lengthy stays at difficult river crossings or stay-overs in the buffer zones separating Indian provinces.

Many scenarios therefore predict that European material will be concentrated in Native communities. Regarding specific contexts in the towns, a common contrast is drawn between burial and nonburial situations.[37] The fundamental question is, what are the different behaviors that account for occurrences of sixteenth-century trade goods in graves, or other kinds of exclusive contexts, versus occurrences in nonexclusive contexts, such as in general community and midden deposits? Occurrences of the first sort seem to be most common in the region. Indeed, it has become nearly axiomatic that burials are where such objects will be found. I will maintain, however, that burials do not have to be the sole context in an Indian setting that is "exclusive." Items of value to the leadership and the community, including exotica from abroad, were likely stored within nondomestic, public buildings, such as temples or council houses.

Sixteenth-century European artifacts could, in fact, occur in either exclusive or nonexclusive contexts on the same Soto-related site or in both. In the one reported case where numerous European objects of diverse kinds were found in only nonexclusive, nonburial contexts, namely, the Martin Site, it was interpreted to represent a prolonged encampment.[38]

How did it get there? A jumble of processes transferred objects of European origin to the Native realm. But a universal, complicating factor, no matter the mode of introduction, is what we call the portability problem. All the things we know to have been exchanged were small and lightweight and, therefore, easily carried from one place to another. Indeed, circulation of newly acquired European goods tends to be another de facto corollary of "contact." Consequently, the locations where early European material is discovered cannot be automatically accepted as the actual points of Spanish-Indian encounters. It becomes, then, the onus of the archaeologist to sort out the dynamics of movement, the path these items followed from point of origin to point of deposition. Unsurprisingly the distinctions become even blurrier at sites or in areas that experienced multiple episodes of contact over many decades.

David Hally and Marvin Smith have tried to tackle the issue, and they define a multitude of mechanisms by which European goods could be acquired and consumed by indigenous people.[39] The varied avenues include direct gift-giving by upper-echelon members of exploring parties, direct gift giving by lower-ranking members of exploring parties, Native scavenging or pilfering under varied circumstances, and battlefield salvage.

Those many pathways account well for the diverse range of objects observed archaeologically, especially for material that ultimately was interred with the Native dead. In other words, regardless of the specific mechanism of acquisition, the Hally and Smith model, consistent with long-standing views, describes a process that begins with purposeful acquisition of European goods by Native people, next involves incorporation of the objects into the Native system as privileged goods, and ends with their near-uniform consumption as funerary objects. In their words, "we are of the opinion that most, if not all, Spanish artifacts recovered from burials in the interior Southeast were interred with their original owners. . . . Because of their association with the powerful Spanish intruders, even items stolen from the Spanish or recovered from the battlefield may have conferred some prestige on their owners, thus motivating those individuals to keep them and display them one last time at their funerals."[40] Thus we are still in need of a model that is well suited to explain the occurrence of European objects in nonburial contexts, particularly when they are not of the classic gift-good type, meaning things like nails and horseshoes.

Under a scenario of prolonged encampment, for example, European things could have gotten around under other pretexts, not to mention the fact that the complex routine of an encamped exploring party would generate all manner of debris beyond what was purposely exchanged with Indians. Entrada members would have simply discarded and lost some objects in the course of making and breaking camp and as gear was assessed and maintained. These are the things the Indians would have most likely scavenged later. In addition, at a bustling camp, gifts would very likely have flowed between members of both groups and across more than one level of status, perhaps in defiance of official policies or customs.

There may be ways for us to address some of these challenges. One is to use the diversity of an assemblage to gauge the nature of an encounter. Richness, or the number of documented artifact categories, may be a factor of encounter intensity or duration, encounter directness, and encounter kind. Hypothetically, a small assemblage composed of only one or two kinds of artifacts would more likely result from a relatively brief or indirect encounter, whereas a large and diverse collection of artifacts might more likely be construed as the outcome of a relatively prolonged or direct interaction. Also, the ratio of probable gift items versus items that were more likely lost or discarded and then scavenged serves as a basis for similar judgments. With the exception of skirmishes, brief encounters would be least apt to generate extraneous debris and, instead, involve more or less exclusive exchange of sanctioned gift items like beads, bells, and iron tools. Encampment situations of a few days or longer duration would, in contrast, be more likely to entail both gift exchanges and general loss and discard of other material.

Were there rules to the game? The circumstances of intercultural encounters, particularly those that represent first or very early ones, as in the sixteenth-century Southeast, can arguably be the most opaque. They constitute unprecedented interactions on both sides of the equation, for which ready cultural mores may not have existed. In cases like these, when norms could easily fail, one should not necessarily expect to discern patterned behavior in the usual sense. Or, old patterns may have been adjusted to meet a new condition. In effect, we would be wrong to ignore the ways that ingrained cultural mores determined the nature of interactions, but we would also be mistaken to dismiss the caveat anthropologists refer to as *agency*.[41] In the environment we are considering, newly acquainted individuals and groups may have been grasping at disparate, essentially experimental solutions. A case in point is the contrast in receptions given to Soto at Capachequi and Ichisi.

Some of the time we can anticipate adaptations of long-standing behaviors to the contact situation. A common assumption, as we have seen, is that virtually any European object acquired by Natives in the sixteenth-century Southeast would have been requisitioned and closely controlled by the Native leadership. The objects would have relatively quickly been taken out of general circulation, hoarded and displayed for status-linked purposes, and then, in the same sense, ultimately deposited as grave furnishings.[42] At work, then, was a kind of status-linked gravitational pull. Certainly this would be a direct outcome of gift exchange since the vast majority of goods entering the system that way were given directly to high-ranking individuals. However, even items acquired by scavenging, say in the wake of conflict or at abandoned encampments, would also presumably enter the elite exchange system quickly and be consumed as high-status burial goods. This argument also implies that, most of the time, prized European objects would not circulate beyond the limits of the sociopolitical unit in which they were originally deposited. In the late prehistoric Southeast, this would be the extent of chiefly provinces.[43]

Soto and his men were perhaps the least predictable as far as behavior is concerned. One gathers from period accounts that Soto often engaged Native people according to immediate contingencies as opposed to a fixed strategy. At any given time his operational rubric accounted for factors as varied as threat level, the condition and mood of his army, the prospect for reward, his store of provisions, and the weather. One can infer that, under pressure to succeed, he operated in a highly changeable fashion simply to get the results he wanted. For this reason we would do well to anticipate variation in the archaeological patterns created by his entrada. However, while Soto and his followers might have operated in a less rule-bound fashion outside familiar society, we must also appreciate that they were not entirely immune to the influence of their own culture. A Western European rationale of some kind would always have been shrouded in the chaos.

At last, our extended interrogation of the Glass Site findings and our dialogue with the debates that swirl around discoveries like it have brought us to the point of an interpretation. The implications of the claims demand that we undertake a rather clinical summary vis-à-vis the expectations I have just reviewed. I will argue that there are grounds to believe the Glass Site represents the location of a Native encounter with the exploring party of Hernando de Soto. I will cast additional evidence as the signal of other encounters, perhaps one before 1550 and certainly one afterward. The Big Bend province, it is safe to say, became caught up in the flow of early colonial affairs.

The Native context is appropriate. The Glass Site is a late Lamar community occupied at least between AD 1450 and 1550. This has been determined from radiocarbon dating results and attributes of the artifacts. Archaeology has also documented a province-like grouping of sites at the Big Bend of the lower Ocmulgee. Internally, their distribution conforms to the classic, late Lamar pattern of dispersed settlement.[44] Thanks in large measure to Frankie Snow's surveys, no fewer than twelve late Lamar sites are concentrated within a closely circumscribed area, and surely many companion sites await discovery. Comparisons with other provinces indicate that the Glass Site bears the hallmarks of a principal town within such a cluster.[45]

The site's location and setting meet expectations for a place that would have attracted an early European exploring party. The Glass Site, and the province over which it reigned, was the kind of target explorers like Soto found attractive. The concentration of people and resources was strategically connected to a wider world by waterways and an established system of trails.

The province lay within the important Altamaha River basin, for ages a major conduit between the Atlantic coast and interior Georgia. Eighty-four miles (135 km) inland the strategic bifurcation of the Altamaha, appropriately dubbed The Forks, presented useful options for east-to-west travelers. The lower or southern branch, the Ocmulgee, would lead eventually to sites concentrated, at times, at Macon Plateau. Several other mound-centered provinces were accessible by the northern arm, the Oconee. Also, during the period of contact, the Altamaha system could have connected places like Ayllón's colony and Catholic missions to Native provinces of Altamaha and Ichisi and Ocute. More than a century later, Mary Musgrove chose the vicinity of The Forks for her trading post.[46]

Riverine access was enhanced by a system of trails, including a local nexus that linked drainages of the Atlantic slope to those of the Gulf system. Paths paralleled either side of the Altamaha's main trunk and its major feeders, the Ocmulgee and the Oconee.[47] The Glass Site is located along the first of these tributaries. Extrapolating from nineteenth-century cartography, we have established that the site also lies near a north-to-south connecting trail, using a river ford formerly known as Blackshear's Landing. It tied together the paths running parallel with the Ocmulgee River on its south and north sides.[48] Then there were trails that took an overland path, linking the Big Bend to the Gulf Coast, and points in between, by running against the grain of Gulf-oriented streams. These include the unnamed path followed by Fray Ore, the Tallahassee trail, and another one that led from an intersection at Philema on the Flint River.[49]

Our own evaluation of the standard sources, the Soto chronicles, Indian trail locations, and the latest archaeology establishes that it is quite possible to plot a feasible path for Soto's entrada that gets it to the lower Ocmulgee, instead of the middle Ocmulgee at Macon, on the right schedule (see appendix). We recognize alternative paths of travel deviating from the well-argued route proposal of Hudson's team, between Anhaica and Cofitachequi, that can explain the evidence at the Glass Site (figure 8.1).

Equally telling is a glaring absence of competing archaeological evidence from elsewhere in the 740 km stretch between today's Tallahassee and the eastern slope of the Appalachians in North Carolina. Not a solitary item of compelling early sixteenth-century vintage has turned up, even in the intensively investigated and purported provincial areas around Macon and the upper Oconee (identified by Hudson, respectively, as Ichisi and Ocute). Not to mention that there was no one home when Soto passed through some of the key mound sites inferred by others to be principal towns within major provinces.

Perhaps, then, we should be unsurprised to find that the debris field in the upper Altamaha basin, consisting of European material, contains things dating from the post-Soto era, even continuing into the eighteenth century. Only the Glass Site so far yields the earliest kind of artifacts, but it and numerous other Native sites upstream of The Forks have also produced objects of later styles.[50] I believe we are witnessing in this evidence the archaeological signature of a known-world effect. Soto put the area's provinces on the map, and thereafter they experienced pulses of historically inspired visitation. Indeed, the precedent of Soto explains several provincial revisits over the ensuing half century or so, almost always where Soto spoke positively of a place, whether in terms of resources or reception.[51] This once-known-then-long-known effect might well explain the setting for Mission Santa Isabel de Utinahica.

The site has produced a persuasive assemblage of European material culture. The Glass Site's European assemblage is dominated by artifacts widely recognized as markers of the earliest Spanish encounters.[52] The objects from the site that are most indicative are two varieties of Nueva Cádiz beads; small,

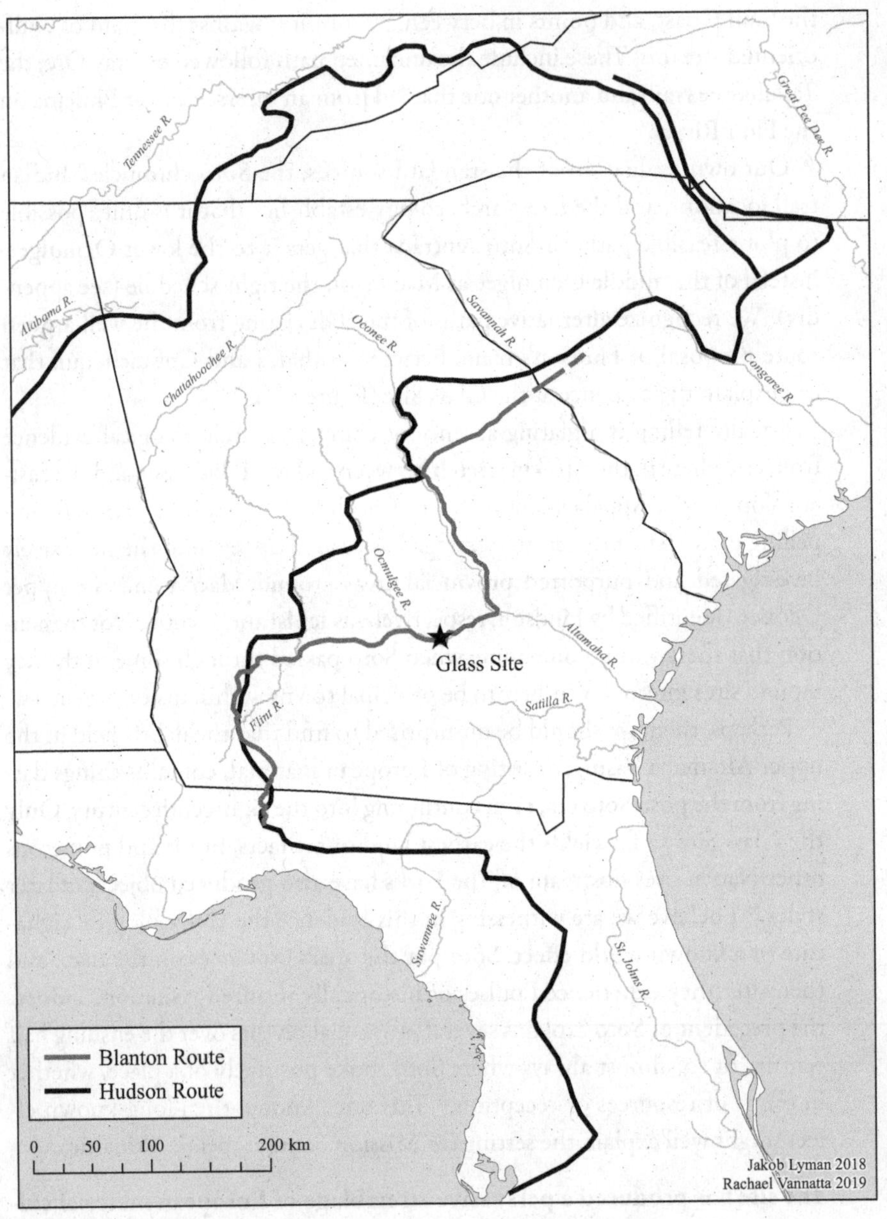

8.1 Proposed adjustment of Soto route intersecting the Glass Site location

seven-layer, faceted chevron beads; a Clarksdale bell; and characteristic types of iron tools.

The Glass Site assemblage is uniquely large and diverse, qualities aligning with expectations of residue associated with a large exploring party consisting of hundreds of individuals, including military men, artisans, priests, and others, plus their hundreds of animals and necessary baggage.

This is the pattern that would be especially predictable where a Native-Spanish encounter was relatively amicable and longer lasting than a one-night stand. At Ichisi, for example, the entrada received an uncharacteristically warm reception from the chief, in marked contrast to the long winter of skirmishes at Anhaica and the series of tense if not violent encounters since departing a month earlier. As Elvas noted, "[Soto] thanked him heartily for his offer and for his good will, as if he had welcomed him and offered him a great treasure."[53] And Rangel observed, "As [the Lord of Ichisi] was the first who came in peace, they did not wish to be tiresome."[54] The ultimate show of appreciation, we are told, after a two-night stopover, was that a Christian cross was erected at the site.[55] The same pattern is also described at Altamaha and Ocute, persisting until the entrada made its turn toward Cofitachequi.

The contexts of European artifacts on the site are appropriate. The Glass Site is unusual because none of the early European material has been recovered in an obvious grave. The situation is not unheard of, however, since the same conditions apply at the site of Soto's first winter encampment excavated in Tallahassee.[56]

To be sure, special contexts linked with upper-status individuals or exclusive activities do not have to be confined to graves. I have suggested that one such context at Glass is the temple structure since buildings like it housed the valued property of the elite, the community, and the province.[57] If one also accepts the argument that the Glass Site was a chiefly compound, it allows us to ask whether the entire community was not an exclusive context, a place where highly regarded objects may have been kept in multiple places. If this were the case, then one would anticipate the village-wide pattern we have documented.[58]

To return to one of our original hypotheses, the distribution of early European material at Glass still falls short of our estimate for the footprint of an encampment of Soto's full contingent. The artifacts do not occur in a space of 2.4 ha (6 ac) or more that could accommodate several hundred men and horses. They instead are confined to the village ring encompassing 1.1 ha. A couple of factors might explain this pattern. First, it is commonly assumed that explorers were careful to protect their limited supply of equipment and other material, thus leaving only sparse postencampment leftovers. Also, we can imagine that an extensive encampment made in and around an Indian community would have been thoroughly scavenged of debris. Together, these kinds of actions would not be conducive to creation of a robust archaeological signature beyond the limits of the community the foreign objects were shunted toward.

At this point you would be wise to ask if there are explanations other than Soto for the oldest European artifacts at the Glass Site. There are, and I will lay them out, but by now you will also expect that there are some wrinkles to consider beforehand.

One of them concerns the nature of earliest Spanish activity in La Florida between about 1513, when Juan Ponce de Leon gave the region its name, and about 1565, when enough had transpired to justify a more permanent and official colonial presence. Outside academic circles few people understand just what a busy era it was. That half century experienced numerous exploratory treks and colonizing ventures, none of which succeeded as originally envisioned. Soto's might have been the most protracted expedition, but it was not the only one to be launched. John Worth has spent as much time as anyone with extant records, and he documents several lesser expeditions over that period, in addition to speculating that a number of others happened under the historical radar.[59]

If you're conjuring up a Wild West kind of image, then you would not be far off. The celebrated Period of Discovery did not unfold as a highly coordinated deployment by European states of closely controlled, disciplined explorers. Beyond the official decrees, the activity comes across as an entrepreneurial free-for-all fueled as much by avarice as thoughtful execution of policy. To the extent the ventures were strategic, cold-blooded competition and extraction were prime incentives. To the extent fact-finding was an objective, accounts were erroneous or veered toward overblown appraisals, especially of potentially extractable resources, precious metals chief among them. There was stocktaking of the territory's suitability for settlement, for sure, but that was usually the secondary interest. In effect, the expeditions amounted to an initial look under the region's hood, and the intelligence that was gleaned eventually influenced official policy. But between the moments of royal approval and the official parsing of news the ventures delivered home, it was left to the explorers to conduct affairs as they saw fit.

As archaeologists we do our best to anticipate the nature of evidence that might result from one event or another, or from one kind of behavior or another. Essentially, we are trained to formulate logical hypotheses about the relationship between things and actions that we can go forth and systematically test. However, given what we know about the divergent character of the earliest ventures, it is really hard to be specific about what is likely to be discovered. Autonomy exercised on the march leaves us with an archaeological record that, in more ways than one, is all over the map. This is as true of southern and eastern Georgia as it is anywhere. All the typical sorts of New World incursions played out there, under different flags, and inclusive of both exploratory and colonizing ventures. And every kind of these actions took place within about 160 km (100 mi) of the Glass Site, even conservatively measured (figure 8.2).

This leads us back to that vexing problem of portability. All the European peregrinations I allude to raise the probability that some of their things were filtering to places like the Glass Site, and from multiple expeditions. Newly coveted foreign goods could theoretically rocket across the landscape as fast as rumors of strange men. In short, there's no question that some of the European material we've found at the Glass Site got there indirectly via Native-to-Native transactions. I do not believe secondhand exchanges to be the most parsimonious explanation for most of the earliest material on the site, but here are a couple of scenarios we must consider.

Acquisition could have begun with scavenging at abandoned European settlements or encampments, followed by dispersal through Native networks. In the Glass case, we must consider in this regard the failed 1526 Ayllón colony on the Atlantic side, or the 1528 encampments of Narváez's struggling party at Apalachee and on the Gulf coast. Then, of course, the same process could apply to the later Soto encampments, including the entrada's sustained winter camp at Anhaica.

Certainly we don't have to look far to find support for this kind of dispersal mechanism. We know that rare, exotic goods were desired as a means of perpetuating an ancient status hierarchy and that those goods were circulating

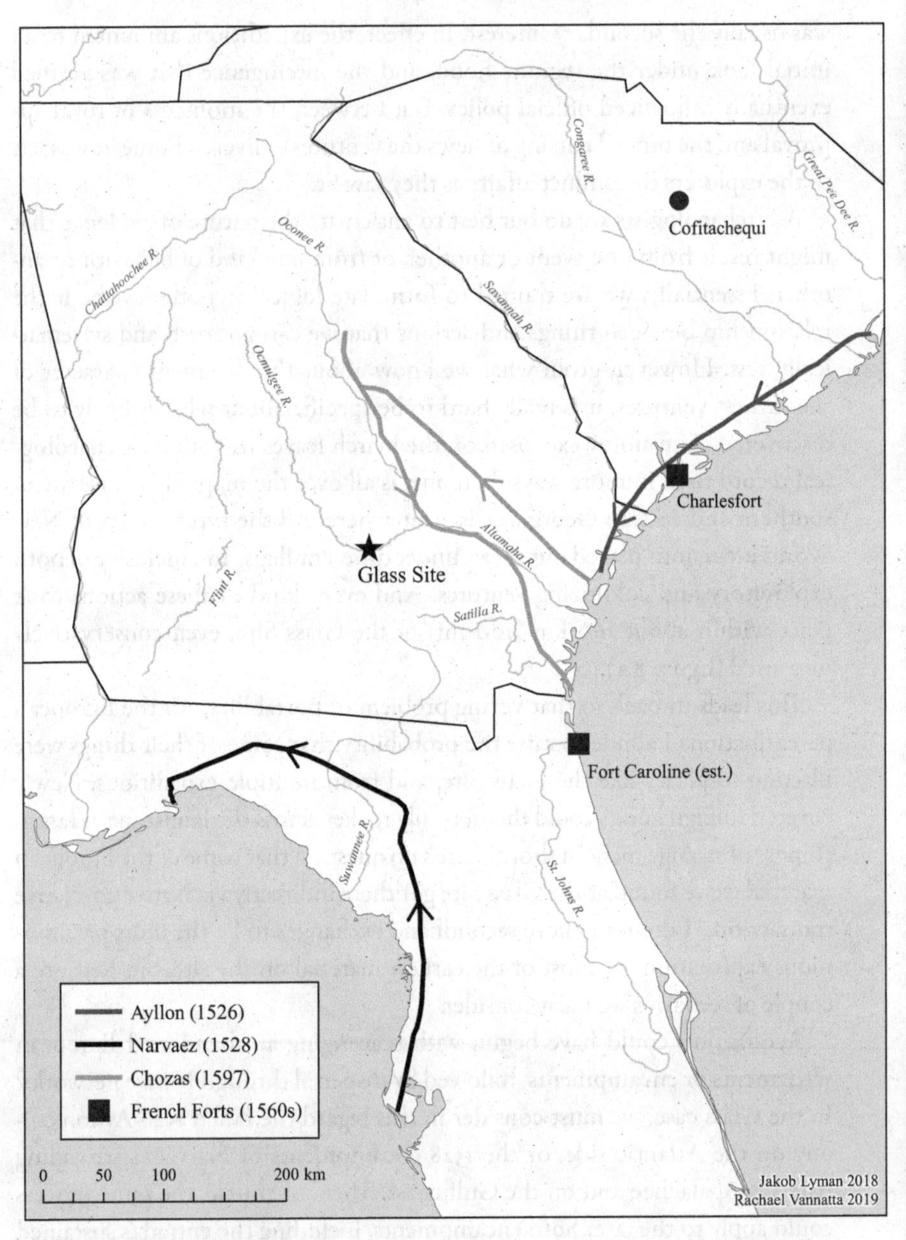

8.2 Estimated paths and locations of other sixteenth-century ventures that potentially have implications for Glass Site findings

over impressive distances. None other than Perico and Marcos, Soto's young guides and interpreters, were described as "traders." Marcos, we're told, had working knowledge of territory to the province of Ocute, 360 km (224 mi) beyond Anhaica, and Perico had apparently ventured at least 550 km (342 mi) southward to Florida from his homeland around Cofitachequi (Yupaha). If we extrapolate from these trading radii, Glass Site traders would theoretically have been in easy reach of not only the Atlantic and Gulf coasts but also the southern Appalachians.

We actually have irrefutable evidence of the movement of things from the Glass Site area deep into Florida. Mitchem and others report that a necklace made of Altamaha lance (*Elliptio shepardianus*) mussels was excavated in a burial at the Weeki Wachee mound site, 370 km (230 mi) south of the Ocmulgee-Altamaha Rivers.[60] Populations of this species of mussel, today barely surviving under protected status, are endemic only to the Altamaha drainage. What might sixteenth-century residents of places like the Glass Site have acquired in return, if anything, for those exported shellfish?

Because southern Georgia was part of a wider field of play, a credible treatment of the Glass case requires me to give equal consideration of contact, in some form, with intruders less heralded than Soto. And if we agree that Soto is archaeologically elusive, then these characters are downright invisible. Make no mistake; their stories are not second-rate consolation prizes. Archaeological evidence of Ayllón or Narváez would be received enthusiastically, to say the least, whether it is found at the Glass Site or elsewhere.

All this history is murky for some valid reasons. Not one of the ventures we know about is well documented. Neither Ayllón nor Narváez nor Soto personally set down in writing anything approaching a thorough account of his experience. That was a job mainly assigned to official scribes or ship captains, who, at best, would routinely record only the things required of them or the things they perceived to be noteworthy, and then only in the sparest of terms. Fuller accounts were sometimes written by ordinary participants in the ventures, in forms ranging from letters to full-blown memoirs. Then there are a handful of second- or thirdhand accounts gleaned from interviews and the like.

If that weren't enough, not a single map is known to exist that is attributable to leading members of the ventures. As far as we can tell, none of them traced a line on parchment to register movements; only a paltry few post hoc maps drafted by others record information about the region. That's hard for most of us to imagine, but with a little reflection it makes sense given what we know about the period's underdeveloped science of cartography—and its vague knowledge of the wider world. Making a map, especially of poorly known waters and totally alien lands, is no simple matter.

As it happens, the closest thing we have to a first-person map is frequently referred to as the "Soto map," but the attribution remains speculative.[61] It outlines the entire Southeast and portrays many rivers and mountain ranges familiar to us. It also includes names of Indian lands. But there is no line to approximate a route of travel or a cartographer's name or date.

All these facts speak loudly about the importance of archaeological inputs. But even as spare as they are in details, it pays to take advantage of the documentary sources we know of. In that spirit, I will now sketch out the state of historical knowledge regarding other potential sources of Glass Site artifacts.

Ayllón's San Miguel de Gualdape. One of the better-known incidents reported by Soto's chroniclers is the first-ever discovery of European artifacts at an Indian town in North America. Members of his army were shocked to stumble across evidence of their own kind at Cofitachequi, in what is now central South Carolina. They asked themselves the question we still debate, "How could this be?"

Soto's party had hustled across Georgia to reach the fabled province. Arriving at Cofitachequi on the first of May 1540, they passed two weeks in the province. Their stay did prove to be momentous, but for none of the reasons they envisaged. The trekkers were starving, and when they weren't devouring Indian stores, they offended and later kidnapped the noble known as the "Lady of Cofitachequi." They also pilfered every holy of holies in the territory, but with no gold or silver to show for it. And it was while ransacking an exclusive mortuary atop an earthen mound that they turned up some startlingly familiar things. They were stunned to find there, as you may recall, an iron ax blade, a dagger, green glass beads, and rosaries stored away in a box of freshwater pearls and other Indian splendor. Rather quickly Soto and his men deduced the origin of the items: the failed colony of Lucas Vázquez de Ayllón, attempted about a decade and half earlier, in 1526.[62]

Most of us believe that their inference was correct. Scholarly scrutiny of the Ayllón venture concludes that its target and first point of landfall was

Winyah Bay, the mouth of the Santee River in South Carolina. Agents of Ayllón dispatched earlier from Santo Domingo to scour the lower Atlantic coast for Indian slaves and to scout for a suitable settlement site had returned with favorable accounts of that area. They referred to the territory by an Indian name, Chicora, but chose to call the local river Jordan.[63] The entrepreneurial Ayllón managed to secure approval for a permanent outpost at the bay and enlisted around six hundred people to sign on. Distributed among six well-supplied ships, his would-be colonials set sail from Santo Domingo in mid-July 1526 and without remarkable incident arrived offshore of Rio Jordan on August 9. Then their luck turned for the worse.

Under rough seas the main vessel became grounded in the shoaly offshore waters. As much as possible was salvaged from it, and a provisional encampment was established. It didn't take long to recognize that their Native hosts were more resistant than welcoming, and just as quickly, the local soil was determined to be unsuited to the kind of agriculture they had envisioned. Within a month an alternative plan was devised. All along, arguments had been made in favor of colonizing a location within the Guale Indian territory, some 170 km (106 mi) south on the coast of today's Georgia, and that concept rapidly developed into Plan B (see figure 8.2). Most of the colonists, especially the women, children, and the ill, made the reverse journey under sail, while a smaller contingent slogged overland down the mainland fringe.

At the designated meeting place, we're told that a community called San Miguel de Gualdape was organized, consisting of simple dwellings and a church. From the beginning the aspiring colony was beset with more troubles. Natives were again shy if not hostile, thus cutting off the ideal option for sustenance. Illness rapidly became a second problem. By 18 October, Ayllón himself was dead. The stress of the experience, coupled with a vacuum of leadership, promptly and predictably bred dissent. The faction that favored complete retreat won, and by November a full evacuation was organized. Stunningly, only 150 of the original 600 had survived to sail back to familiar ports. San Miguel was no more.

Precisely where Ayllón's colonizers rejoined to carve out their settlement is one of the region's enduring mysteries. The uncertainty is not for lack of research. Surviving records have been studied intensively by scholars like Paul Hoffman, and archaeologists have long been alert for physical clues. Two things in particular stymie the hunt. One, of course, is unspecific historical sources. Numerous books and maps refer to Ayllón's colony and places associated with it, but they don't come close to pinpointing a location. A good example is the 1526 Vespucci map that bears a label, "Tierra Nueva de Ayllón," laid across a sizable space. Hoffman has overcome some of the locational issues by parsing a ship captain's log, and it is he who put the colony's site at Sapelo Sound.[64] The other major handicap is the brief duration of the settlement. Six weeks is not a lot of time for modestly sheltered newcomers to indelibly imprint the landscape.

For our purposes, the question is whether Gualdapain goods made their way to the interior, as far away as places like the Glass Site. If we accept Soto's discovery of Ayllón artifacts at Cofitachequi, as we should, it makes sense that those items originated from the original landing point. The landing and the Chicora province are 190 km (118 mi) apart, linked directly by the Santee drainage. In the same way, the Glass Site is located about 175 km (109 mi) up the Altamaha drainage from the presumed site of San Miguel at Sapelo Sound. If coast-to-interior movement happened at the first place, it was even more likely to have occurred from the final site.

The two or three mechanisms by which this most likely occurred will be familiar. One, of course, would be customary patterns of exchange or trade. Ayllón's people surely parlayed locally for Indian food and other kinds of cooperation using objects like beads and simple tools. There is no reason to believe that those same Ayllón-related goods would not later be distributed more distantly via the ancient Indian-to-Indian network. Also postabandonment, it is near certain the Indians would have scavenged all manner of things from the settlement and, conceivably, launched them into the wider sphere of trade. And, finally, there is reason to believe some of the desperate colonists defected and cast their lot with the Natives, perhaps well into the interior.[65] It is likely that they, too, would have introduced objects of European make into the Indian system.[66]

Thus the possibility exists that objects originating with this earliest of Georgia adventures might present themselves to an archaeologist digging at an influential Indian town 110 miles upstream. Any of the things we have recovered at the Glass Site, short of the obvious late-dating beads, could have been in Ayllón's baggage. However, I would be most persuaded of an Ayllón connection with Big Bend people if an even wider range of artifacts had turned up, such as ceramic and glasswares, that had to be prominent in the supplies of ambitious colonizers.

The expedition of Pánfilo de Narváez. Ayllón's lucky survivors were probably still reeling from their horrific experience when another colonizing venture was launched. Contrary to plan, it degenerated into a warm-up act for Soto's grander undertaking a decade hence. Just about anyone today with even an inkling of the story knows it from the celebrity it launched for Cabeza de Vaca. But that extraordinary tale is . . . another story.[67]

A one-eyed veteran of New World conflicts and, in fact, a character familiar to Ayllón, Pánfilo de Narváez embarked in 1527 from Spain with plans to settle and pilfer the northern Gulf coast of Mexico. Lured by the prospect of quick riches, he also assembled a force of up to six hundred. Between desertion and storms, Narváez ultimately departed Cuba with three ships and perhaps four hundred men. In mid-April 1528, when they were hardly under way, stormy weather battered the small fleet and forced it so far off course that it landed just above Tampa Bay rather than the other side of the Gulf.[68]

Essentially lost but responsible for hundreds, Narváez took a page from the Ayllón book and split his contingent between the land and the sea (see figure 8.2). A cohort of three hundred or so, led by Narváez, charted a path northward, up the peninsula. Among other things, their journey provided a preview of the Apalachee province (Anhaica) of Soto fame. In the meantime, the waterborne contingent sailed along the coast with the aim of rendezvous. None of it turned out well.

Having lost track of Narváez and his company, despite weeks of scanning the coastline, the ship captains feared the worse and elected to return home. Meanwhile, Narváez managed to slash and burn his way to Apalachee (at Tallahassee), twenty-five miles inland from the searching ships. The Indian community he and his men occupied seems to have been a second-tier town in the province. The Spaniards were underwhelmed by it, no doubt because their standard for a rich place was the likes of Montezuma's Aztec capital. Frustrated and ill, Narváez led his people out of Apalachee toward the coast, hoping mightily to end the ordeal. The path to open water was complicated by expanses of tidal marshes and the winding creeks that drain them. When at last they reached an inlet at the Gulf in early August, not a sail in sight, they executed a plan to build their own rescue boats.

In pure survivalist mode, they cobbled together large, seagoing barges that, with luck, could deliver them to Mexico. Horses had to be slaughtered for food and for material, and makeshift forges rendered iron gear into spikes and fittings. Weeks of frantic construction yielded several questionable boats, and in September around 250 people shoved off for points west. Soon thereafter another storm swamped most of the boats, and many who made shore were killed by Indians. A handful of castaways survived to begin what, in its own right, is one of the great survival stories of all time.

The relevance of this series of events for our discoveries is the same as it is with Ayllón's venture. We must ask, knowing what we do about the portability of Spanish baggage, whether any material trace of Narváez's group migrated as far northward as the Glass Site. If panhandle Florida marks the northernmost point of the expedition's travel, it would place Europeans 160 km (100 mi) southwest of the lower Ocmulgee River basin, comfortably within a range of Native-to-Native interaction. Likewise, had any deserters managed to survive and operate within the area, their movements could have introduced "trade" goods. The Indians' network of trails offered ready avenues of movement, and some led directly from the Gulf region toward the Glass Site's realm. If nothing else, the early bead types at the Glass Site could have originated with Narváez, none more so than the olive-shaped type in blue and white.

The French connection. Well after Soto, competing interests under a different flag were also affecting the Native world in and around southern Georgia. France was provoked by Spain's burgeoning presence in the Southeast and between 1562 and 1565 asserted its own interests. The first move was establishment of Charlesfort at Port Royal on South Carolina's coast, south of the spot Ayllón had chosen for his first landing (see figure 8.2). And like Ayllón's attempt at colonization, theirs also quickly fell apart. Doubtful that the leader, Jean Ribault, would make good on his promise of resupply and crippled by internal bickering, the anxious Protestants gave up and set sail for home, just eleven months after arriving.[69]

Even in the face of that disaster, a Ribault associate, René Goulaine de Laudonnière, accepted charge of a second attempt to secure a claim. He set up a fortified settlement called Fort Caroline in 1564 at the "River May," but unlike Charlesfort, this location has yet to be definitively identified. Competing arguments place it as far south as Jacksonville in Florida or as far north as Darien in Georgia.[70] In any event, over its yearlong history the hundreds in the new settlement faced one setback after another as food ran short and local Indians were alienated.

Naturally, the actions of the French were more than Spain could tolerate. About the time Ribault managed to arrive at Fort Caroline with a flotilla full of supplies for Laudonnière, the Spanish governor of La Florida, Pedro Menendez de Aviles, took swift and punitive action to quash the colony. Capitalizing on the distraction of a hurricane, he launched a brutally successful attack on Fort Caroline by land, destroying for good any French designs on the southern Atlantic coast. Later Menendez shifted his regional capital from Santa Elena, built essentially over the former site of Charlesfort, to St. Augustine, purportedly not far from Fort Caroline.[71]

We know, then, that the French were plying the local Indians with their own tradable goods, over about a five-year period. They understood as well as the Spanish that gifts of glass beads and metal "trinkets" were a way to curry favor. For us, the questions concern where and how much the French gave away, especially from the base at Fort Caroline, and whether they were uniquely French in any recognizable way.

The probability that Glass Site residents acquired French goods is not terribly remote. A natural link from the heart of the French sphere of operation to the lower Ocmulgee exists in the form of rivers. The headwater streams of the Satilla River are born within 10 km south- and westward of the site, in today's Coffee and Ben Hill counties, and the river eventually empties at Woodbine near Cumberland Island (see figure 8.2). Beads and iron weapons excavated from a mound near the river's mouth have already been attributed to French activity.[72] That outlet of the Satilla is 65 km north of the proposed fort location near Jacksonville, and from the Glass Site the distance is about 160 km (100 mi) as the crow flies. Alternatively, if the stream the French called the River May proves to be the Altamaha, as some are proposing, then it, too, gave ready access to the Big Bend.

But what about that question of recognition? Could an archaeologist today differentiate a bead originating in a French transaction from one passed along by a Spaniard? Because the major European powers all relied heavily on places like Venice for glass beads, the chances are not good. Likewise, various sources, including archaeological ones, indicate that the metal tools in a French colony could be similar to those in a Spanish one. I know from colleagues who excavated at the site of Charlesfort and Santa Elena that differences in French and Spanish goods are minor.

More challenging is accounting for a type of striped glass bead at the Glass Site that is most familiar on French-associated sites located elsewhere, and apparently of very late sixteenth- or seventeenth-century vintage. As far as I can tell, it is the first of its kind to turn up in Georgia. A search for analogues leads only to points westward, such as at Mission San Luis de Apalachee at Tallahassee or beyond to places like Mobile.[73] Those sources implicate the system of trails described earlier, including the one that could have led Soto to Glass from Apalachee. Post-Soto, that network continued to accommodate a flow of people and things from south and west more than a century later, but under a radically different and "shattered" cultural milieu.[74] This is to say that, at this point, any ties to French goings-on, even indirectly, most likely existed later rather than earlier in the site's history.

The Big Bend province and the Glass Site did not exist in a vacuum. Even in the absence of European intrusions, their inhabitants were not provincial, literally speaking. I have described ample evidence of the interactions they enjoyed with other Native groups in all directions. For us archaeologists, the connections are sometimes expressed stylistically, as with shared ceramic decorations, or by things like shell artifacts that were both shipped and received. These are the signs of a connected existence that seems always to have existed in Native America.

By virtue of location, the province and the site were situated somewhat uniquely in the postcontact world. The Big Bend area is equidistant to hotspots of earliest European incursion on the Atlantic and Gulf coasts, and a multitude of aquatic and terrestrial conduits enabled knowledge of and interaction with it. Preconditioned by an ancient pattern of external relations, the province, not surprisingly, also became a magnet for goods originating from diverse European sources. Quite different from the reputation it bears today, this part of Georgia was, in those olden days, a desirable location that important roads led into and out of.

Hernando de Soto drove a small army directly through the heart of the interior's piney woods, far from the security of the coasts. He was drawn to places of consequence, like the Big Bend area. It would only be remarkable, then, to discover that there are *no* places in that area, like the Glass Site, with artifacts of the kinds he was dispensing. Most of the other early European ventures skirted the interior of La Florida, however, including South Georgia. Beyond Soto, this gives reason to imagine that only a trickle of foreign people and goods might reach the lower Ocmulgee. But not only could it have happened—it apparently did.

IX

Making Meaning

After more than a decade, the Glass Site experience has given me a certain empathy for Soto and his kind. Like his, my path has at once been unpredictable, challenging, and anxious. Like him, I set out to find one thing but discovered another. And the outcomes of my work, like his expedition, may become a subject of endless debate.

Still, I believe the archaeological endeavor I've shared with you can make a useful difference in the way we understand a slice of history. To that end, I have given honest commentary, mostly for the benefit of the less initiated, on the day-to-day practice of archaeology and history. I have sought to demystify the process, to explain how it works—and sometimes doesn't—and how it can be steered by quirks of luck and happenstance. Along the way, I have also tried to explain the good, the bad, and the ugly of archaeological evidence itself. We pity the modern-day detective assigned to a cold case, but that's the only kind an archaeologist knows, and in the extreme.

The book is also concerned with the production of knowledge, with how it is generated and then consumed. I devote much of this chapter to that topic. It is useful to ask why discoveries happen when they do, and why they are received and applied the way they are. Some say every good discovery has its time, but what does that really mean?

Progress is a matter of penetrating barriers and of crossing thresholds. And although *barrier* can imply a physical obstacle, it might also be something else. In retrospect, I believe archaeological and historical advances in the realm of the Big Bend province have been handicapped as much by human predispositions as by material conditions. The way a new discovery will be received is not preordained.

I cannot deny that the most obvious impediment to archaeology in southeastern Georgia *is* of a physical sort. The sultry forest that cloaks so much of the territory has obscured a remarkable past. Nothing about the stories I am trying to relate was ever fixed in a robust, decisive "history." Only occasionally did these earliest of historical events ever perk to the surface of the common narrative. Why? To believe any of those parts of the story—fleeting events occurring before about 1700—often means seeing them. Only as Frankie took advantage of industrialized forestry, when the green cloak was removed, were the first palpable and enduring breakthroughs made. Since then, my campaign to move a lot of South Georgia earth has exposed to view some of the story's finer texture. Theoretically at least, the new results will further heighten general awareness and interest.

At the same time, less tangible barriers might have been—and still may be—equally formidable. From the outside looking in, South Georgia is a forbidding corner of the region saddled with an unflattering reputation. Outsiders see few good reasons to venture below the "gnat line." And if they do, they're advised to make the trip pedal down, windows up, and AC blasting. Monotonous, pine-dominated forestland, broken only by dank and mysterious swamps and crisscrossed here and there by sandy, washboard roads, does not create a scene the average person equates with promise and prosperity.

The same prejudices seem to have infected scholarly appraisals, beyond the celebrations of some notable naturalists, including Frankie Snow. The freighted notions of "pine barrens" and "crackers" haven't inspired the numerous shelves of scholarly works that other places have, particularly as they pertain to the national identity. A second-class reputation has effectively condemned a huge area to historical obscurity, much the same way it has retarded economic development. Those same forces account for the puzzlement elicited by my claims of flourishing Indian villages and Spanish mission outposts. The here and now has been serving to define the there and then.

Reactions to new discoveries, especially unanticipated ones like ours, are fascinating to track. New and novel information is not universally embraced out of the gate. It requires a longer period of independent evaluation and digestion before verdicts are announced. This, most of the time, is the healthy trajectory of good scholarship. Updates from the Glass Site have been greeted this way, and then some. What I was reporting stirred the proverbial pot and upset some comfortable notions about what lay under the pine straw in Telfair County. Sound method and theory and careful analysis were not a guarantee of acceptance.

At the root of debates over Soto's path, whether they concern the Glass Site or not, are the persistent effects of the two major route reconstructions, those of the Swanton and Hudson teams. For a great many nonprofessionals, especially in South Georgia, the path of Soto was fixed in 1939, by a federal government commission no less, and they'll fight you over a challenge to that version of history. This is especially true in those proud communities that can boast an official highway marker saying, in so many words, "Soto slept here." For years I would jokingly dare students to make a nighttime raid on the Wilcox County courthouse in Abbeville to pluck up the town's Swanton-inspired marker and move it to Jacksonville, where we were actually finding Soto evidence. It was a potentially dangerous prospect that fortunately had no takers.

Over in Sumter County there's an entire town named De Soto. At least it used to be a town, one of many—like Alma—established at the end of the nineteenth century around a railroad stop. Today it's a forlorn collection of buildings, but in faded glory, a water tower, emblazoned "De Soto" in tall letters, urges passersby to wonder that it might still matter. Lots of people know the place and will not be persuaded that the rusting tank is misleading.

These anecdotes all speak to the power of something called collective memory. People have a way of latching on to ideas, especially optimistic ones, and those ideas can sometimes so infuse everyday thinking that they ossify into essential elements of identity. It is the way of myth making, as true on a local level as it is nationally. Community building requires points of intersection, and opinions about history can become the germinal features that undergird and define passionate pride in a place. Origin myths and heroic legends, in and of themselves, are not problematic. They are universal and even necessary. But once they infuse the local psyche and become definitional, they tend not to be at all fluid. Alternative facts are not greeted kindly. Indeed, educators and scholars constantly combat the primacy of received wisdom. New contributions might be technically credible, but they still may be greeted by fierce resistance. It is no wonder, then, that so many Soto legends seem never to die. History made is sometimes history made immovable.

There is a certain irony in the attachment some locales have to Soto legends since Georgia's long and important period of Spanish history is effectively invisible in the wider conversation. I have enjoyed the role of the spoiler in talks to civic clubs and school groups, posing the question, "Who is responsible for the first recorded history in Georgia?" Lots of hands shoot up, and with rare exception the answer I get is "James Oglethorpe," the Englishman who in 1733 gridded off a colonial port town called Savannah. But that was two centuries after the Spaniards had charged into the wilderness and later sustained a string of Catholic missions. In this instance, the crux of the problem—the ignorance of the history—is what scholars refer to as the "Black Legend," a rather systematic and vindictive policy of underplaying, if not erasing, the Spanish opening before an English triumph.[1] Another instance of winners writing the story.

Prevailing sentiments must not be allowed to speak for the past entirely. One of the most powerful challenges to the status quo can be physical evidence. Concrete results intrinsically have a voice that is formidable if not unassailable. That is why archaeological findings may have special power to eclipse entrenched lines of reason. On the matter of Soto, Charles Hudson himself almost always closed his analyses with a bit of scholarly fine print, acknowledging that he was doing the best he could with a set of improved but still imperfect evidence. He was particularly emphatic about the role of archaeology, pointing out that its findings would be the final arbiter of anyone's reconstruction, especially where the documents were dimmest.

As laudable as that stance may be, it cannot be taken as a given. Paradoxically, new information can actually complicate the wider perspective on the matter. I read recently about the way DNA analysis is revolutionizing our understanding of human evolution. But especially in that arena, new discoveries often illuminate only a tiny sliver of the story. It is progress measured in drips and not by floods. But as the mountain of disparate details builds, it can actually become less and less clear to the ordinary researcher how to connect the swarm of dots. Comprehension of complexity contributes to both the excitement and the chagrin of the scientists devoted to it.

The same effect is sometimes at work in Soto scholarship. New discoveries—like ours—are made, but the business of puzzling out the "real" story is no simple matter. To use a fashionable term, there's plenty of nuance to navigate. Long gone are the days when one might believe "the conquest" was as simple as veni, vidi, vici. The Spanish agenda was not fixed, and neither were Indian responses. Causes and effects evolved in accordance with market forces, state-level agendas, religious doctrine, individual personalities, localized customs, the mounting toll of the march, the vagaries of weather, and so on. As we grow to appreciate the inherent complexity of our own subject, the variability we observe in the archaeological evidence tied to Soto is made less mystifying. There are some regular aspects to it, to be sure, but for every theme we discern, from site to site, there seems also to be at least one divergence.

In the case of the Glass Site, I have and will continue to argue that a healthy portion of the evidence does link us to Soto. My colleagues have formulated a sensible rationale for assessing old and new claims of Soto sites, and I have applied their criteria. Until other tangible evidence is introduced, the bottom line is this: we can't have it both ways. Either the criteria for evaluation and the results they yield are valid, or they are not. If the Glass Site is not recognized as a likely Soto site, then there are precious few other sites in the entire region, if any, that qualify.

In practice we must, once again, accept that any route proposal, including the Hudson team's, is a best approximation. Theirs, to a significant degree, is grounded, literally, in archaeological evidence. The majority of the sites bearing up under the criteria I have described lie within a fifty-mile buffer of Hudson's path. That is fairly persuasive support. There are lengthy stretches, however, that do not have archaeological anchors, at least in the form of early sixteenth-century Spanish artifacts. This is especially true in the segment we are concerned with. Specifically, the projected locations of Ichisi at Macon and Ocute on the Oconee have produced no tangible evidence of early Spanish encounters, despite the fact they are two parts of the state that have been most intensely explored by archaeologists.[2] At the end of the day, I dare say the Glass Site discoveries would have influenced the route reconstructions of both Swanton and Hudson—had they been known.

What you are witnessing is the reality that documentation of Soto, and early explorers and colonists like him, is an ultimate test for historical archaeology. Think about the fact that today there are no more than ten claims of Soto finds that enjoy any kind of consensus. And they amount to no more than 2 percent of all the encampments the entrada made between Tampa Bay and Texas. On top of that, a great many of the widely accepted archaeological claims of Soto-related sites are accidental discoveries. Glass is in this category. There has been more than one purposeful and well-organized search for the same kind of evidence we have found—with nothing to show for the effort. Well-known examples are intensive hunts for Cofitachequi, Mabila, and Chicasa, places that should have especially robust archaeological signatures.[3] At the end of the day, what does this track record say about the entire scholarly enterprise, the state of the art, so to speak?

We've learned, at the very least, how difficult it is to track a relatively brief, one-off historical event—really a moving chain of events—even if it did involve hundreds of actors and shiploads of movable matériel. It is a truth that betrays a deep lack of fundamental knowledge. We are still living with an inability to predict, over large chunks of the region, where Soto-related sites will be. And predictive capacity is the universal measure of mature scholarship.

This, obviously, is a condition we want to improve. Doing so means continued, honest appraisal of all that we've learned and application of the lessons in the design of newer and better search strategies. I don't have a magic formula to divulge that can guarantee success, but I do submit that the Glass Site experience offers useful lessons. It pays to recognize the factors that were operating in our favor, intentional and otherwise.

Landscape conditions. Every one of the sites on our original short list was documented by Frankie Snow. He could record and sample so many sites only because they had been laid bare by the unprecedented scale of forest clearance and land disturbance begun in the 1970s. The surface of South Georgia, and what lay just beneath it, had never before been so visible.

Frankie's results are an endorsement for intensive, large-area survey. Scholars like Stephen Kowalewski at the University of Georgia and several of his colleagues began to argue in the 1970s that the traditional hunt-and-peck approach to site discovery, focusing on small areas and large sites, was inadequate. Only full and intensive examination of huge swaths of territory would provide a comprehensive and accurate glimpse of a human landscape, capturing the full spectrum of activities and settlements.[4] David Hurst Thomas transferred this kind of approach from his successful survey work in the desert West to St. Catherines Island. It proved equally revelatory in the University of Georgia's Wallace Reservoir survey on the Oconee River. Independently, Frankie recognized the same benefit that mainline archaeologists had and, under unique conditions, achieved comparable results. I am not advocating a new campaign of clear-cutting across South Georgia, but I am in favor of requirements that allow us to learn something more from the exposures when they happen.

Local expertise. I was fortunate that Frankie was among the local sources I could consult. The way he applied his scientific training to Big Bend archaeology is legendary, and I was keen to know what he had to say about it. I have witnessed the dismissive attitudes of colleagues in their dealings with informants who lack formal archaeological credentials. It is a shortsighted position that cuts off a stream of information that is impossible to replicate: a lifetime of intimate, local knowledge. There are many knowledgeable sources out there in addition to archaeologists, and collaboration beyond the academy can yield tremendous dividends. People like Frankie, particularly in the remoter parts of the region, are precious resources and rise to the status of "recognized scholars" in their own right.

Systematic research approach. The project's design capitalized on high-quality, local knowledge, but it was also undertaken as an independent evaluation of that information. My goal was to avoid blind assumptions, as credible as some of the original information might have been, and to guard against a self-fulfilling prophecy. We subjected all the sites on the short list to an identical, minimum level of evaluation, consisting of standard shovel testing and unit excavation. Doing so enabled easy comparative analysis and satisfied basic scientific protocols.

Intensive recovery. In a way, it is no wonder that we have assembled an unusually large collection of early European artifacts. We worked deliberately and hard to find them. Few other sites of its kind have been as thoroughly and systematically sampled as the Glass Site has—specifically with the goal of documenting European objects, and with near-equal priority given to the plow zone and underlying, intact deposits. More commonly, archaeological projects investigate only prominent features such as mounds, only the "richest" portions of large communities, or only large subsurface features exposed after the plow zone is stripped away. While I recognize that our approach renders the results from less thoroughly investigated sites less comparable, we also believe that approach improves prospects for deciphering the archaeological record at sites of initial European-Indian contact.

The project's methodology, aimed originally at mission-related evidence, held fast for the duration. I will list what I believe to be the generally unique aspects of the strategy we employed in our documentation of Indian-European contact at the Glass Site:

- Commitment to a multiyear, interdisciplinary program of research
- Commitment to a multisite, comparative study
- Intensive, systematic shovel testing of an entire habitation area
- Intensive, systematic metal detector survey of a habitation and large portions of the surrounding area
- Employment of geophysical prospecting in selected areas
- Uniform sampling of all contexts, including plow zone
- Processing of all excavated matrix, except in shovel tests, by water screening through 1/8-inch or smaller hardware cloth

Special expertise. Successful implementation of the intensive recovery strategy required special expertise. I don't know any archaeologist in full command of all the skill and equipment necessary to undertake every facet of the job. In my case, many of the new technologies that have become a routine part of field and lab work had not even been developed when I was learning the practice. All kinds of efficiencies were realized when I surrounded myself with experts like Jeffrey Glover (mapping), Spencer Barker (metal detecting), and Chet Walker (geophysics). As cliché as it is to say, a team will always accomplish more than an individual. And teamwork can be pretty fun, too.

Steady support. The project succeeded because it was supported well. Steady institutional support was given by Fernbank Museum of Natural History. The museum's leadership was committed to the archaeological project, and in addition to giving me freedom to design and schedule the work, it devoted significant effort to marshaling funding on an annual basis. Fernbank is also the dedicated repository of the project's collections and the principal venue for reporting and exhibiting findings. External funding secured through Fernbank was augmented by a grant from the National Geographic Society. I have happily enjoyed continuation of the Fernbank affiliation since 2013, when I accepted a university faculty position. Continuity matters.

I also had the extraordinarily enthusiastic support of landowners. The Glass family was unwavering in its encouragement and material aid. Similarly, the Georgia Department of Natural Resources was quick to issue permits for access to its property across the river.

Dedicated volunteers have been the cornerstone of the project, including participants in the early educational programs that ranged from high school students to public school teachers. Very literally, the field and the lab work would not have succeeded without their involvement. Dozens of volunteers, from teenagers to retirees, have excavated, sifted, washed, and sorted alongside paid staff. Truth be told, some of these "untrained" volunteers have become so skilled and have such a remarkable work ethic that they are the perfect role models for students.

Luck. It has been said that it is better to be lucky than to be good. I don't buy fully into the notion, but I also don't deny there is a place for something like good karma. And we had it. At the outset, none of us anticipated the kinds of finds we began to make—apart from Julian Williams, perhaps. But the key is to recognize an opportunity when you see it. Beyond acquiring the knowledge to understand what a surprise discovery might mean, it is equally necessary to build flexibility into a research program that will allow a project to capitalize on them. Blind adherence to a research agenda is not always beneficial.

With a little reflection, you will probably agree that the beads and the brass and the iron from the Glass Site don't speak in perfect unison. The strongest signal emanating from the site, to my ear, does pertain to Soto, but I have to concede that his signal is distorted by some interference. In the background is an archaeological babble that is the product of more than one cross-cultural encounter. Further still, the collective evidence is muddled by the passage of time underground and by a scientific process that yields only a subset of evidence.

Those circumstances are not at all peculiar to this story; the Glass Site and the artifacts from it do not suffer from unique, fatal flaws. The background noise in particular is a reflection of the wider, early-contact archaeological landscape in the Southeast. I should hope my struggle with it is a healthy object lesson for future pursuits of the topic. Channeling a Rumsfeldian perspective, I'll argue we're only beginning to know what we don't know with respect to the business of charting paths of exploration and, more importantly, to the convoluted, cultural milieu of the attendant encounters.

Although archaeological and historical pictures are always a bit messy, for this era they are especially fractious. That fact need not cripple ongoing scholarship. The key, as I have learned, is to embrace rather than resist the complexity that so defines the era. This can mean accepting the reality that our arguments will, more often than not, be buttressed with circumstantial evidence than by truly definitive proofs. It makes good policy, I'm afraid, to greet steadfast declarations from archaeologists with a bit of skepticism.

With time, a measure of consensus has formed around the origins of the European material at Glass, even outside the circle of people intimately involved in the project. Many archaeologists and nonprofessionals alike are persuaded that the most plausible explanation for the bulk of the European material is the entrada of Hernando de Soto. Right now, the Glass Site is very possibly our best archaeological candidate for the site of a Soto encounter between panhandle Florida and the Appalachian front in North Carolina. But because no one expected to see what we have revealed, the results have played out as a bit of archaeological gate crashing. They have upset aspects of an earlier consensus.

No question, the Glass Site findings are provocative. On a personal level even, they required a reckoning with what I thought I had learned and understood. In this book I have described the evidence from the site and the struggle to apprehend its meaning. The conclusions I have drawn, as tentative as they may sometimes be, are the product of careful analysis. They are the best I can offer at this point, but they are also elastic. All of us should be prepared to reconsider them under challenges from new findings. My interpretation amounts to a working hypothesis, and like all good hypotheses it is testable.

Certainly there is more to be learned from the Glass Site. Indeed, the entire story of first encounters between indigenous southeastern populations and Europeans is still a work in progress. Most of the sites that were created by those events remain undocumented, and archaeology will prove, more than ever, to be the source of critical new information. Quoting Charles Hudson and his associates: "We have reconstructed the route of the de Soto expedition from beginning to end, though we are more confident of some parts of it than of others. Some segments can be verified or improved through archaeological research, and we expect adjustments to be made for some years to come."[5]

Based on my Glass Site experience and what I've learned about the history of other discoveries, I believe future breakthroughs are as likely to be serendipitous as intentional. But I hasten to say that the chain of events is not likely to be entirely accidental. Historically speaking we are increasingly aware of cause-and-effect relations that, even over decades, inspire seemingly disparate events to play out in exactly the same places. Historical events are subject to their own kind of stratification. But regardless, a key truism for making any progress will be this: looking matters. Archaeology is not a passive vocation, and the absence of effort does a lot to explain an absence of evidence.

A respected strategy for documenting new Soto sites is referred to as the "long string" approach.[6] It argues for well-informed, systematic searching over long stretches of the route, as opposed to sniffing out solitary encampments or other points of encounter. The concept at work is that confidence in a path is bound to be raised if a series of archaeological sites is identified within extended segments of the entrada's march.

Post-Glass, I have tried to adopt that strategy. My attention is now focused on an area farther southwest in Georgia that appears to correspond to the Indian province of Capachequi. This area combined with the Big Bend investigation is a continuing effort I call the Points of Contact project. Using an approach similar to the one I developed for Glass and its related sites, I have begun to explore several connected locations in the Capachequi area. From a scholarly standpoint, Capachequi is perhaps the least contested province location on Soto's march out of Florida. There are few other places he could have reasonably passed through at the beginning of his northward trek that spring, and the local landscape and the sites we know about match details in the accounts very well.[7]

Interestingly, my excavations at two large Capachequi towns, on and off since 2008, have yielded results more or less opposite those I had in the Big Bend area. On the Ocmulgee, I set out to find a seventeenth-century mission and wound up with Soto evidence. In Capachequi territory, I have seventeenth-century, mission-related artifacts but nothing I can solidly tie to Soto's three-day stopover. Suffice it to say, these very different experiences exemplify what we face.

Plenty of rational people would flee the challenge of bringing meaning to archaeological evidence. Who could blame them? But archaeologists tend to be stubborn optimists, and the best of them crave a good challenge. Sometimes the challenges even become obsessions; I can say so from personal experience. I have learned to embrace rather than complain about the nature of archaeological evidence. And I also treat it as a precious gift. We should be grateful that traces of ancient activity survive at all, and we are right to cherish the privilege to work with it. The business of tracing the human story, from the ground up, is as magical as it is necessary.

APPENDIX

Description of a Proposed Modification to Soto's Route between Capachequi and Cofaqui

This appendix consists of an excerpt from the 2011 technical report describing our Glass Site results up to that time.[1] The excerpt specifically presents the lengthy section Wes Patterson and I wrote to explain our argument for an alternative path for Soto's entrada between the Indian provinces of Capachequi and Cofaqui. Because the implications of Soto route reconstructions can have far-reaching significance, and because they can also be contentious, I have an obligation to provide the details of our proposal for readers who want to evaluate it closely.

Because the purpose of evaluating an alternative route was to test the feasibility of a Soto pause at the Glass Site, we examined segments ahead of and beyond the Deer Run (Capachequi) and Glass Site locations to ensure that our proposal dovetailed with the proposed, overall path. Additionally, the corresponding portion of the Hudson route was entered into the GIS, allowing us to directly compare their route with our alternative. In formulating our alternative, we deliberately followed Indian trails wherever it was reasonable to do so. In the end, about 100.8 km (63 mi), or around 20 percent, of our route corresponds to recorded trails. An average daily travel distance of approximately 20 miles per day was assumed. This is a slightly faster rate than the 17 miles/day used by Hudson and his colleagues, but it only calls for travel one-half a mile per hour faster and/or a longer period of travel time each day. Ultimately, when both proposals are compared, our alternative segment is only slightly longer at about 311 miles, compared to the Hudson distance of around 300 miles. Thus in absolute terms, our alternative is not remarkably different from the Hudson route, but there are some significant differences in the details between them. (More details concerning our methodology are provided in a closing note.)

We begin the evaluation in the southernmost section under consideration, although our proposal for that area is in general agreement with that of the Hudson team. We believe that the Soto party, after departing 3 March 1540 from its extended winter encampment at Anhaica in present-day Tallahassee, traveled nearly due north to the south bank of the River Guacuca (Ochlockonee) close to its confluence with Hadley Creek, a distance of about 22.6 miles. The crossing point of the Ochlockonee we have chosen corresponds with a known Indian trail crossing. Over the course of the next two days, between 4 and 5 March, the party covered about 40 miles on a northwesterly course until it reached the River Capachequi (Flint) not far east of its junction with Ichawaynochaway Creek, where another known trail crossing existed. Its crossing of the River Capachequi was a difficult one, presumably because the river was running high as is the norm in the early spring.[2] The chronicles tell how the struggle to cross the river consumed five days, between 6 and 10 March, and involved stringing chains together for securing people, horses, and supplies. On 11 March we believe they closely followed the east side of the Ichawaynochaway and then Chickasawhatchee Creek for a total distance of about 27 miles. This leg of the journey brought them squarely within the Native province of Capachequi, widely believed to have encompassed the area of the Deer Run site. The portrayal of the area in the chronicles is similar to the scene encountered in that territory today, one of expansive wetlands and red-hued uplands.

We propose that the first Capachequi village that the Soto group encountered, on 11 March, was among a cluster of late-dating sites at the confluence of Spring and Chickasawhatchee Creeks and, potentially, the noted Red Bluff Earthlodge Site itself. Certainly the wetland-dominated landscape of that locale matches the description in the chronicles. Then we believe it would have been more than feasible for the group to push farther up Spring Creek late in the same day, eventually reaching the Deer Run Site or another one close by. The entrada collected itself there for about five days but under tense conditions. The Indian community it chose to occupy had been hastily abandoned, but apparently the Spanish were under constant surveillance. At one point, a small party of foraging Spanish was attacked, and at least one member was killed and three others badly wounded.[3]

Beyond Capachequi our proposed route begins to diverge significantly from that of Hudson's team, but for a time it conforms reasonably closely to the path proposed by the earlier Swanton commission. Following its tense stay at Capachequi, we believe the entrada made its way along a generally east-trending path toward the Flint River. The first day of travel, on 16 March, took it from Capachequi to an impressive "white spring." Many natural springs issue from sinkholes and springheads in this karstic region, making it nearly impossible to determine which the Soto chroniclers were referring to, but we offer that they may have stopped at Palmyra Spring just west of Kinchafoonee Creek and north of present-day Albany, Georgia, having covered a stretch of about 23 miles. Continuing its eastward travel the next day for about 9 miles, the group arrived at another crossing point of the River Capachequi (Flint) between Piney Woods and Mill creeks. The river's high water had not subsided over the previous week, and the crossing was again described as very difficult. Our reading of the chronicles indicates that the traverse was attempted at two nearby locations where a total of five different bridges were built, four of which failed. The river was finally crossed on 22 March, after five days of labor, not far upstream of the place of the initial crossing attempt. After the party crossed, the march was short, and a night was spent in the pine woods.

The next day, 23 March, Soto proceeded northward for about five miles, moving parallel to the river on its east side. This brought the group to a large village in the province of Toa. By our estimation the village the chronicles describe was located at the point where Philema Branch enters the Flint from the west side. Local informants have recovered impressive quantities of Fort Walton–Lamar ceramics from a site there, thereby meeting expectations of a major site occupied at the time of Soto's passage and coinciding with the location of historically known Philma's Town.[4] It is on this point, the location of the large Toa town, that our route and that of the Hudson team significantly part ways.

The Philema Branch Site (also called the Chokee Site) was unknown to Hudson and his colleagues, who were pressed to identify a suitable site for the Toa community elsewhere in the Flint basin. Their candidate location some 35.5 miles farther upstream was the archaeological site of Hartley-Posey or Neisler, reportedly with terminal occupations during the mid-sixteenth century.[5] While that site seems to bear evidence of sixteenth-century Native occupation, getting there from the Albany area requires that either the five-day bridge-building ordeal be ignored or believing that a long trek of between 30–40 miles was covered in hardly more than a day. Indeed, Hudson and his colleagues later revised their estimation for Toa's location, moving it southward to the vicinity of Marshallville and closer to the crossing point we favor.[6]

We believe it is more reasonable to correlate Toa's location with the Philema Branch site for several reasons. First, as noted, it very strongly meets our archaeological expectations of a candidate Toa site. Second, it does not require excessive travel distances for Soto's cumbersome army according to the calendar schedule we are given for its travel. And third, the location coincides with an important nexus of Indian trails, directly across the Flint from Philma's Town at a place formerly called Pindertown or Kennards, from which one of the paths continued eastward directly toward the Glass Site.[7]

We are told that under cover of night on the day Toa town was reached (23 March), Soto led a contingent of forty cavalrymen on a lengthy reconnaissance of the territory ahead. We argue that their hasty advance was aimed along the east-oriented Indian trail (Ten Mile Trail) leading away from the network junction at Toa (Pindertown), instead of on the northerly path along the Flint that Hudson and his colleagues favored.[8] The chronicles imply that Soto pushed this mounted vanguard along the trail for nearly a week before finally pausing to rest at a village in the province of Ichisi, where he waited for the main body of his group to rejoin them. It was an arduous ride for the group since, in addition to the forced pace, the men were required to ford several streams in a season when they perennially run high.

After some eighteen hours of hurried travel, Soto's party encountered the first "bad crossing" in the early evening of 24 March that we suggest was at today's Deep Creek some 25 miles east of Toa and the Flint. Over the course of 25 March, the reports mention two additional difficult crossings. One they describe as the broad branch of a river we believe to be the Alapaha, only 8 miles farther along the trail from Deep Creek. Archaeologically this area is poorly known, but we have confirmed reports from collectors of a substantial late-dating (Lamar) settlement at the Sand Sink Site, precisely where the trail makes its Alapaha River crossing. We propose that this site, or one associated with it nearby, marks the location of the island village the army attacked after crossing.

About 17 miles farther along to the northeast is a crossing at House Creek that may mark the second tough crossing of the day. There, one man and two horses are reported to have drowned. Soon after the crossing, the reports describe a second village affiliated with the province of Ichisi. At this place the cavalry contingent chose to rest for two days. Because it coincides with the intersection of several trails and the location of a prominent "boiling" spring (Ossiwitchee Spring) where archaeological sites are clustered, we propose that this stopping point was at today's Bowens Mill. It was at this encampment that Soto had his first parlay from the provincial chief via a messenger.

It is about here, incidentally, that the direction of travel of our proposed route diverges significantly from that of Swanton.[9] This is not to say that the two proposals are synchronized up to this point but only that their sharpest differences begin near the Ocmulgee. Indeed, contrary to our reconstruction, Swanton's team correlated sections of the Flint River with the province of Ichisi and then argued that Soto's party marched overland toward the Ocmulgee at present-day Abbeville, Georgia, to find the province of Altamaha. But what is pertinent here is the fact that Abbeville lies just upstream of Bowen's Mill, where we have them on 25 March.

Moving on, the reconnaissance party pushed deeper into Ichisi starting 29 March, and during that day it negotiated yet another bad stream crossing. We believe this crossing coincided with today's Sturgeon Creek, approximately 9 miles east of Bowens Mill. Continuing further the group reached a third Ichisi community late on the 29 March where, once again, it paused to rest and to allow the body of the group to gain ground. Here, too, we are unable to link a known archaeological site with the village. (Frankie Snow does report Lamar Sites from Red Bluff westward, upriver, to Ossiwitchee Spring at Bowens Mill.) However, by this point the mounted advance was deep within the Ocmulgee River basin and probably very close to its south bank near today's Red Bluff.

On the morning of 31 March, the group broke camp and very soon reached a "great river," a stream we, like others, believe to have been the Ocmulgee. The accounts tell us that the party used Indian dugout canoes and made a relatively easy crossing. On the opposite side, it arrived at the principal town of Ichisi occupied by its chief. The reception the Spaniards received was cordial, and the group elected to pause at this settlement for two full days. We argue that this principal town was located at the Glass Site.

The case we make for correlating the Glass Site with this Ichisi village is based on several lines of evidence. There is, first, the obvious archaeological evidence there of not only a substantial Indian community but also a sustained Spanish presence. Second, the Glass Site is located very close to a well-known crossing of the Ocmulgee at Blackshear's Landing, formerly an Indian trail crossing. This trail trends north and south and has a junction with the east-west trail just south of the river and then another connection with a prominent east-west trail paralleling the north side of the river. Finally, we can comfortably put the Soto entrada at the Glass Site using reasonable daily estimates of travel and on the same schedule that he is reported to have arrived at Ichisi. In short, we place the province of Ichisi in the Big Bend of the Ocmulgee as opposed to the area of the Lamar Site, some 87 miles upstream nearer the fall line.

Like our predecessors, we agree that the next leg of the route probably involved travel through the Oconee River valley, and we have extended our reconstruction beyond the Glass Site to include it. Because so little archaeological study has occurred along the lower part of the Oconee in the Coastal Plain, we are hard pressed to identify candidate sites or clusters of sites that would correspond to places identified in the chronicles. But like the situation we inherited along the lower Ocmulgee, a lack of information does not mean there is no potential for evidence of early interaction. The questions will be resolved only with appropriate archaeological investigations, and we view our proposal for that segment as the basis for launching such research.

Soto and his group took leave of the principal Ichisi town on 2 April 1540 and spent that night in "open country." The next day they came to a significant stream that we propose was the Oconee River. They observed some deserted Indian huts there and were met by messengers from Altamaha who led them a bit farther to a larger town in the province where a night was spent. On Sunday, 4 April, they made their crossing in dugout canoes with the help of Indian guides, probably at the ford just west of present-day Mount Vernon and a distance of about 44 miles by trails from the Glass Site. The Soto party lingered in Altamaha for a few days, erecting another cross in acknowledgment of the hospitable treatment it received. Here Soto also learned of the great chief Ocute and summoned him.

Departing Altamaha with the cacique Ocute on 8 April and spending one night in huts along the trail, the party reached a principal town in the Ocute province on 10 April where it remained for about two days. From Ocute it traveled to the province of Cofaqui, arriving there after only a day's travel. This community potentially corresponds with the location of the Shinholser Site, not far south of present-day Milledgeville, Georgia.

Although evidence is sparse, the lower Oconee Valley is not completely without indications of late prehistoric, Lamar culture activity. Besides the obvious, intensive habitation at Shinholser near the fall line, primarily of an earlier date, there are reports of Lamar components at lesser-known places downstream. A good example is the Sawyer Site (9LS1) near Dublin, Georgia.[10]

In addition, there are references in the chronicles that potentially correspond to geographical features in this area. First, in Biedma's description of reaching the province of Altamaha, he comments that after passing through "Chisi" the party encountered a "river that did not flow to the south like the other that we had crossed. It flowed east, to the sea."[11] This is interesting, as our route suggests that the province of Altamaha would have been near the confluence of the Ocmulgee and Oconee Rivers, which forms the Altamaha River and flows into the Atlantic Ocean. Along with his description of this eastward flowing river, Biedma references Lucas de Ayllón, whose attempted colony of 1526 was likely located near the mouth of the Altamaha River.[12] The confluence of the Ocmulgee and Oconee Rivers is geographically positioned such that it fits Biedma's description well, being relatively close to the Atlantic, especially compared to Hudson's placement of the province of Altamaha much further north on the Oconee River. Second, Garcilaso refers to a town above Altamaha as "Achalaque,"[13] which is phonetically similar to "Ochwalkee," the name of the creek that joins the Oconee River where we have placed the entrada's crossing point. Considering the usual difficulties associated with a reading of the chronicles, these descriptions appear to be consistent with our route's placement of the entrada at this particular place and time, requiring a minimal amount of interpretive liberties.

Some closing comments are also in order regarding our reconsideration of the long-favored Ocute province formulation of Smith and Kowalewski.[14] The enduring strength of this argument, which correlates a series of Lamar-affiliated mound sites on the upper Oconee River with historically documented territories in the province of Ocute, has given it a kind of tacit authenticity that we must respect. However, as is evident from our proposal, we are not yet persuaded of the certainty of the proposal. In short, we seek to better support our claim that Soto's entrada did not significantly penetrate the Georgia Piedmont and, therefore, did not visit any Indian communities along the upper Oconee.

First, we wish to argue that the mound-centric route reconstructions of the path may be built on a false premise, and especially that big mounds can be red herrings. In other words, and in large measure based on the perspective gained from the Glass Site experience and the Martin Site case, it is abundantly clear that major Indian-Spanish encounters were occurring at nonmound communities or at communities with small earthworks. This, we believe, means that the field of candidate contact sites is far larger than we tend to assume. As has been the case in many locales, including the Capachequi and Glass Site areas, recent archaeological investigations have recorded principal towns without imposing mounds. We can imagine, then, that relevant sites exist along the lower Ocmulgee in spite of the relative scarcity of large, late-dating mound sites. And there is the issue of erroneous dating of large mound centers. Just as John Chamblee discounted mid-sixteenth-century occupation at Pine Island near Capachequi, Mark Williams has marshaled evidence to suggest that the Shinholser Site was unoccupied at that time.[15]

Second, the currently favored Ocute argument is handicapped by a complete absence of diagnostic early sixteenth-century Spanish artifacts.[16] It is true that numerous glass beads have been recovered from Lamar sites along the upper Oconee, but all of them either clearly date to a later period or are of types that cannot be precisely dated, like monochrome turquoise-colored beads.[17] To be sure, the same is true of Spanish artifacts from middle and lower Oconee sites, but the point here is that the question of the route must remain open until more compelling evidence is recovered.

Appendix Note: Methodology

Our focus on that portion of the route necessitates that three locations be central to our estimation of it: (1) Anhaica, or the Governor Martin site, located near Tallahassee, Florida; (2) Capachequi, a province located in the Ichawaynochaway-Chickasawhatchee area, which would have included the Deer Run Site; and (3) Ichisi, one village of which we propose is represented by the Glass Site. The locations of these sites were compiled as GIS files using their latitude and longitude in decimal degrees. The locations of all other referenced sites were entered by cross-referencing hydrological features common to our base maps and their locations on printed maps. As Indian trails would have proven invaluable to the entrada's movement from place to place, the locations of trails recorded on early nineteenth-century Georgia land-lottery surveys for the areas around and between these locations were also transferred to GIS files.

When dealing with the land-lottery maps, it is important to keep in mind that the survey methods of that era were far less accurate than today's methods. The land-lottery surveys were completed using a compass and chain method, the compass being used to measure direction in degrees and a one-hundred-link chain to measure distance in chains (1 chain = 66 ft). Surveyed counties were divided into districts, and the districts were divided into lots with stakes or "witness trees" serving as the corners. This method of survey was subject to an estimated error of 1 foot for every 50 to 100 feet measured, compared to current error rates estimated at 1 foot of variance in every 50,000 feet.[18] Still, the maps do provide benefits over using secondary compilations of early roads and trails overlain on modern base maps, such as have been published by Marion Hemperly.[19] First, they record a greater number of trails than the later maps, and, second, the ability to georeference the original plats allows for greater accuracy of placement, even considering the inaccuracies of the early records.

To begin the evaluation process, we downloaded digital copies of the land lottery district plats from the Georgia Virtual Vault.[20] Survey plats for the original Wilkinson (1807, 202.5 ac lots), Irwin and Appling (1820, 490 ac lots), Early (1820, 250 ac lots), Dooly (1821, 202.5 ac lots), and Lee (1827, 202.5 ac lots) counties were all examined for trails recorded by surveyors. The portions of the images with recorded trails were then georeferenced using a data set generously provided by rGa & Associates, and each trail was digitized as a line feature. During this process, it quickly became evident that trails were incompletely recorded on the survey plats. However, it also became clear that a complex network of Indian trails existed prior to Euro-American settlement in the early nineteenth century that, theoretically, approximated an ancient network that would have been available for the Soto expedition's use. Also, it is often simple to extrapolate the course of trails on plats that do not display them because adjoining plats offer connectable endpoints. The end result is a partial representation of the Native terrestrial transportation network that can be displayed together with site locations and other data in an informative manner.

The path posited by Hudson and his colleagues serves as the basic benchmark for our own reconstruction.[21] In their proposal, the authors put forth four generalizations that guided the investigation: (1) that Soto relied heavily on Indian guides and Indian trails; (2) that they maintained an average rate of travel of 5 leagues (17.25 mi) per day; (3) that the expedition's course was regulated by the location of Native population centers where they hoped to find food and valuable resources; and (4) that they would have traveled through the southeastern Coastal Plain as quickly as possible. The first and third of these assumptions are well supported by historical evidence. And it is in the third supposition that the authors cite most of their archaeological evidence, keying on Mississippian mound sites known or suspected to have been occupied during Soto's day. It is true that many large late-prehistoric sites were marked by large mounds, but it is also true that many were not. Indeed, we believe that the Glass and Deer Run sites are a counterpoint to that line of reasoning. We also will report how sixteenth-century dates assigned to certain mound sites thirty years ago have been adjusted.

The second generalization of Hudson and his colleagues, that the entrada covered an average of 5 leagues each day, is difficult to confirm due to the nature of the chronicles. Two league measurements were in use by the Spanish during this time period in the New World: the legua comun (3.45 mi) and the legua legal (2.63 mi), and it is unclear which of them the chroniclers of the Soto expedition were referring to on the rare occasion distances are provided at all. The Hudson team chose a distance measure (legua comun) based on analogy with other early Spanish expeditions in La Florida, though the records of these expeditions are subject to the same shortcomings as the Soto chronicles. Ultimately, an accurate measure of the expedition's average daily rate of travel is difficult to make, and it could be argued that such a figure may have limited utility, knowing the expedition's rate of travel likely varied due to many factors, including terrain, weather, and interactions with Native peoples, both unfriendly and friendly.

Perhaps more useful is a consideration of the amount of time that could have feasibly been devoted to daily travel. At the time of year the entrada was traveling through Georgia, 11.5 to 12.5 hours of daylight would have been available to them.[22] Considering the time required to make and break camp and perhaps pause occasionally while on the march, the entrada could potentially have been on the move for close to 10 hours each day. Considering that a human being walking 2 mph is a slow pace and 3.5 mph is brisk,[23] one can appreciate the range of distances that might be traveled depending on terrain, the amount of time spent traveling, and so on. The five-league per day standard used by Hudson and his colleagues would have required the entrada to travel a little over 2 mph over a period of 8 hours, or a bit more than 1.5 mph over 10 hours. Thus, it would seem, given optimal conditions, the Soto party would have been capable of covering more ground than our predecessors estimated.

Notes

CHAPTER I. On a Mission

1. Hudson 1997:466.

2. A series of technical reports and articles has been prepared through the course of the project that contain details supportive of the arguments I make in this book. See Blanton 2007, 2009; Blanton and Snow 2009, 2010; Blanton et al. 2011, 2013.

CHAPTER II. Possessed by Passions

1. Mary Musgrove, a woman of Creek-English heritage, emerged in the eighteenth century as an influential advocate for the Creek Nation and a formidable businessperson. With her second husband, Jacob Matthews, she established a trading post on the Altamaha at Mount Venture in the late 1730s. See Hahn 2012; Sweet 2009.

2. Clarence Bloomfield Moore, an independently wealthy Philadelphian, in 1898 explored from his steamboat, *Gopher*, numerous Indian mounds along the Altamaha River, and his report of the expedition became a guide for some of my own explorations. See Larson 1998.

3. The National Historic Preservation Act of 1966 mandated that cultural resources, including archaeological sites, be taken into account when federally funded or permitted projects are undertaken. By the 1970s, implementation of the law had led to an explosion of new archaeological projects nationwide. This federal action was preceded a generation earlier by activities of the New Deal's Works Progress Administration, which sponsored numerous large-scale archaeological projects, including at Macon Plateau, where Ocmulgee National Monument now exists. For information on the New Deal era's archaeology, see Means 2013.

4. Thomas 1987, 1988, 1991, 1993, 2008; Thomas and Larsen 1979, 1982, 1986.

5. Hally 2008; Smith 2000.

CHAPTER III. Never Say Never

1. For information about Santa Catalina de Guale, see Thomas 1987, 1988, 1991, 1993.

2. Braley 1995; Geiger 1937; Hann 1996; Lawson 1987, 1991; Milanich 1996; Worth 1995, 1998.

3. Geiger 1937; Hann 1996; Worth 1998.

4. Thomas 1987.

5. Geophysics refers to a variety of noninvasive methods designed to collect information about belowground conditions. They include magnetometry, ground-penetrating radar, and soil resistance. In its own way, each method records local variation in near-surface soil conditions that, in turn, signifies the presence of "anomalies" which can sometimes be archaeological features such as foundations, ditches, and graves. Properly processed, the results may be viewed as images.

6. Snow 1977, 1990; Snow and Stephenson 1998; Stephenson and Snow 2004.

7. The Lamar Site (9BI2) is located in the Ocmulgee River floodplain about a mile from the earlier-dating Mississippian center at Macon Plateau. It was first excavated by Jesse Jennings, Gordon Wiley, and James Ford, and reported first in Kelly 1938.

8. Hudson 1994a, 1997; Hudson, Smith, and DePratter 1984; Hudson, Worth, and DePratter 1990.

9. Swanton 1985.

10. Hally 2008; Smith 1975, 2000.

11. Toner 2006.

CHAPTER IV. A Temple in the Pines

1. Hoffman 1994a:45–46; Hudson 1997:146–147; Larson 1980:228–229; Snow 1977:48–49.

2. Hudson et al. 1984:67.

3. Archaeologists in the United States apply the Smithsonian trinomial system to designate unique archaeological sites. A site is identified by the state's number in alphabetical order, a two-letter abbreviation for county location, and a unique number indicating the order in which it was recorded in the specified county; thus the Glass Site—9TF145—is the 145th site officially recorded in Telfair County, Georgia. I began to refer to the site by the name Glass in 2010. Frankie originally named it the Lampkin Branch Site after a nearby stream, and he also assigned it the number 9TF145. In time I believed it was appropriate to rename it the Glass Site as a way of recognizing the landowners and their support of the project. This was especially meaningful upon the death in 2012 of Pat Glass Thorpe and her husband, Wilson. They became sole owners of the property after we started the project and were perennially enthusiastic about the work.

4. Descriptions of Altamaha Line-Block ceramics may be found in DePratter 1979; Saunders 2000, 2009; Thomas 2009.

5. Blanton and Snow 2010.

6. Hudson 1976:Chapter 3.

7. Two kinds of large buildings are known to have occupied late Mississippian towns, temples and council houses, and I reviewed archaeological and historical descriptions of them to determine which of the two kinds ours might be. I choose to describe the large Glass Site structure as a temple since it falls short of the mammoth sizes of most council houses, which were designed to accommodate even hundreds of people. Blanton et al. 2011:15–18; Blanton et al. 2013; Rodning 2002.

8. Qtd. in Grantham 2002:60.

9. Grantham 2002:75.

10. Sacred structures at southeastern Indian villages often housed, among other things, a perpetually burning fire that symbolized the sun. It was extinguished and rekindled only once a year in conjunction with the annual busk renewal known widely as the Green Corn ceremony. Hudson 1976:317; Rodning 2010; Swanton 1979:773.

11. Waselkov and Braund 1995:125–126, 149.

12. Goodyear et al. 1980.

CHAPTER V. A Round Town

1. Bleed and Scott 2009, 2011; Scott 2013.

2. Hally 2008:525–534; Nass and Yerkes 1995:71, 76; Sullivan 1995:114.

CHAPTER VI. Calling Cards of a Conquistador

1. Venetian glassmakers, concentrated at places like Murano, dominated much of the world glass market from as early as the thirteenth century. Glass bead production was raised to an art form during the period of exploration. Francis 2009a; Pendleton and Francis 2009.

2. Deagan 1987; Francis 2009a, 2009b; Little 2008, 2010; Mitchem and Leader 1988; Pendleton and Francis 2009; Smith 1983, 1987.

3. Chevron beads were dispersed to many European colonial territories, especially in the Americas and Africa. They have been discovered across North America where Spain, France, the Netherlands, and England pursued colonial interests, especially in the sixteenth and seventeenth centuries. In the Southeast, small, seven-layer, faceted chevrons are reported from at least twenty-six sites, ranging from Arkansas to the Carolinas. Little 2008, 2010; Smith 1983, 1987; Smith and Good 1982.

4. Nueva Cádiz beads were named for the sixteenth-century pearl-fishing center in Venezuela, where they were documented by archaeologists in numbers. Fairbanks 1968; Francis 2009a:66; Little 2010.

5. Worldwide, Nueva Cádiz beads are less common than chevron beads, but they do occur in most of the same places as early varieties of chevrons. In the Southeast Nueva Cádiz beads of different types are reported from at least 23 sites. Little 2008, 2010; Smith 1983, 1987; Smith and Good 1982.

6. A surprising abundance of Nueva Cádiz beads is documented at the site of James Fort in Virginia, almost exclusively in the earliest contexts (1607–10). The two leading explanations surround later production of the beads in the area of Amsterdam by transplanted Italian glassmakers or acquisition of antique beads by Virginia Company planners. Lapham 2001; Little 2010; Francis 2009b.

7. These beads are known as Type 24 in Smith and Good 1982.

8. Beads of this kind are very rare, and other than the Glass Site, they have been documented at only four sites in Florida, including the Tatham Mound and St. Marks Cemetery. Little 2008; Mitchem and Leader 1988; Smith and Good 1982.

9. Hoffman 1994b; Marrinan et al. 1990; Swanton 1985:Chapter 12.

10. Brain 1975; Mitchem 1990; Waselkov 2009. Similar sets of artifacts are documented at sites linked with Coronado's near-simultaneous expedition into the American West from 1540 to 1542: for example, see Mathers and Haecker 2011; Mathers et al. 2011; Schmader 2011.

11. Blair et al. 2009:158–159; Dalton-Carriger and Blair 2013.

12. Brain 1979; Good 1972; Mission San Luis 2011; Smith 1992; Waselkov 2005.

13. Brown 1977, 1979; Mitchem and McEwan 1988.

14. Brown 1977, 1979; Mitchem and McEwan 1988.

15. Clarksdale bells are relatively numerous in Florida and at sites in the Mississippi River valley, but they also occur at points in between, including in contexts dated to the late sixteenth century. See Brain 1975; Brown 1977, 1979; Hudson 1997:74; Mitchem and McEwan 1988; South et al. 1988.

16. Mitchem 1989; Mitchem and Leader 1988.

17. Translations of the feather gift differ in the details, but as Hudson does, some understand it to have been a feather adorned somehow with silver. Hudson 1997:164; Swanton 1985:55; Worth, trans. 1993a:272.

18. Biscayan axes are reportedly named for a region in Spain or France called Vizcaya, or Biscay, that supplied manufacturers with iron ore.

19. Marvin Smith generously provided me with copies of his records of southeastern metal artifacts. His years-long compilation documents Biscayan-style axes at the following sites: Hightower Site, Alabama (n=2); ICE308, Alabama; Pine Island, Alabama; Brown Farm, Georgia; Dunn's Creek, Florida; Phillip Mound, Florida (Benson 1967). See Sempowski 2001 for examples of axes with hafting eyes removed.

20. Hudson 1997:177–178; Swanton 1985:171; Worth, trans. 1993a:279, 1993b:231. See also discussion of Ayllón's colony in Chapter XIII of this book.

21. Some of the better documentation of iron tools, including simple ones, and contexts of exchange is found in the inventory of Juan Pardo's 1560s expeditions from Santa Elena into the interior; see DePratter and Smith 1987; Hudson 2005b. In northwestern Georgia, similar artifacts in potential Soto-related contexts are documented at the King and Little Egypt Sites (Hally 2008:222–223; Moorehead 1932:153–154; Smith 1975, 1992).

22. From personal communication with Chester DePratter and James Legg, I learned that simple celts, similar to some examples at Glass, were fashioned by blacksmiths at Santa Elena (South Carolina) by repurposing segments of iron barrel hoops and other scrap metal.

23. Byne and Stapley 1915.

24. Most iron awls from sixteenth- and seventeenth-century New World sites are simple sharpened rods, sometimes even modified spikes and nails. Examples with flatter cross sections and/or more complex forms are rare. Awls vaguely similar to the Glass Site specimen are reported in Deagan and Reitz 1995.

25. Hutchinson 2006; Mitchem and Weisman 1984; Mitchem et al. 1985.

26. The single reported large, round-section chisel in the region is from burial context in the Tatham Mound in Florida. Hutchinson 2006; Mitchem 1989, 1991; Mitchem and Hutchinson 1987.

27. Larson 1958.

28. Bullen 1952; Griffin and Smith 1948; Larson 1958; Moore 1896; Sears et al. 1994:60–65; Willey 1954.

29. Hudson 1997:240; Swanton 1985:213; Worth, trans. 1993a:294

30. Little 2008; Smith 1987; Waselkov 2009.

31. Finger rings are common on early Spanish and French sites dating from the seventeenth century. The classic type consists of a thin band to which is attached a seal-like disk bearing Catholic iconography. Simple, wide bands are less common but not unknown on sixteenth and seventeenth-century sites in the Southeast (Deagan 2002; Thomas 1988, 1991).

32. The metal tip of a crossbow bolt is called a quarrel. Quarrels were made from iron, copper, and copper alloys. The common form consists of a shank designed to be crimped onto the wooden shaft, and a solid, four-sided tip. Ewen and Hann 1998; South et al. 1988.

33. See Wells 1998 for discussion of nail types. The naval stores industry was a mainstay of South Georgia commerce during the nineteenth and early twentieth centuries. Prized longleaf yellow pine and cypress trees were extracted on a vast scale. "Rafts" of

logs were floated down streams like the Ocmulgee to ports and mills. Small, temporary camps were established to accommodate the loggers, rafters, and others involved in the enterprise. U.S. Army Corps of Engineers 1909.

34. Carat-headed nails are documented from early Spanish-related sites in Florida (Ewen and Hann 1998:83–84, 87) and New Mexico (Mathers and Haecker 2011; Schmader 2011).

35. An arquebus is a primitive, smooth-bore firearm with a matchlock-style mechanism. Several men in Soto's entrada carried them. See Hudson 1997:69; Worth, trans. 1993a:274.

CHAPTER VII. A Big Bend Province

1. The Lamar Culture was first defined by Kelly (1938) based on his work at the Lamar site and its environs, and from related findings elsewhere in the region. Generally, it spans the period AD 1350–1800 and represents the terminal stage of Mississippian culture in Georgia. More recently, David Hally (1994) has written a comprehensive summary of the culture's history and archaeology. See also Williams and Shapiro 1990.

2. Anderson 1996; Hally 1994, 1996.

3. Rudolph and Blanton 1980; Williams and Shapiro 1996:139.

4. Snow 1990:89.

5. One the first and most obvious questions I had about the Glass Site concerned the choice of location. I looked at contemporary soil-survey data compiled by the U.S. Department of Agriculture's Soil Conservation Service (U.S. Department of Agriculture 2003). We discovered that the soil at the Glass Site is exceptionally well suited to corn agriculture. Blanton et al. 2011:105–110.

6. Blanton et al. 2011:89–90, 92–105; Hemperly 1989.

7. Evidence at Etowah for a Soto encounter exists mainly in the form of metal artifacts, including an iron celt (Smith 1987, 2000). For a discussion of Etowah's history see, King 2003.

8. Hally 2008:157–158; Hudson 1976:221.

9. Hally 2008:537. See also Narroll 1962 on concept.

10. Hally 2008:525–534; Nass and Yerkes 1995:71, 76; Sullivan 1995:114.

11. Braun 1983.

12. Hensler 2018.

13. Snow 1990.

14. Blanton 2016.

15. Windham 2010, 2011.

16. Hudson 1976:280.

17. For a representative discussion of faunal evidence for elite Mississippian dietary practices, see Jackson and Scott 2003.

18. Mark Williams (2010) has proposed that the Glass Site population moved to the lower Ocmulgee from the Little River valley (in the Piedmont) in the sixteenth century.

19. Numerous scholars have examined the patterns of development and decline for Mississippian sites and cultures. A good source of broad information on the topic is John Scarry's edited volume (1996).

20. The formal concept of a Mississippian cultural pattern developed in the 1930s. It was based on reports of archaeological cultures from the Mississippi River Valley to the deeper Southeast that shared "traits" such as platform mounds, shell-tempered pottery, and an elaborate ceremonial complex. A helpful overview of Mississippian culture in the Southeast is Hally and Mainfort 2004.

CHAPTER VIII. Elusive Closure

1. Quotation from Hudson 1997:466. See also Hudson et al. 1984:75; Hally et al. 1990:121.

2. Blanton and Snow, 2010; Blanton et al. 2011; Blanton et al. 2013.

3. Hudson 1997:138–142; Milanich and Hudson 1993.

4. Hudson 1997:129–130; Swanton 1985:165; Worth, trans. 1993b:225.

5. Juan Ortiz was a member of the Narváez expedition later taken captive by Natives in southern Florida. He was rescued by chance by Soto, and he served the entrada as an interpreter. Hudson 1997:85–87.

6. Ewen and Hann 1998; Hudson 1997:Chapter 5; Swanton 1985:160.

7. Hudson 1997:150; Swanton 1985:167, 173; Worth, trans. 1993a:269.

8. Hudson 1997:163; Swanton 1985:176–177; Worth, trans. 1993b:229.

9. Hudson 1997:150; Swanton 1985:167; Worth, trans. 1993a:269.

10. Hudson 1997:156; Swanton 1985:167; Worth, trans. 1993b:228. As noted elsewhere, opinions differ in route reconstructions about the locations of Capachequi and Toa, and in the chronicles there are inconsistencies in first reports of the cave-like structures. Regardless, my ongoing work in the area of Capachequi has documented the construction there, by Indians, of wattle-and-daub buildings at the time of Soto's expedition.

11. Swanton 1985:176, 178–179.

12. Hudson 1997:504, Endnote 47; Worth, trans. 1993a:262.

13. Hudson 1997:162, 164; Swanton 1985:168–169; Worth, trans. 1993a:272.

14. Hudson 1997:166; Swanton 1985:169; Worth, trans. 1993a:273.

15. Swanton 1985.

16. Lawson 1987, 1991; Worth 1994, 1995.

17. Swanton 1985:177.

18. Swanton 198:174.

19. Chamblee 2006. See also Worth 1989 for description of Capachequi-area sites.

20. The village and mound site at Hartford have been thoroughly studied by Frankie Snow and Keith Stephenson, and their findings demonstrate that it is affiliated with the Swift Creek culture (AD 100–800).

21. Swanton 1985:179.

22. Swanton 1985:183–184.

23. Hudson 1997:466–472; Hudson et al. 1984:75.

24. Hudson 1994b; Hudson et al. 1984.

25. Hudson et al. 1984:67.

26. Hally 1994; Kelly 1938.

27. The University of Georgia, under contract with the Georgia Power Company, undertook in the 1970s a comprehensive survey and ambitious excavations within the basin of the proposed Wallace Reservoir hydroelectric project. Today the impoundment is known as Lake Oconee. Dozens of technical reports and articles were generated to describe the results of the landmark project.

28. Hudson 1994b, 1997:465; Hudson et al. 1984:70; Smith and Kowalewski 1980; Williams 1994.

29. Worth 1988.

30. Hudson et al. 1984:70.

31. Williams 2010; Worth 1988.

32. Blanton and Snow 2010; Blanton et al. 2011; Blanton et al. 2013.

33. Spanish material culture studies, see in-text citations.

34. Little 2008; Smith 1987.

35. Ewen 1990, 1996; Ewen and Hann 1998: 52–53, 105–108.

36. Ewen and Hann 1998:53, 105–108.

37. Hally and Smith 2010; Hudson et al. 1984:65; Smith 1987.

38. Ewen and Hann 1998:106.

39. Hally and Smith 2010.

40. Hally and Smith 2010:62–63.

41. Lightfoot 1995.

42. Smith 1987.

43. Hally 1994:167.

44. Rudolph and Blanton 1981; Williams 1994; Williams and Shapiro 1996.

45. Hally 1994:153–159.

46. Hahn 2012; Sweet 2009.

47. Blanton et al. 2011:89–105; Hemperly 1989.

48. Blanton et al. 2011:102; Cadle 1991; U.S. Army Corps of Engineers 1909.

49. Blanton et al. 2011:101–102; Hemperly 1989.

50. Several sites on the Ocmulgee and Oconee Rivers have yielded very late sixteenth- and seventeenth-century artifacts in Indian contexts. In particular, late-style glass beads are known from the Joe Bell Site (9MG28), 9HK8, Shinholser (9BL1), and Macon Plateau, among others. Williams 2010.

51. Soto's Coosa province became the stuff of legend based on his glowing reports, and in 1560 a party from Tristan de Luna y Arellano's desperate colonizing party returned to it in hope of finding much-needed food; see Priestley 2010. In similar fashion, Juan Pardo from 1566 to 1568 pursued both riches and food in the Appalachians by launching expeditions from Santa Elena and also by establishing a fort in the province of Joara; see Beck et al. 2016.

52. Little 2008:34–51; Mitchem 1991; Smith 1987:44–52.

53. Hudson 1997:160–165; Swanton 1985:168–169, 176; Robertson 1993:76–77.

54. Hudson 1997:162, 164; Swanton 1985:168–169; Worth, trans. 1993a:272.

55. Hudson 1997:162, 164; Swanton 1985:168–169; Robertson 1993:77; Worth, trans. 1993a:272.

56. Ewen 1990, 1996; Ewen and Hann 1998.

57. Waselkov and Braund 1995:173; Worth, trans. 1993a:279–280.

58. Williams 1995.

59. Worth 1993, 1994.

60. Mitchem et al. 1985.

61. Hudson 1997:453–455; Swanton 1985:11, Map No. 1.

62. Hudson 1997:177–178; Swanton 1985:171; Worth, trans. 1993a:279, 1993b:231.

63. Hoffman 1990, 1994a; Peck 2001.

64. Hoffman 1990:Appendix.

65. Blanton et al. 2011:91; Hoffman 1990:75–77.

66. Small numbers of sixteenth-century Spanish artifacts, such as Nueva Cádiz and faceted chevron beads and iron objects, have been excavated from time to time from burial mounds on Georgia's barrier islands. These sites include the Taylor Mound and the Kent Mound, both on St. Simons Island. Pearson 1977. Also, a single Nueva Cádiz bead was recovered from a seventeenth-century burial in the church at Santa Catalina de Guale (Blair et al. 2009).

67. Cabeza de Vaca 1871; Hoffman 1994b.

68. Hoffman 1990, 1994a; Marrinan et al. 1990; Swanton 1985:Chapter 12.

69. Stanley South, later with Chester DePratter, discovered and excavated at Parris Island, South Carolina, the early Spanish capital enclave of Santa Elena (South 1988), where they also documented evidence of the French outpost of Charlesfort (DePratter et al. 1996)

70. The precise location of Fort Caroline has been a subject of perpetual debate. Beginning in 2014, a group of researchers proposed that the River May referred to

in French sources is today's Altamaha River, and therefore the fort site will be found on the lower reaches of the same stream. Archaeological confirmation of the claim is waiting. See Fort Caroline Archaeology Project 2018.

71. Bennett 2001.

72. In 2005 a cultural resource management survey in Camden County, Georgia, documented a mound site, and a test excavated into the mound recovered an impressive array of mid- to late sixteenth-century artifacts. Ultimately attributed to Indian-French interactions, the inventory of European artifacts in the mound test included over two hundred glass beads—including faceted chevrons—and numerous iron artifacts such as a halberd blade, a hatchet blade, and a knife. However, because the glass bead collection from this site also contains many types not present at the Glass Site, it does not stand out as equivalent. Thomas Whitley, 2008, personal communication.

73. Brain 1979; Good 1972; Hann and McEwan 1998; Smith 1992; Waselkov 2005.

74. Ethridge and Shuck-Hall 2009.

CHAPTER IX. Making Meaning

1. The Black Legend concept was given prominence by Juderías 1914; see also Deagan 1990.

2. European artifacts, including beads, have turned up on Native sites farther up the Ocmulgee and Oconee Rivers, but they are universally of later-dating types. For example, I excavated a number of turquoise glass beads from a late Lamar site in Hancock County that conform precisely to the kinds of beads one expects of mission-era interactions (Blanton 1995.) The same is true of the beads from Wallace Reservoir (Lake Oconee) sites and from excavations around Macon, where the contexts tend to be seventeenth to eighteenth century (Williams 2010). See also Walker 1994 for a history of archaeological investigations in the Macon area.

3. Knight, ed. 2009.

4. Stephen Kowalewski and his associates demonstrated the utility of complete survey coverage over large areas with projects in Oaxaca, Mexico. Fish and Kowalewski 1990.

5. Hudson, DePratter, and Smith 1990:84.

6. Knight 2009.

7. Hudson 1997:149–150; Hudson et al. 1984; Swanton 1985:166–167, 172–17.

APPENDIX

1. Blanton et al. 2011:92–105.

2. U.S. Geological Survey 2011.

3. Hudson 1997:150; Robertson 1993:74–75.

4. Hemperley 1989:82.

5. Worth 1988.
6. Hudson, Worth, and DePratter 1990.
7. Hemperley 1989:82.
8. Hudson et al. 1984.
9. Swanton 1985.
10. Williams and Shapiro 1996.
11. Worth, trans. 1993b:229.
12. Worth, trans. 1993b:229.
13. Worth, trans. 1993a:262.
14. Smith and Kowalewski 1980. See also Hally 1994; Hudson 1984.
15. Chamblee 2006; Williams 1994.
16. Smith and Kowalewski 1980; Williams 2010.
17. Blanton 1995.
18. Corbin and Corbin 2007.
19. Hemperly 1989.
20. Georgia Virtual Vault 2011.
21. Hudson et al. 1984.
22. U.S. Navy 2011.
23. Ainsworth et al. 1992.

References

Ainsworth, Barbara E., William L. Haskell, Arther S. Leon, David R. Jacobs Jr., Henry J. Montoye, James F. Sallis, and Ralph S. Paffenbarger Sr.

1993 Compendium of Physical Activities: Classification of Energy Costs of Human Physical Activities. *Medicine and Science in Sports and Exercise* 25:71–80.

Anderson, David G.

1996 Chiefly Cycling and Large-Scale Abandonments as Viewed from the Savannah River Basin. In Scarry 1996:150–191.

Beck, Robin A., Christopher B. Rodning, and David G. Moore (editors)

2016 *Fort San Juan and the Limits of Empire*, University Press of Florida, Gainesville.

Benson, Carl A.

1967 The Philip Mound: A Historic Site. *Florida Anthropologist* 20:118–127.

Bennett, Charles E.

2001 *Laudonnière & Fort Caroline: History and Documents*. University of Alabama Press, Tuscaloosa.

Blair, Elliot H., Lorann S. A. Pendleton, and Peter Francis Jr.

2009 *The Beads of St. Catherines Island*. Anthropological Papers of the American Museum of Natural History Vol. 89. American Museum of Natural History, New York.

Blanton, Dennis B.

1995 Investigation of Upland Piedmont Lamar Site 9HK64. *Early Georgia* 23(2):1–30.

2007 *In Search of Mission Santa Isabel de Utinahica: Season I Progress Report*. Fernbank Museum of Natural History, Atlanta. Copies available from Fernbank Museum of Natural History, Atlanta.

2009 *In Search of Mission Santa Isabel de Utinahica: Season II Progress Report.* Fernbank Museum of Natural History, Atlanta. Copies available from Fernbank Museum of Natural History, Atlanta.

2016 *Mississippian Smoking Ritual in the Southern Appalachian Region.* University of Tennessee Press, Knoxville.

Blanton, Dennis B., and Robert A. DeVillar (editors)

2010 *Archaeological Encounters with Georgia's Spanish Period, 1526–1700.* Special Publication No. 2. Society for Georgia Archaeology, Athens.

Blanton, Dennis B., Rachel Hensler, Jeffrey B. Glover, Wes Patterson, Frankie Snow, and Chester P. Walker

2011 *Points of Contact: The Archaeological Landscape of Hernando de Soto in Georgia.* Fernbank Museum of Natural History. Submitted to National Geographic Society, Grant No. 8765-10. Copies available from Fernbank Museum of Natural History, Atlanta.

Blanton, Dennis B., Wes Patterson, Jeffrey B. Glover, and Frankie Snow

2013 *Point of Contact: Archaeological Evaluation of a Potential De Soto Encampment in Georgia.* Fernbank Museum of Natural History, Atlanta. Copies available from Fernbank Museum of Natural History, Atlanta.

Blanton, Dennis B., and Frankie Snow

2009 Early Sixteenth-Century Spanish Activity on the Lower Ocmulgee River: New Findings and New Questions. Paper presented at the Sixty-Sixth Annual Meeting of the Southeastern Archaeological Conference, Mobile, Alabama.

2010 New Evidence of Early Spanish Activity on the Lower Ocmulgee River. In Blanton and DeVillar 2010:9–18.

Bleed, Peter, and Douglas D. Scott

2009 *Fields of Conflict: Battlefield Archaeology from Imperial Rome to Korea.* Potomac Books, Washington, D.C.

2011 The Archaeology of Historic Battlefields: A History and Theoretical Development in Conflict Archaeology. *Journal of Archaeological Research* 19(1):103–134.

Brain, Jeffrey

1975 Artifacts of the Adelantado. *Proceedings of the Conference on Historic Site Archaeology Papers* 8:129–38.

1979 Glass Beads from the Tunica Treasure. *Lower Mississippi Survey Bulletin* 7. Peabody Museum of Archaeology and Ethnology. Cambridge, Massachusetts.

Braley, Chad O.

1995 *Historic Indian Period Archaeology of the Georgia Coastal Plain.* Georgia Archaeological Research Design Paper No. 10. University of Georgia Laboratory of Archaeology Series Report No. 34. University of Georgia, Athens.

Braun, David P.

1983, Pots as Tools. In *Archaeological Hammers and Theories*, pp.107–134. Academic Press, New York.

Brown, Ian W.

1977 Historic Trade Bells. *Proceedings of the Conference on Historic Sites Archaeology Papers* 10:69–82.

1979 Bells. In *Tunica Treasure*, edited by Jeffrey P. Brain, pp. 197–205. Papers of the Peabody Museum of Archaeology and Ethnology Vol. 71. Harvard University, Cambridge, Massachusetts.

1980 Trade Bells. In *Burr's Hill: A 17th-Century Wampanoag Burial Ground in Warren, Rhode Island*, edited by Susan G. Gibson, pp. 92–95. Studies in Anthropology and Material Culture Vol. 2. Haffenreffer Museum of Anthropology, Brown University, Providence, Rhode Island.

Bullen, Ripley P.

1952 *Eleven Archaeological Sites in Hillsborough County, Florida*. Report of Investigations No. 8. Florida Geological Survey, Tallahassee.

Byne, Arthur, and Mildred Stapley

1915 *Spanish Ironwork*. Hispanic Society of America, New York.

Cabeza De Vaca, Álvar Núñez

1871 *Relation of Alvar Nunez Cabeça de Vaca*. Translated from the Spanish by Buckingham Smith. Printed by J. Munsell for H. C. Murphy, Albany, New York.

Chamblee, John

2006 Landscape Patches, Macroregional Exchanges and Pre-Columbian Political Economy in Southwestern Georgia. PhD dissertation, Department of Anthropology, University of Arizona, Tucson.

Clayton, Lawrence A., Vernon James Knight Jr., and Edward C. Moore (editors)

1993a *The De Soto Chronicles: The Expedition of Hernando de Soto to North America in 1539–1543*, Vol. 1. University of Alabama Press, Tuscaloosa.

1993b *The De Soto Chronicles: The Expedition of Hernando de Soto to North America in 1539–1543*, Vol. 2. University of Alabama Press, Tuscaloosa.

Corbin, Charles C., and Tripp Corbin

2007 Georgia Land History. Unpublished manuscript, Keck & Wood, Duluth, Georgia.

Dalton-Carriger, Jessica, and Elliot H. Blair

2013 Compositional Analysis of Glass Trade Beads from the Interior Southeast. Paper presented at the Southeastern Archaeological Conference, Tampa, Florida.

Deagan, Kathleen

1987 *Artifacts of the Spanish Colonies of Florida and the Caribbean, 1500–1800*, Vol. 1: *Ceramics, Glassware, and Beads*. Smithsonian Institution Press, Washington, D.C.

1990 Sixteenth-Century Spanish-American Colonization in the Southeastern United States and the Caribbean. In Thomas 1990:225–250.

2002 *Artifacts of the Spanish Colonies of Florida and the Caribbean, 1500–1800*, Vol. 2: *Portable Personal Possessions*. Smithsonian Institution Press, Washington, D.C.

Deagan, Kathleen, and Elizabeth Reitz

1995 *Puerto Real: The Archaeology of a Sixteenth-Century Spanish Town in Hispaniola*. University Press of Florida, Gainesville.

Deagan, Kathleen, and David Hurst Thomas (editors)

2009 *From Santa Elena to St. Augustine: Indigenous Ceramic Variability (A.D. 1400–1700)*. Anthropological Papers of the American Museum of Natural History Vol. 90. American Museum of Natural History, New York.

DePratter, Chester B.

1979 Ceramics. In Thomas and Larsen 1979:109–132.

DePratter, Chester B., and Marvin T. Smith

1987 Sixteenth Century European Trade in the Southeastern United States: Evidence from the Juan Pardo Expeditions (1566–1568). *Notebook* 19(1–4):52–61.

DePratter, Chester B., Stanley South, and James Legg

1996 The Discovery of Charlesfort. *Transactions of the Huguenot Society of South Carolina* 101:39–48.

Ethridge, Robbie, and Sheri M. Shuck-Hall (editors)

2009 *Mapping the Mississippian Shatter Zone: The Colonial Indian Slave Trade and Regional Instability in the American South*. University of Nebraska Press, Lincoln.

Ewen, Charles R.

1990 Soldier of Fortune: Hernando de Soto in the Territory of the Apalachee, 1539–1540. In Thomas 1990: 83–92.

1996 Continuity and Change: De Soto and the Apalachee. *Historical Archaeology* 30(2): 41–53.

Ewen, Charles R., and John H. Hann

1998 *Hernando De Soto among the Apalachee: The Archaeology of the First Winter Encampment*. University Press of Florida, Gainesville.

Fairbanks, Charles

1968 Early Spanish and Colonial Beads. *Conference on Historic Sites Archaeology Papers* 2:3–21.

Fish, Suzanne K., and Stephen A. Kowalewski (editors)

1990 *The Archaeology of Regions: A Case for Full Coverage Survey*. Smithsonian Institution Press, Washington, D.C.

Flint, Richard, and Shirley Cushing Flint (editors)
1997 *The Coronado Expedition to Tierra Nueva: The 1540–1542 Route across the Southwest.* University Press of Colorado, Boulder.
2003 *The Coronado Expedition from the Distance of 460 Years.* University of New Mexico Press, Albuquerque.
2011 *The Latest Word from 1540: People, Places, and Portrayals of the Coronado Expedition.* University of New Mexico Press, Albuquerque.
Fort Caroline Archaeology Project
2018 The Fort Caroline Archaeology Project. http://www.tfcap.org, accessed April 30, 2018.
Francis, Peter, Jr.
2009a The Glass Beads of the *Margariteri* of Venice. In Blair et al. 2009:65–71.
2009b The Glass Beads of the *Paternostri* of Venice. In Blair et al. 2009:73–80.
Galloway, Patricia (editor)
2005 *The Hernando de Soto Expedition: History, Historiography, and "Discovery" in the Southeast.* University of Nebraska Press, Lincoln.
Geiger, M.
1937 *The Franciscan Conquest of Florida (1573–1618).* Catholic University of America, Washington, D.C.
Georgia Archives
2011 Georgia's Virtual Vault. District Plats of Survey. Electronic document, Georgia Archives, https://vault.georgiaarchives.org/digital/collection/dmf, accessed March 2011.
Good, M. E. K.
1972 *Guebert Site: An 18th Century Historic Kaskaskia Indian Village in Randolph County, Illinois.* Central States Archaeological Society, Wood River, Illinois.
Goodyear, Albert C., James L. Michie, and Barbara Purdy
1980 The Edgefield Scraper: A Distributional Study of an Early Archaic Stone Tool from the Southeastern U.S. Paper presented at the Thirty-Seventh Annual Southeastern Archaeological Conference, New Orleans.
Grantham, Bill
2002 *Creation Myths and Legends of the Creek Indians.* University Press of Florida, Gainesville.
Griffin, John W., and Hale G. Smith
1948 *The Goodnow Mound, Highlands County, Florida.* Contributions to the Archaeology of Florida, No. 1. Florida Park Service, Tallahassee.
Hahn, Steven C.
2012 *The Life and Times of Mary Musgrove.* University Press of Florida, Gainesville.

Hally, David J.
1994 An Overview of Lamar Culture. In Hally, ed. 1994:144–174.
1996 Platform-Mound Construction and the Instability of Mississippian Chiefdoms. In Scarry 1996:92–127.
2008 *King: The Social Archaeology of a Late Mississippian Town in Northwestern Georgia*. University of Alabama Press, Tuscaloosa.

Hally, David J. (editor)
1994 *Ocmulgee Archaeology, 1936–1986*. University of Georgia Press, Athens.

Hally, David J., and Robert C. Mainfort Jr.
2004 Prehistory of the Eastern Interior after 500 B.C. In *Handbook of North American Indians: The Southeast*, edited by Raymond D. Fogelson, pp. 265–285. Smithsonian Institution, Washington, D.C.

Hally, David J., and Marvin T. Smith
2010 Sixteenth-Century Mechanisms of Exchange. In Blanton and DeVillar 2010:53–66.

Hally, David J., Marvin T. Smith, and James B. Langford Jr.
1990 The Archaeological Reality of de Soto's Coosa. Thomas 1990:121–138.

Hann, John H.
1996 *A History of the Timucua Indians and Missions*. University Press of Florida, Gainesville.

Hann, John H., and Bonnie G. McEwan
1998 *The Apalachee Indians and Mission San Luis*. University Press of Florida, Gainesville.

Hemperly, Marion R.
1989 *Historic Indian Trails of Georgia*. Garden Club of Georgia, Athens.

Hensler, Rachel
2018 Variation of Native American Ceramics in the Big Bend Region of the Lower Ocmulgee River Valley, Georgia, AD 1540 to AD 1715. PhD dissertation, University of Kentucky, Lexington.

Hoffman, Paul E.
1990 *A New Andalucia and a Way to the Orient: The American Southeast during the Sixteenth Century*. Louisiana State University Press, Baton Rouge.
1994a Lucas Vázquez de Ayllón's Discovery and Colony. In Hudson and Tessar 1994:36–49.
1994b Narváez and Cabeza de Vaca in Florida. In Hudson and Tessar 1994:50–73.

Hudson, Charles M.
1976 *The Southeastern Indians*. University of Tennessee Press, Knoxville.
1994a The Hernando de Soto Expedition, 1539–1543. In Hudson and Tessar 1994:74–103.

1994b The Social Context of the Chiefdom of Ichisi. In Hally, ed. 1994:175–180.

1997 *Knights of Spain, Warriors of the Sun: Hernando de Soto and the South's Ancient Chiefdoms*. University of Georgia Press, Athens.

2005a The Historical Significance of the Soto Route. In Galloway 2005:313–326.

2005b *The Juan Pardo Expeditions: Exploration of the Carolinas and Tennessee, 1566–1568*. University of Alabama Press, Tuscaloosa.

Hudson, Charles, Chester B. DePratter, and Marvin T. Smith

1990 Hernando de Soto's Expedition through the Southern United States. In Milanich and Milbrath, eds. 1990:77–98.

Hudson, Charles, Marvin T. Smith, and Chester B. DePratter

1984 The Hernando de Soto Expedition: From Apalachee to Chiaha. *Southeastern Archaeology* 3(1):65–77.

Hudson, Charles, and Carmen Chaves Tesser (editors)

1994 *The Forgotten Centuries: Indians and Europeans in the American South, 1521–1704*. University of Georgia Press, Athens.

Hudson, Charles, John E. Worth, and Chester B. DePratter

1990 Refinements in Hernando de Soto's Route through Georgia and South Carolina. In Thomas, ed. 1990:107–120.

Hutchinson, Dale L.

2006 *Tatham Mound and the Bioarchaeology of European Contact*. University Press of Florida, Gainesville.

Hutchinson, Dale L., and Jeffrey M. Mitchem

1996 The Weeki Wachee Mound, An Early Contact Period Mortuary Locality in Hernando County, West-Central Florida. *Southeastern Archaeology* 15(1):47–65.

Jackson, H. Edwin, and Susan L. Scott

2003 Patterns of Elite Faunal Utilization at Moundville, Alabama. *American Antiquity* 68(3):552–572.

Juderías, Julián

1914 *La leyenda negra y la verdad histórica* [The black legend and the historical truth]. Madrid, Tip. de la Revista de Archivos.

Kelly, Arthur R.

1938 A Preliminary Report on Archaeological Exploration at Macon, Georgia. *Bureau of American Ethnology Bulletin No. 119*, Smithsonian Institution, Washington, D.C.

King, Adam

2003 *Etowah: The Political History of a Chiefdom Capital*. University of Alabama Press, Tuscaloosa.

Knight, Vernon James, Jr.

2009 Seeking Methods That Work. In Knight, ed. 2009:139–149.

Knight, Vernon James, Jr. (editor)

2009 *The Search for Mabila: The Decisive Battle between Hernando de Soto and Chief Tascalusa*. University of Alabama Press, Tuscaloosa.

Lapham, Heather

2001 More Than "A Few Blew Beads": The Glass and Stone Beads from Jamestown Rediscovery's 1994–1997 Excavations. *Journal of the Jamestown Rediscovery Center*, Vol. 1.

Larson, Lewis H.

1958 Southern Cult Manifestations on the Georgia Coast. *American Antiquity* 23(4):426–430.

1980 *Aboriginal Subsistence Technology on the Southeastern Coastal Plain during the Late Prehistoric Period*. University Press of Florida, Gainesville.

Larson, Lewis H. (editor)

1998 *The Georgia and South Carolina Expeditions of Clarence Bloomfield Moore*. University of Alabama Press, Tuscaloosa.

Lawson, Samuel J., III

1987 La Tama de la Tierra Adentro. *Early Georgia* 15:1–18.

1991 Tama. *Soto States Anthropologist* 91(1):28–38.

Lightfoot, Kent G.

1995 Culture Contact Studies: Redefining the Relationship between Prehistoric and Historical Archaeology. *American Antiquity* 60(2):199–217.

Little, Keith J.

2008 European Artifact Chronology and Impacts of Spanish Contact in the Sixteenth-Century Coosa Valley. PhD dissertation, Department of Anthropology, University of Alabama, Tuscaloosa.

2010 Sixteenth-Century Glass Bead Chronology in Southeastern North America. *Southeastern Archaeology* 29:222–232.

Marrinan, Rochelle A., John F. Scarry, and Rhonda L. Majors

1990 Prelude to de Soto: The Expedition of Pánfilo de Narváez. In Thomas 1990:71–82.

Mathers, Clay, and Charles Haecker

2011 Between Cibola and Tiquex: A Vazquez de Coronado Presence at El Morro National Monument, New Mexico. In Flint and Flint 2011:286–307.

Mathers, Clay, Dan Simplicio, and Tom Kennedy

2011 "Everywhere They Told Us He Had Been There": Evidence of the Vazquez de Coronado Entrada at the Ancestral Zuni Pueblo of Kedhiba:wa, New Mexico. In Flint and Flint 2011:262–285.

Means, Bernard K. (editor)

2013 *Shovel Ready: Archaeology and Roosevelt's New Deal for America*. University of Alabama Press, Tuscaloosa.

Milanich, Jerald T.

1990 The European Entrada into La Florida: An Overview. In Thomas 1990:3–30.

1996 *The Timucua*. Blackwell, Oxford, England.

Milanich, Jerald T., and Charles Hudson

1993 *Hernando de Soto and the Indians of Florida*. University Press of Florida, Gainesville.

Milanich, Jerald T. and Susan Milbrath

1990 Another World. In Milanich and Milbrath, eds. 1990:1–26.

Milanich, Jerald T. and Susan Milbrath (editors)

1990 *First Encounters: Spanish Explorations in the Caribbean and the United States, 1492–1570*. University Press of Florida, Gainesville.

Mission San Luis

Mission San Luis Collections. Electronic document, Mission San Luis, accessed March 2011. http://www.missionsanluis.org/research/collection/showDrawer.cfm?id=32.

Mitchem, Jeffrey M.

1989 Redefining Safety Harbor: Late Prehistoric/Protohistoric Archaeology in West Peninsula Florida. PhD dissertation, Department of Anthropology, University of Florida, Gainesville.

1990 Artifacts of Exploration: Archaeological Evidence from Florida. In Milanich and Milbrath, eds. 1990:99–109.

1991 Initial Spanish-Indian Contact in West Peninsular Florida: The Archaeological Evidence. In Thomas 1990:49–60.

Mitchem, Jeffrey M., and Dale Hutchinson

1987 *Interim Report on Archaeological Research at the Tatham Mound, Citrus County, Florida: Season III*. Florida State Museum, Gainesville.

Mitchem, Jeffrey M., and Jonathan M. Leader

1988 Early Sixteenth Century Beads from the Tatham Mound, Citrus County, Florida: Data and Interpretations. *Florida Anthropologist* 41:42–60.

Mitchem, Jeffrey M., and Bonnie McEwan

1988 New Data on Early Bells from Florida. *Southeastern Archaeology* 7:39–49.

Mitchem, Jeffrey M., Marvin T. Smith, Albert C. Goodyear, and Robert R. Allen

1985 Early Spanish Contact on the Florida Gulf Coast: The Weeki Wachee and Ruth Smith Mounds. In *Indians, Colonists, and Slaves: Essays in Memory of Charles H. Fairbanks*, edited by Kenneth W. Johnson, Jonathan M. Leader, and Robert C. Wilson, pp. 179–220. Florida Journal of Anthropology Special Publication No. 4. Gainesville Letter Shop, Gainesville, Fla.

Mitchem, Jeffrey M., and Brent R. Weisman

1984 Excavations at the Ruth Smith Mound (8CI200). *Florida Anthropologist* 37:100–112.

Moore, Clarence Bloomfield

1896 Certain River Mounds of Duval County, Florida. *Journal of the Academy of Natural Sciences of Philadelphia*, 2nd Series 10(4):449–501.

Moorehead, Warren K.

1932 *Etowah Papers*. Yale University Press, New Haven, Connecticut.

Narroll, Raoul

1962 Floor Area and Settlement Population. *American Antiquity* 27:587–589.

Nass, John P., and Richard W. Yerkes

1995 Social Differentiation in Mississippian and Fort Ancient Societies. In Rogers and Smith 1995:58–80.

Pearson, Charles

1977 Evidence of Early Spanish Contact on the Georgia Coast. *Historical Archaeology* 11:74–83.

Peck, Douglas T.

2001 Lucas Vasquez de Ayllón's Doomed Colony of San Miguel de Gualdape. *Georgia Historical Quarterly* 85(2):183–198.

Pendleton, Lorann S. A., and Peter Francis

2009 Introduction to Bead Manufacture and Origins. In Blair et al. 2009:53–57.

Priestley, Herbert Ingram

2010 *The Luna Papers, 1559–1561*. 2 Vols. University of Alabama Press, Tuscaloosa.

Robertson, James Alexander (translator)

1993 The Account by a Gentleman from Elvas. In Clayton et al. 1993a:19–220.

Rodning, Christopher B.

2002 The Townhouse at Coweta Creek. *Southeastern Archaeology* 21:10–20.

2010 Architectural Symbolism and Cherokee Townhouses. *Southeastern Archaeology* 29(1):59–79.

Rogers, J. Daniel, and Bruce D. Smith (editors)

1995 *Mississippian Communities and Households*. University of Alabama Press, Tuscaloosa.

Rudolph, James L., and Dennis B. Blanton

1980 A Discussion of Mississippian Settlement in the Georgia Piedmont. *Early Georgia* 8:14–37.

Saunders, Rebecca

2000 *Stability and Change in Guale Indian Pottery, A.D. 1300–1702*. University of Alabama Press, Tuscaloosa.

2009 Stability and Ubiquity: Irene, Altamaha, and San Marcos Pottery in Time and Space. In Deagan and Thomas 2009:83–112.

Scarry, John F. (editor)

1996 *Political Structure and Change in the Prehistoric Southeastern United States.* University Press of Florida, Gainesville.

Schmader, Matt

2011 Thundersticks and Coats of Iron: Recent Discoveries at Piedras Marcadas Pueblo, New Mexico. In Flint and Flint 2011:308–347.

Scott, Douglas D.

2013 *Uncovering History: Archaeological Investigations at the Little Bighorn.* University of Oklahoma Press, Norman.

Sears, William H., Elsie O'R. Sears, and Karl T. Steinen

1994 *Fort Center: An Archaeological Site in the Lake Okeechobee Basin.* University Press of Florida, Gainesville.

Sempowski, Martha L., and Lorraine P. Sanders

2001 *Dutch Hollow and Factory Hollow: The Advent of Dutch Trade among the Seneca (3 Parts).* Charles F. Wray Series in Seneca Archaeology Volume 3, Research Records No. 24. Rochester Museum and Science Center, Rochester, New York.

Shelby, Charmion (translator)

1993 *La Florida.* In Clayton et al. 1993b:25–559.

Smith, Marvin T.

1975 European Materials from the King Site. *Southeastern Archaeological Conference Bulletin* 18:63–66.

1983 Chronology from Glass Beads: The Spanish Period in the Southeast, 1513–1670. *Proceedings of the 1982 Glass Trade Bead Conference*, Research Records No. 16, Rochester Museum and Science Center, Rochester, New York.

1987 *Archaeology of Aboriginal Culture Change in the Interior Southeast: Depopulation during the Early Historic Period.* University Press of Florida, Gainesville.

1992 Glass Beads from the Council House at San Luis. In *Archaeology at San Luis: The Apalachee Council House*, by Gary Shapiro and Bonnie G. McEwan, pp. 107–117. Florida Archaeology No. 6, Pt. 1. Florida Bureau of Archaeological Research, Tallahassee.

2000 *Coosa: The Rise and Fall of a Southeastern Mississippian Chiefdom.* University of Alabama Press, Tuscaloosa.

Smith, Marvin T., and Mary Elizabeth Good

1982 *Early Sixteenth Century Glass Beads in the Spanish Colonial Trade.* Cottonlandia Museum, Greenwood, Mississippi.

Smith, Marvin T., and Stephen A. Kowalewski
1980 Tentative Identification of a Prehistoric “Province” in Piedmont Georgia. *Early Georgia* 8(1–2):1–13.
Snow, Frankie
1977 *An Archaeological Survey of the Ocmulgee Big Bend Region*. Occasional Papers from South Georgia No. 3. South Georgia College, Douglas.
1990 Pine Barrens Lamar. In Williams and Shapiro 1990:82–93.
Snow, Frankie, and Keith Stephenson
1998 Swift Creek Designs: A Tool for Monitoring Interaction. In *A World Engraved: Archaeology of the Swift Creek Culture*, edited by Mark Williams and Daniel T. Elliott, pp. 99–111. University of Alabama Press, Tuscaloosa.
South, Stanley
1988 Santa Elena: Threshold of Conquest. In *The Recovery of Meaning*, edited by Mark Leone and Parker B. Potter, pp. 27–72. Smithsonian Institution Press, Washington, D.C.
South, Stanley, Russell K. Skowronek, and Richard E. Johnson
1988 *Spanish Artifacts from Santa Elena*. Anthropological Studies No. 7. South Carolina Institute of Archaeology and Anthropology, University of South Carolina, Columbia.
Stephenson, Keith, and Frankie Snow
2004 Swift Creek to Square Ground Lamar: Situating the Ocmulgee Big Bend Region in Calibrated Time. *Early Georgia* 32(2):127–160.
Sullivan, Lynne P.
1995 Mississippian Household and Community Organization in Eastern Tennessee. In Rogers and Smith 1995:99–123.
Swanton, John R.
1979 *The Indians of the Southeastern United States*. Smithsonian Institution Press, Washington, D.C.
1985 *Final Report of the United States De Soto Expedition Commission*. Classics of Smithsonian Anthropology. Smithsonian Institution Press, Washington, D.C.
Sweet, Julie Anne Sweet
2009 Mary Musgrove: Maligned Mediator or Mischievous Malefactor. In *Georgia Women: Their Lives and Times*, Vol. 1, edited by Ann Short Chirhart and Betty Wood, pp. 11–32. University of Georgia Press, Athens.
Thomas, David Hurst
1987 *The Archaeology of Mission Santa Catalina de Guale, 1. Search and Discovery*. Anthropological Papers of the American Museum of Natural History Vol. 63(2).

1988 *St. Catherines: An Island in Time*. Georgia History and Culture Series. Georgia Endowment for the Humanities, Atlanta.

1991 The Archaeology of Mission Santa Catalina de Guale: Our First Fifteen Years. In *The Missions of Spanish Florida*, edited by B. G. McEwan, pp. 107–125. The Florida Anthropologist Vol. 44(2–4). Florida Anthropological Society, Tallahassee.

1993 *Historic Period Indian Archaeology of the Georgia Coastal Zone*. Georgia Archaeological Research Design Paper No. 8. University of Georgia Laboratory of Archaeology Series Report No. 31. University of Georgia, Athens.

2009 Late Aboriginal Ceramics from St. Catherines Island (cal. A.D. 1400–1700), In Deagan and Thomas 2009, pp. 49–82.

Thomas, David Hurst (editor)

1990 *Columbian Consequences: Archaeological and Historical Perspectives on the Spanish Borderlands East*, Vol. 2. Smithsonian Institution Press, Washington, D.C.

2008 *Native American Landscapes of St. Catherines Island, Georgia. Anthropological Papers of the American Museum of Natural History*. Vol. 88 (1–3). American Museum of Natural History, New York.

Thomas, David Hurst, and Clark Spencer Larsen

1979 *The Anthropology of St. Catherines Island: 2. The Refuge-Deptford Mortuary Complex*. Anthropological Papers of the American Museum of Natural History Vol. 56(1). American Museum of Natural History, New York.

1982 *The Anthropology of St. Catherines Island: 4. The St. Catherines Period Mortuary Complex*. Anthropological Papers of the American Museum of Natural History Vol. 57(4). American Museum of Natural History, New York.

1986 *The Anthropology of St. Catherines Island: 5. The South End Complex*. Anthropological Papers of the American Museum of Natural History Vol. 63(1). American Museum of Natural History, New York.

Toner, Mike

2006 Bead Hints at Old Mission. *Atlanta Journal-Constitution*, July 1.

U.S. Army Corps of Engineers

1909 Map section. Ocmulgee River survey. Washington, D.C.

U.S. Department of Agriculture

2003 *Soil Survey of Bleckley, Dodge, and Telfair Counties, Georgia*. U.S. Department of Agriculture, Washington, D.C.

U.S. Geological Survey

2011 USGS National Water Information System. Electronic document accessed March 2011. https://waterdata.usgs.gov/nwis.

U.S. Navy

2011 Sun or Moon Rise/Set Table for One Year. Electronic document, accessed March 2011. https://aa.usno.navy.mil/data/docs/RS_OneYear.php.

Walker, John W.

1994 A Brief History of Ocmulgee Archaeology. In Hally, ed. 1994:15–35.

Waselkov, Gregory A.

2005 *Old Mobile Archaeology*. University of Alabama Press, Tuscaloosa.

2009 What Do Spanish Expeditionary Artifacts of Circa 1540 Look Like and How Often Are They Preserved? In Knight, ed. 2009:94–106.

Waselkov, Gregory A., and Kathryn E. Holland Braund (editors)

1995 *William Bartram on the Southeastern Indians*. University of Nebraska Press, Lincoln.

Wells, Tom

1998 Nail Chronology: The Use of Technologically Derived Features. *Historical Archaeology* 32(2):78–99.

Willey, Gordon R.

1954 Burial Patterns in the Burns and Fuller Mounds, Cape Canaveral, Florida. *Florida Anthropologist* 7(3):79–90.

Williams, Mark

1994 Growth and Decline of the Oconee Province. In Hudson and Tesser 1994:179–196.

1995 Chiefly Compounds. In Rogers and Smith 1995:124–134.

2010 Notes and Queries on Spaniards and Indians in the Oconee Valley. In Blanton and DeVillar 2010:35–52.

Williams, Mark, and Gary Shapiro

1996 Mississippian Political Dynamics in the Oconee Valley, Georgia. In Scarry 1996:128–149.

Williams, Mark, and Gary Shapiro (editors)

1990 *Lamar Archaeology: Mississippian Chiefdoms in the Deep South*. University of Alabama Press, Tuscaloosa.

Windham, R. Jeannine

2010 Faunal Exploitation and Feasting at the Glass Site. In Blanton and DeVillar 2010:19–34.

2011 Zooarchaeological Remains from 9TF145. Appendix A in Blanton et al. 2011.

Worth, John E.

1988 Mississippian Occupation of the Middle Flint River. MA thesis, Department of Anthropology, University of Georgia, Athens.

1989 Mississippian Mound Centers along Chickasawhatchee Swamp. *LAMAR Briefs* 13:7–9.
1993 Prelude to Abandonment: The Interior Provinces of Early 17th-Century Georgia. *Early Georgia* 21(1):24–58.
1994 Late Spanish Military Expeditions in the Interior Southeast, 1595–1628. In Hudson and Tesser 1994:104–122.
1995 The Early Seventeenth Century Locations of Tama and Utinahica. In Braley 1995:A-1–A-8.
1998 *The Timucuan Chiefdoms of Spanish Florida*. 2 vols. University Press of Florida, Gainesville.

Worth, John E. (translator)
1993a Account of the Northern Conquest and Discovery of Hernando de Soto. In Clayton et al. 1993a:247–306.
1993b Relation of the Island of Florida. In Clayton et al. 1993a:221–246.

Index